A Soldier's Kipling

A Soldier's Kipling

Poetry and the Profession of Arms

Edward J. Erickson

Pen & Sword
MILITARY

First published in Great Britain in 2018 by
Pen & Sword Military
an imprint of
Pen & Sword Books Ltd
47 Church Street
Barnsley
South Yorkshire
S70 2AS

Copyright © Edward J. Erickson 2018

ISBN 9781526718532

A CIP catalogue record for this book is
available from the British Library

Typeset in 10.5/13.5 Ehrhardt MT by SRJ Info Jnana System Pvt Ltd.
Printed and Bound in the UK by TJ International.

Pen & Sword Books Ltd incorporates the imprints of Pen & Sword Archaeology,
Atlas, Aviation, Battleground, Discovery, Family History, History, Maritime,
Military, Naval, Politics, Railways, Select, Social History, Transport, True Crime,
and Claymore Press, Frontline Books, Leo Cooper, Praetorian Press,
Remember When, Seaforth Publishing and Wharncliffe.

For a complete list of Pen & Sword titles please contact
PEN & SWORD BOOKS LIMITED
47 Church Street, Barnsley, South Yorkshire, S70 2AS, England
E-mail: enquiries@pen-and-sword.co.uk
Website: www.pen-and-sword.co.uk

Contents

This book is dedicated
to my students at the
United States Marine Corps Command and Staff College
from whom I have learned so much,
in particular
Major Will Norcott, Royal Marine Commandos
Major Sandra Patterson, New Zealand Army
Major Dina Poma-Barnes, Unites States Marine Corps
Major James Small, United States Army

Acknowledgements

I would first and foremost like to compliment and acknowledge the contributions to the completion of this book made by the students who took my Kipling elective at the Marine Corps Command and Staff College in Quantico, Virginia. They are Major Will Norcott, Royal Marine Commandos, Major Sandy Patterson, New Zealand Army, Major Dina Poma–Barnes, United States Marine Corps, and Major James Small, United States Army. Although few in number their many sage insights, comments, and thoughts helped me understand these verses in ways that I had not seen. Their observations about how practitioners of the Profession of Arms, fresh to Kipling, interpret his work were monumentally important in developing how I have understood and presented these verses. All four of them are combat veterans and all four had served in Afghanistan, some multiple times. Major Patterson's family served in India under the Raj until 1947. I have used their ideas mercilessly and without attribution, and I can't thank them all enough! Like Kipling, who observed similarities between his own appropriation of stories with that of the ancient Greek poet Homer, I hope that Will, Sandy, Dina, and James will grant me a wink and a nod when they read this book.

'When 'Omer smote
'is bloomin' lyre...'
Introduction to the 'Barrack-Room Ballads' in
The Seven Seas

When 'Omer smote 'is bloomin' lyre,
    He'd 'eard men sing by land an' sea;
An' what he thought 'e might require,
    'E went an' took – the same as me!

The market-girls an' fishermen,
    The shepherds an' the sailors, too,
They 'eard old songs turn up again,
    But kep' it quiet – same as you!

They knew 'e stole; 'e knew they knowed.
    They didn't tell, nor make a fuss,
But winked at 'Omer down the road,
    An' 'e winked back – the same as us!

I would also like to acknowledge the authors and members of the Kipling Society, whose wonderfully complete website contains a wealth of valuable information and insights about these poems. I am especially grateful to Alastair Wilson and John Seriot of the Kipling Society for going the distance and reading the entire manuscript in detail and providing exquisitely comprehensive and eye-opening comments. Thank you Alastair and John! Several members of the Kipling Society have also read parts of my manuscript and I owe them my thanks as well, they are: Meredith Dixon, John McGivering, and John Radcliffe. The superb work of Andrew Lycett has also been of great value in understanding Kipling and his world. I absolutely could not have mined the numberless small details required for this book by myself.

I am also indebted to the Director of the Marine Corps Command and Staff College, Colonel Mike McCollough, United States Marine Corps, and the Dean of Academics, Dr Doug McKenna, for allowing me to create a graduate course titled 'Rudyard Kipling's Small Wars' as an elective offering to the students of the college.

Finally, I owe a great debt of gratitude to my patient and beautiful wife, Jennifer Collins, and to my faithful editor and friend at Pen and Sword, Rupert Harding, for their endless encouragement and constant support.

List of Maps

List of Plates

Foreword

Lieutenant General Paul E. Funk (US Army, Retired)

Long before I was a soldier, I was a fan of Rudyard Kipling. In seventh grade in public school in the town of Roundup, Montana, our English teacher, Mr Feldman, read 'Gunga Din', 'Tommy' and 'If' to the class in dramatic accents. Later, as our army family drove cross-country (this happened a lot in those days of the Vietnam War) my dear wife, Danny, would read those poems and Kipling's other masterpieces to our three children. My sons, Paul II and Jim, really loved those poems and the way their Mom read them (she was great, and I confess that I loved being read to as well)! Becky was quite a bit younger and may not have listened quite as raptly. It made the time pass much more quickly. The boys memorized some of the poems and recited them at school and even for some of our house guests.

Fast forward to 1989 when I was privileged to command the United States Army's Third Armoured Division in Germany, where I served with our author Ed Erickson. Major Erickson was then an artilleryman in the superb 'Spearhead' Division. Apparently, Ed recognized me (and later my son, Paul II) as a 'kindred Kipling soul'. Our service continued through Operation Desert Storm, where the great soldiers of the Spearhead Division helped crush Saddam Hussein's army in 1991. In particular, the 'Gunners' of our Division Artillery, led by outstanding leaders such as Major Erickson, performed magnificently in what was our army's greatest 'First Battle.'

A Soldier's Kipling, Poetry and the Profession of Arms is a title truly borne out in the author's profession! Unabashedly focused upon those who do the real fighting (and almost all the dying), it is direct and plain 'soldier thought' and insights which come through his interpretation of Rudyard Kipling's work.

The sequence cleverly follows the outline of nearly every junior soldier's life, and, in my view, is brilliant. I have always felt that Kipling understood soldiers and soldiering better than many others, including many senior leaders in the profession of arms itself.

The book is a real treat to read and is a tribute to Ed Erickson's intellect, passion and understanding of soldiers. I have a personal connection to '"Snarleyow"' (I was raised around horses in Montana), and could anyone not see the loyalty and humanity of 'Gunga Din', or the brilliance of 'If' (which is possibly my favourite)? We should all remember that the 'Bear' is most dangerous when she is weakened (talk about current events), and there are all kinds of lessons for today's soldiers (or those who would try to understand them) throughout. I hope that you'll enjoy Ed's interpretations of Kipling as much as I have.

Preface

Kipling and Me

As a young boy in upstate New York my favourite movies on television were about the British Army on India's Northwest Frontier – *Soldiers Three, Gunga Din, Lives of a Bengal Lancer,* and *Wee Willie Winkie* were chief among them. In my young mind's eye I had already created a stereotyped British non-commissioned officer built on the work of British character actor Victor McLagen, who played Sergeant Donald MacDuff in *Wee Willie Winkie.* So when I found Rudyard Kipling's *Departmental Ditties and Barrack Room Ballads* on a bookshelf in our home it immediately attracted my attention and I found to my delight that if I read a poem aloud as Kipling wrote it, *Gunga Din* for example, I was speaking like Sergeant MacDuff!

Kipling's verse fit neatly and right into my carefully imagined boy's world of toy soldiers, wartime uniforms with rolled up cuffs, and hilltop forts built of branches and rocks. From my earliest days stories of soldiers and campaigns captivated me and I was immediately enthralled by Kipling's vivid choice of words and phrases. As I grew I developed a passion for military and naval history, and I found and read more of Kipling's poetry. And many of Kipling's verses were about wars and soldiers I'd never heard of, and so I read more about Britain's small wars. Later films such as *Zulu,* a wonderful movie about the heroic defence of Rorke's Drift by the South Wales Borderers in 1879, cemented my love of British military history and Kipling into a lifelong interest.

When I grew up I joined the United States Army and I brought Kipling with me to every station I went to. That's when the deeper meanings of what Kipling had to say about the profession of soldiering and war began to resonate strongly in my consciousness. I began to develop a more mature understanding of what Kipling had to say about the profession of arms. While a captain and serving as an ROTC instructor at St Lawrence University I developed an elective course that I titled 'Kipling's Empire'. We read and discussed the poems and the history. Later I would occasionally run into senior officers, such as Major General Paul Funk, the commander of the 3rd Armoured Division, who would quote Kipling. Over the years and over the course of a career of garrison and combat duties I grew to appreciate Kipling's verse at a very elemental and fundamental level. I had often thought about writing a book like this, but it was not until I offered an elective course at the Marine Corps Command and Staff College called 'Rudyard Kipling's Small Wars' that the themes began to self-organize in my head.

A Soldier's Kipling

It is hard today, given our contemporary sensibilities about discrimination and fairness, to separate the chauvinistic and imperialistic rhetoric of Rudyard Kipling's verse from what he meant to convey in his own time. And, because of his apparent casual racism and evident belief in the superiority of Britain to other nations, people today find it hard to take his work seriously. While we are pleased to retell and profit from his children's stories, such as *The Jungle Book* and the *Just So Stories*, our contemporary world rejects much of his work about the British Empire and its army as ethnocentric justifications for imperialism. In fact the reverse is true, and should the reader read this book through to the very end, he or she will discover that Kipling (while most certainly an ardent imperialist) was sensitive to the plight of the underdog, appreciative of the lives, languages, and culture of non-western peoples, and deeply critical of the self-centred behaviour and aspirations of his fellow Britons living in the industrialized home islands. Kipling's work, especially his verses about soldiers and war, deserve a second look and reflection.

A Soldier's Kipling, Poetry and the Profession of Arms explores a selection of Rudyard Kipling's military poetry relating to how the British Army waged its campaigns during what are called 'Queen Victoria's Little Wars'. It is relevant today to reflect on the idea that the British Army of Kipling's time was a volunteer, long-service, professional army. Moreover, it had a volunteer reserve force of citizen-soldiers, who were called on to expand the army in times of need. This army was unique in nineteenth-century Europe and, in many ways, much like our western armies of today. Many of its soldiers were recruited from the lower classes of British society and joined for work or to escape hopeless circumstances. Its officer corps was something of a transgenerational family-centric caste system. Once trained, the regiments of the British Army were subject to prolonged deployments to the fringes of the empire, for garrison duty or for war. In these ways, then, the British Army of Victoria's time was much like the British and American armies of today.

The reign of Queen Victoria began in 1837 and lasted until 1901, and it was a period of unrivalled prosperity and influence for Britain. Sometimes the period is known as *Pax Britannia*, but in truth it was a period of almost continuous and seemingly endless small wars. These wars were rarely in easily accessible or pleasant places, occurring mostly in isolated, distant, and climactically uncomfortable locations. Victoria's wars were often fought in jungles, wintry mountains, deserts, or endless plains, against all manner of enemies – some civilized and many savage. The army's campaigns of this era were sequential in serial order and sometimes even overlapped. It was not at all uncommon for the British Army to have to return to fight a war several times against the same enemy, and many of its wars bear the prefix 'Second' or 'Third'. Today we call this phenomenon a period of 'persistent war'. Like the composition of the British Army, the wars of the Victorian era were similar to those of the present time. Contemporary soldiers find themselves fighting in theatres like Afghanistan, Iraq, Mali, the Philippines, Somalia, Syria, and Yemen – sometimes for a second and third time. There is certainly relevance and reflection to be found here for modern soldiers.

Kipling's military poetry offers insights into the profession of arms and how, in the past, professional regulars approached the problem of training soldiers for combat and then taking those soldiers to fight in distant expeditionary campaigns against savage foes. Although he was not a soldier himself, Kipling also wrote about many other timeless themes relevant to the profession of arms. This book presents selected poems by Kipling, organized around themes familiar to professional soldiers (the term professional soldiers being easily applied to all members and genders of the military and naval forces). My intent for the reader of *A Soldier's Kipling* is not to tutor or instruct, but to generate an appreciation for Rudyard Kipling's military poetry and for the timeless themes about the nature of soldering and the profession of arms contained in those verses.

It has become an item of popular belief and conventional wisdom that the post-modern world of the twenty-first century is far more complex and less rule-bound than the worlds of the past. There is certainly some truth to this, and we readily accept the idea that 'Gen-Xers' and 'Millennials' face a world that is inherently more ambiguous and complex than the world that their parents faced. Contemporary military literature is filled with bumper-sticker-like phrases like 'fourth-generation war', 'persistent war', and 'non-linear war', leading to the conclusion that war today is somehow much different and far more difficult for the practitioners of military arts than it was in the past. The corollary to this line of thought is that the problems of being a soldier in this new world are also somehow different and more difficult than during those wars of the past. Frankly I question the idea that today's world is more complex and more ambiguous for the people living in it than the world was for people living in past times.

While the world may be increasingly complicated in terms of soldiering, I reject entirely the idea that the nature of soldiering has changed. My position comes from the close study of the great military theorist Karl von Clausewitz, who advanced the concept in his monumental study *On War* that the *nature of war* is enduring and unchanging (uncertainty, friction, the fog of war, and chaos for example) and that the *character of war* changes constantly and continuously (weapons, tactics, and organizations for example). I do not think that it is a stretch to suggest that the nature and character of soldiering exist in a similar equation. Combining these thoughts, I believe that Kipling's verse presents themes about both the nature and the character of military service. If this book has a thesis of any sort it is that the nature of soldiering today is not much different than soldiering in Kipling's time, although the character of the profession has changed enormously.

Kipling and Soldiers

Rudyard Kipling was a journalist born in Bombay, India in 1865 to a professional family employed by the government. His father was an architectural sculptor and young Rudyard was sent off to public school in England to be educated. He attended the United Services College, which was also known by the unusual name of a nearby village, Westward Ho!. The college was set up to prepare young men to enter the army, navy, or civil service. Unable to afford university Kipling returned to India aged seventeen and a friend of his father's arranged for him to work as a journalist for the *Civil and Military Gazette* in Lahore. Thus his background had prepared him to work in the imperial system, and his choice of a profession brought him into close and frequent contact with his readers, who were soldiers and civil servants. Kipling's world and his world view were framed by the fact that in the mid-1880s Britain was at the apogee of imperial power and its empire seemed as though it would last for a thousand years. It was Queen Victoria's empire – it was a world of certainty, place, and obligation, in which Englishmen knew not only who they were, but also that Britannia ruled the globe.

Kipling himself was not a soldier, although he was carried briefly on the rolls of the 1st Punjab Volunteer Rifles. Rather it was his background and his education which prepared him to be with soldiers, and his work as a reporter and journalist took him into close contact with soldiers. Lahore was a garrison town for the Indian Army, and Kipling lived with and worked among British soldiers and, as importantly, among the Indian soldiers of the 'martial races'. In 1886 Kipling was the *Civil and Military Gazette*'s reporter writing about the expeditionary campaign in upper Burma when he learned that a Westward Ho! classmate, Lieutenant Robert Dury, had been killed (leading Kipling to write *Arithmetic on the Frontier*). He travelled frequently in the Punjab and to the parts of the frontier threatened by banditry and violence. Kipling made it his business to understand British India and to understand the men and women who made it what it was. He left India in 1889 for London and was soon to become an acclaimed and world-famous author.

It is evident from his work that Kipling felt an abiding affection for soldiers and that he held them in great admiration. But to clarify this, he held these notions only as far as he observed and understood the separation that distanced field soldiers from the behind-the-lines staffs and self-serving officers who plagued the army. I think that Kipling understood what William Shakespeare meant when Harry spoke of a 'band of brothers' and of 'warriors for the working day' in *Henry V.* Soldiers, for Kipling, fought in the front line toe-to-toe with the enemy and, when not fighting, they stoically endured both the hardships of the long campaign and the tedium of barracks life. They stood their ground against savage enemies and did so without complaint. During his time in India, Kipling paid attention to soldiers; he listened to and remembered their stories, and he formed life-long ideas about what it was like to be a soldier. Kipling's archetypal soldier was a wily underdog with a local accent who understood how the game was played off the playing fields of Eton. He was mischievous, devious, and frequently drunk in garrison, but he was a deadly fighter and courageous under fire. Kipling's *Soldiers Three* – Terence Mulvaney from Ireland, the Cockney Stanley Ortheris, and Jock Learoyd from Yorkshire – exemplify the soldiers of Kipling's army.

Later, during his time in South Africa during the Second Anglo-Boer War, Kipling would recast his ideas about soldiering to include criticisms of the decisions and motivation of generals, and about their relief for incompetence. He would write about married reservists and about the problems that soldiers faced when deploying for combat, and about the problems they faced when re-entering civil society – both structural and personal. Kipling was particularly incensed by the shabby treatment that many returning veterans received when returning home to Britain. Finally he would write about the difficulty organizations such as the British Army face when trying to reform and adapt to a changing tactical world. Throughout all of this Kipling remained steadfast in his admiration for 'Tommy Atkins', the archetypal British soldier.

Rudyard Kipling was a popular author and had an active audience in Britain and in the United States. As the reader will note, in almost every case Kipling published the poems presented herewith in the well-known weekly gazettes and daily newspapers of his time. Often the poems appeared initially with a title, which then changed in subsequent versions. Kipling would also frequently add or change verses between the initial media version and his final book version. After appearing in magazines and newspapers the poems were then collected up by his editors and republished in Britain and the United States. The most notable of these collections in terms of military poetry are *Departmental Ditties and Other Verses, Barrack-Room Ballads and Other Verses, The Seven Seas*, and *The Five Nations*.

Reading *A Soldier's Kipling*

Well-informed readers may find versions of Kipling's poems in print and on line which differ from the versions of Kipling's poems presented herein. I have used *Rudyard Kipling's Verse, Definitive Edition*, published by Doubleday and Company, Inc., Garden City, New York in 1940, as the standardized basis for presenting the poems in this book. I have maintained the spelling, punctuation, grammar, structure, and form of Kipling's poems as they are found in that volume. I have also maintained the words and parts of words which Kipling placed in italics, as these appear in the definitive edition as well. Overall, I believe that the 1940 definitive edition of Kipling's verse (printed a year earlier in Britain) to be the truest in content and most authentic to Kipling's intended message.

A Soldier's Kipling is organized thematically along the chronological lines of a soldier's career and professional life – training for war, going to war, fighting a war, coming home from war, and learning from war. We begin the book with poems about how the army turns civilians into soldiers and, in particular, how the army relies on non-commissioned officers to do this. We then turn to the process of deployment to distant theatres of war and the effect that it has on soldiers and their families. There are two chapters dedicated to the experience of combat and two chapters about how soldiers regard their enemies, their fellow fighting men, and their sister services. For combat veterans I think that Chapter Seven, 'Thomas Atkins Comes Home' will resonate strongly and personally, as Kipling delves into the experience of returning home from war. The later chapters cover how armies and nations process the lessons of war, as well as the subject of patriotism as it is imagined and as it is personally experienced as a consequence of war. The final chapter is off topic, but contains a number of my personal Kipling favourites about life.

I would be remiss if I did not share with the reader how I think the book should be read. I present each poem with footnoted terms and vocabulary, and with a follow-on component. The explanatory component discusses any context and history necessary for the reader to understand the time, place, and events that Kipling refers to. This is followed by my reflections, thoughts and views on how particular verses connect to the profession of arms today. This is, in my view, the heart of the book. Finally, I have highlighted and explained noteworthy lines and stanzas about the profession of arms, which I think might resonate strongly with modern practitioners of the art of war.

If you have never read much Kipling, I suggest that you read the entire poem *aloud* as a first step, trying to capture the accents and inflections of Kipling's verse. Then read the footnotes and the sections on the profession of arms. Then read the entire poem aloud a second time… and maybe even a third time if the themes and topics particularly interest you. Kipling's verse gets better over a number of readings and his observations about the nature of soldiering and the profession of arms are timeless. I hope that you'll enjoy reading and thinking about *A Soldier's Kipling, Poetry and the Profession of Arms* as much as I have enjoyed writing it.

Chapter 1

Becoming Tommy Atkins – Learning to Soldier

Introduction

This chapter focuses on the enduring themes inherent in the remaking of civilians into soldiers. Kipling highlights the unique nature and character of the requirements of the profession of arms as experienced by those in the trade itself. The British Army of Kipling's day was composed of long-service professionals who were all volunteers, and it was not a conscripted mass army structured on the Continental model. Moreover, the British Army was an army at war, engaged in fighting in distant theatres continuously during the period between Waterloo in 1815 and Mons in 1914. Soldiers enlisting in the British Army during Queen Victoria's reign could expect to see combat and their training reflected that dynamic. In this respect Kipling's Army was very similar to modern all-volunteer armies composed of highly-trained professionals who, upon enlistment, have to be remade into soldiers.

Integral and vital to the process of training soldiers are non-commissioned officers. In truth it is the corps of non-commissioned officers (composed of corporals through sergeants major) who bear the primary responsibility for training soldiers and ensuring that they perform as they are trained in the heat of combat. Kipling's use of the phrase 'the backbone of the army' defines the importance of non-commissioned officers and the phrase has become a part of our modern military vocabulary. He details the repetitive nature of basic training and the key role that non-commissioned officers play in this essential process. He also examines the relationship that enlisted men have

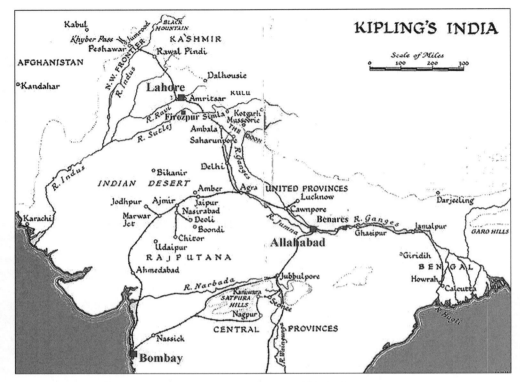

Kipling's India. This map shows the British Raj as Kipling knew it at the turn of the nineteenth/twentieth century. Map courtesy of the Kipling Society.

with their junior officers and highlights the importance of developing respect and affection across the enlisted–officer abyss.

Kipling also explored the relationship of soldiers to their civilian counterparts, which in his time was contentious at best. Today we call this the military–civilian divide, by which we mean that ordinary citizens have little appreciation for what soldiers do, and nor do they have a vested interest in the conditions under which soldiers live or die. Most citizens of countries like Great Britain and the United States today have never served in uniform and have no direct experience of war whatsoever. In fact, many of them might not even know a serving soldier and, while they publicly support the Forces with donations and good will, they are unwilling personally to don the 'widow's uniform' and fight. Within our own memory there have even been periods when soldiers have been reviled by, and excluded from, civil society. Kipling understood this dilemma and raged against it.

Over the past twenty or so years the phrase 'persistent war' has crept into the modern vocabulary of security specialists to describe a prolonged period of military deployments around the globe. While Kipling certainly would not have used the phrase 'persistent war' himself, he would recognize immediately the pattern of rotating battalions and brigades from home station garrisons to distant combat zones. And he would immediately recognize the similarity of what some call today 'the long war' to the 'little wars' paradigm of Queen Victoria's reign.

What was it was like to serve in Victoria's army as an enlisted man, and how did that man relate to his civilian counterparts, as well as to his fellows, sergeants, and officers? For those interested in the late-Victorian British Army I recommend *Mr Kipling's Army, All the Queen's Men* by Byron Farwell as a place to start. The poems I have selected for this chapter are 'To Thomas Atkins', 'Tommy', 'The Men that Fought at Minden', 'The 'eathen', and 'The Shut-Eye Sentry'. Other similar poems, which may be found on the Kipling Society's superb website, and which I recommend to the reader, are 'Belts', 'Cells', 'Danny Deever', 'The Service-Man', and 'The Widow's Party'.

To Thomas Atkins

Prelude to 'Barrack Room Ballads' which follow

This is the dedication to *Barrack Room Ballads*, published in 1892. The voice is Kipling's own.

> I have made for you a song
>   And it may be right or wrong,
> But only you can tell me if it's true.
>   I have tried for to explain
>   Both your pleasure and your pain,
> And, Thomas, here's my best respects to you!
>
>   O there'll surely come a day
>   When they'll give you all your pay,
> And treat you as a Christian ought to do;
>   So, until that day comes round,
>   Heaven keep you safe and sound,
> And, Thomas, here's my best respects to you!

British soldiers in Kipling's time were not treated especially well by the government. They lived in sub-standard and often unheated barracks, they were poorly paid, and were treated shabbily by their civilian counterparts.

Kipling understood the uniqueness of the profession of arms and he recognized that those who have never served in uniform will never quite 'get it right'. His *Barrack Room Ballads* reflect Kipling's observations on the nature of being a soldier and, in the author's opinion, as this chapter and those which follow also show – Kipling understands and 'gets' the pleasure and the pain of being a soldier right.

***

Tommy

This is one of Kipling's most well-known poems – it was first published under the title 'The Queen's Uniform' in the *Scots Observer* in March 1890 and collected in *Departmental Ditties, Barrack-Room Ballads and Other Verses* in that same year. The voice is that of a British Army regular soldier.

I went into a public-'ouse to get a pint o' beer,[1]
The publican 'e up an' sez, "We serve no red-coats here."
The girls be'ind the bar they laughed an' giggled fit to die,
I outs into the street again an' to myself sez I:
 O it's Tommy this, an' Tommy that, an' "Tommy, go away";
 But it's "Thank you, Mister Atkins", when the band begins
 to play,
 The band begins to play, my boys, the band begins to play,
 O it's "Thank you, Mister Atkins", when the band begins
 to play.

I went into a theatre as sober as could be,
They gave a drunk civilian room, but 'adn't none for me;
They sent me to the gallery or round the music-'alls,
But when it comes to fightin', Lord! they'll shove me in the stalls!
 For it's Tommy this, an' Tommy that, an' "Tommy, wait outside";
 But it's "Special train for Atkins" when the trooper's on
 the tide,
 The troopship's on the tide, my boys, the troopship's on
 the tide,
 O it's "Special train for Atkins" when the trooper's on the tide.

Yes, makin' mock o' uniforms that guard you while you sleep
Is cheaper than them uniforms, an' they're starvation cheap;
An' hustlin' drunken soldiers when they're goin' large a bit
Is five times better business than paradin' in full kit.
 Then it's Tommy this, an' Tommy that, an' "Tommy, 'ow's
 yer soul?"
 But it's "Thin red line of 'eroes" when the drums begin to roll,

---

[1] For American readers, a public house is a bar or a saloon open to the public.

The drums begin to roll, my boys, the drums begin to roll,
O it's "Thin red line of 'eroes" when the drums begin to roll.

We aren't no thin red 'eroes, nor we aren't no blackguards too,
But single men in barricks, most remarkable like you;
An' if sometimes our conduck isn't all your fancy paints,
Why, single men in barricks don't grow into plaster saints;
   While it's Tommy this, an' Tommy that, an' "Tommy, fall
   be'ind",
   But it's "Please to walk in front, sir", when there's trouble in
   the wind,
   There's trouble in the wind, my boys, there's trouble in the
   wind,
   O it's "Please to walk in front, sir," when there's trouble in the
   wind.

You talk o' better food for us, an' schools, an' fires, an' all:
We'll wait for extry rations if you treat us rational.
Don't mess about the cook-room slops, but prove it to our face
The Widow's Uniform is not the soldier-man's disgrace.
   For it's Tommy this, an' Tommy that, an' "Chuck him out, the
   brute!"
   But it's "Saviour of 'is country" when the guns begin to shoot;
   An' it's Tommy this, an' Tommy that, an' anything you please;
   An' Tommy ain't a bloomin' fool – you bet that Tommy sees!

Thomas Atkins, or 'Tommy', is a slang term for the British soldier. Its origins are obscure but it seems to have been chosen by the War Office at the end of the Napoleonic Wars for use in the Soldier's Account Book as an example name for filling out specimen forms. The original generic Tommy was illiterate and signed his forms with an 'X', but in the 1830s Thomas Atkins learned to write and could sign his name to a specimen form. By the middle of the Victorian era, Tommy was commonly used by the British public as a nickname for British enlisted soldiers and non-commissioned officers. Quotes from the poem 'Tommy' have been widely appropriated and are often seen as epigraphs to highlight the civil-military divide.

In spite of this divide the average Briton was proud of his empire's forces and was very aware of the army and navy's victories and triumphs. Tennyson's poem 'The Charge of the Light Brigade' embedded the phrase 'thin red line of heroes' in the public consciousness to describe the stand of the 93rd Highlanders at Balaclava during the Crimean War.

In the 1880s, the British army was coming out of a long period of apathetic government oversight and neglect. Pay was very low and soldiers were charged for losses of equipment and damages to army property. Compared to modern soldiering barracks life was harsh, with no central heating, poorly prepared food, and few outlets for healthy off-duty activities; however, few families in Britain's working class and certainly no poor families enjoyed these amenities either. The men the army recruited were often unemployed and sometimes even criminals on the run. Rich recruiting grounds were found in the slums of the rapidly industrializing cities as well as in destitute and remote rural counties where men could not find work. When Tommy received his meagre pay he went to town and spent much of it on alcohol and fallen women. Queen Victoria, however, a widow since the death of Prince Albert in 1861, increasingly took an active interest in her soldiers, which helped to improve their lot in garrison and in war zones.

By Kipling's time, enlightened leaders in the British Army had begun to regard Tommy as an asset to be cared for and improved. Reading rooms and literacy classes for the illiterate opened. Barracks were improved with better heating and lighting, and better food was introduced. Soldiers were encouraged to live a more moral life.

The problem of what is called the civil-military divide is a common subject of discussion in the staff colleges of the world's armies today. It follows a sine curve-like pattern, which ebbs and flows with the public's support of a nation's wars and military spending. In American history, for example, the civil-military divide widened precipitously as public support for the Vietnam War declined. Famously, American soldiers returning from that war suffered such indignities as being spat on in the airport. Today, in the wake of terrorism and turmoil in the Middle East, members of the fighting forces in the West are generally treated well by their fellow civilian citizens.

Poetry and the Profession of Arms

> I went into a public-'ouse to get a pint o' beer,
> The publican 'e up an' sez, "We serve no red-coats here.

Kipling's most quoted line from 'Tommy' illustrates the contempt that the public once had for men in uniform. Kipling led a one-man, life-long crusade to raise the public's awareness of, and appreciation for, British soldiers.

> We aren't no thin red 'eroes, nor we aren't no blackguards too,
> But single men in barracks, most remarkable like you;
> An' if sometimes our conduck isn't all your fancy paints,
> Why, single men in barracks don't grow into plaster saints

Kipling reminds us that most soldiers are – at least in the sense that every individual in uniform is not really a battlefield hero – not much different from ordinary citizens. But neither are soldiers sinister criminals. And he also notes that young single men are unlikely to conform to model behaviour:

> For it's Tommy this, an' Tommy that, an' "Chuck him out, the brute!"
> But it's "Saviour of 'is country" when the guns begin to shoot;
> An' it's Tommy this, an' Tommy that, an' anything you please;
> An' Tommy ain't a bloomin' fool -- you bet that Tommy sees!

The public under-appreciates its fighting forces until they are needed for war. The scorn that is sometimes heaped on those who serve does not go unnoticed and unremarked by those in uniform.

***

'The Men that Fought at Minden'
In The Lodge of Instruction[1]

Kipling's poem, reflecting on the idea that every soldier starts at the bottom of the profession, was published in the *Pall Mall Gazette* on 9 May 1895 and collected in *The Seven Seas*. The voice is that of an experienced senior soldier giving advice to new recruits.

> The men that fought at Minden, they was rookies in their time –
>   So was them that fought at Waterloo!
> All the 'ole command, yuss, from Minden to Maiwand,
>   They was once dam' sweeps like you!
>
> Then do not be discouraged, 'Eaven is your 'elper,
>   We'll learn you not to forget;
> An' you mustn't swear an' curse, or you'll only catch it worse,
>   For we'll make you soldiers yet!
>
> The men that fought at Minden, they 'ad stocks[2] beneath their chins,
>   Six inch 'igh an' more;
> But fatigue it was their pride, and they *would* not be denied
>   To clean the cook-'ouse floor.

---

[1] This is a side reference to Freemasonry. Kipling had been a Freemason in India and while membership was discouraged in the services many of its vernaculars were widely known.
[2] Stocks: a hard six-inch leather device worn to protect the neck.

The men that fought at Minden, they had anarchistic bombs
    Served to 'em by name of 'and-grenades;[3]
But they got it in the eye (same as you will by-an'-by)
    When they clubbed their field-parades.[4]

The men that fought at Minden, they 'ad buttons up an' down,
    Two-an'-twenty dozen of 'em told;
But they didn't grouse an' shirk at an hour's extry work,
    They kept 'em bright as gold.

The men that fought at Minden, they was armed with musketoons,[5]
    Also, they was drilled by 'alberdiers;[6]
I don't know what they were, but the sergeants took good care
    They washed be'ind their ears.

The men that fought at Minden, they 'ad ever cash in 'and
    Which they did not bank nor save,
But spent it gay an' free on their betters – such as me –
    For the good advice I gave.

The men that fought at Minden, they was civil – yuss, they was –
    Never didn't talk o' rights an' wrongs,
But they got it with the toe (same as you will get it – so!) –
    For interrupting songs.

The men that fought at Minden, they was several other things
    Which I don't remember clear;
But *that's* the reason why, now the six-year men are dry,
    The rooks will stand the beer!

Then do not be discouraged, 'Eaven is your 'elper,
    We'll learn you not to forget;
An' you mustn't swear an' curse, or you'll only catch it worse,
    For we'll make you soldiers yet!

Soldiers yet, if you've got it in you –
    All for the sake of the Core;

---

[3] 'and-grenades: grenadiers in infantry regiments carried hand grenades in the 1700s, but these were
obsolete in Kipling's time (they were revived in the First World War for trench warfare and continue
to be used today).

[4] clubbed their field parades: when a man got out of step in the ranks it sometimes caused the ranks to
club together or compress into a group.

[5] musketoons: large-bore matchlock muskets.

[6] 'alberdiers: in the 1600s sergeants carried a long pike-like weapon with a spike and axe head called
a *halberd*.

Soldiers yet, if we 'ave to skin you –
  Run an' get the beer, Johnny Raw[7] – Johnny Raw!
Ho! run an' get the beer, Johnny Raw!

The Battle of Minden was a famous British victory during the Seven Years War (1759), in which French cavalry were routed by British infantry. The British victory at Waterloo in 1815 saw similar feats of heroism. In both cases the French were defeated, but the battles were closely fought and 'near run' victories. On the other hand, the British were defeated at Maiwand (1880) during the Second Afghan War. Of the 2,500 British officers and men who fought there, some 60 per cent became casualties and two Victoria Crosses were awarded during the retreat to Kandahar. Britons in Kipling's time would recognize these battles as today's readers might recognize Normandy's Pegasus Bridge or Gallipoli's V Beach.

The subtitle 'In the Lodge of Instruction' reflects Kipling's affection for primitive and masculine cultures in which young men must endure a rite of passage. This poem is about the nature of becoming a soldier and he reminds us that even the most grizzled and experienced veterans were once recruits who had to learn everything from scratch. Part of becoming a soldier involved repetitive and largely meaningless tasks, such as cleaning barracks and polishing equipment, as well as not complaining about conditions. Towards the end of training young recruits bought beer for their sergeants; gatherings turned into informal opportunities to inculcate more hard-won battlefield wisdom about soldiering.

Poetry and the Profession of Arms

The men that fought at Minden, they was rookies in their time –
So was them that fought at Waterloo!
All the 'ole command, yuss, from Minden to Maiwand,
They was once dam' sweeps like you!

Every professional soldier was, at one time, a rookie who started at the bottom, be they a private or a lieutenant. Kipling would caution against the arrogance of position based on longevity or experience and reminds us that nothing has changed from the 1700s to today.

***

---

[7] Johnny Raw: a nickname used for the newest untrained soldier.

The 'eathen

A classic poem about the duties and the role of non-commissioned officers published in *MacClure's Magazine* in September 1896 and collected in *The Seven Seas*. The voice is that of a senior sergeant reflecting on the nature of his service.

> The 'eathen in 'is blindness bows down to wood an' stone;
> 'E don't obey no orders unless they is 'is own;
> 'E keeps 'is side-arms awful: 'e leaves 'em all about,
> An' then comes up the Regiment an' pokes the 'eathen out.
>
>> All along o' dirtiness, all along o' mess,
>> All along o' doin' things rather-more-or-less,
>> All along of abby-nay, kul, an' hazar-ho,[1]
>> Mind you keep your rifle an' yourself jus' so!
>
> The young recruit is 'aughty – 'e draf's from Gawd knows where;
> They bid 'im show 'is stockin's an' lay 'is mattress square;
> 'E calls it bloomin' nonsense – 'e doesn't know, no more –
> An' then up comes 'is Company an' kicks 'im round the floor!
>
> The young recruit is 'ammered – 'e takes it very hard;
> 'E 'angs 'is 'ead an' mutters – 'e sulks about the yard;
> 'E talks o' "cruel tyrants" which 'e'll swing for by-an'-by,
> An' the others 'ears an' mocks 'im, an' the boy goes orf to cry.
>
> The young recruit is silly – 'e thinks o' suicide.
> 'E's lost 'is gutter-devil; 'e 'asn't got 'is pride;
> But day by day they kicks 'im, which 'elps 'im on a bit,
> Till 'e finds 'isself one mornin' with a full an' proper kit.
>
>> Gettin' clear o' dirtiness, gettin' done with mess,
>> Gettin' shut o' doin' things rather-more-or-less;
>> Not so fond of abby-nay, kul, nor hazar-ho,
>> Learns to keep 'is rifle an 'isself jus'so!
>
> The young recruit is 'appy – 'e throws a chest to suit;
> You see 'im grow mustaches; you 'ear 'im slap 'is boot.[2]
> 'E learns to drop the "bloodies" from every word 'e slings,
> An 'e shows an 'ealthy brisket when 'e strips for bars an' rings.[3]

---

[1] *Abby-nay*: Not now; *kul*: Tomorrow; *hazar-ho*: Wait a bit.

[2] slap 'is boot: Sergeants carried a swagger cane which they slapped on their boot to emphasize a point.

[3] bars an' rings: regimental gymnasiums had exercise equipment such as bars and rings.

The cruel-tyrant-sergeants they watch 'im 'arf a year;
They watch 'im with 'is comrades, they watch 'im with 'is beer;
They watch 'im with the women at the regimental dance,
And the cruel-tyrant-sergeants send 'is name along for "Lance."[4]

An' now 'e's 'arf o' nothin', an' all a private yet,
'Is room they up an' rags 'im to see what they will get.
They rags 'im low an' cunnin', each dirty trick they can,
But 'e learns to sweat 'is temper an 'e learns to sweat 'is man.

An', last, a Colour-Sergeant, as such to be obeyed,
'E schools 'is men at cricket, 'e tells 'em on parade,
They sees 'im quick an 'andy, uncommon set an' smart,
An' so 'e talks to orficers which 'ave the Core at 'eart.

'E learns to do 'is watchin' without it showin' plain;
'E learns to save a dummy, an' shove 'im straight again;
'E learns to check a ranker that's buyin' leave to shirk;
An 'e learns to make men like 'im so they'll learn to like their work.

An' when it comes to marchin' he'll see their socks are right,
An' when it comes: to action 'e shows 'em how to sight.
'E knows their ways of thinkin' and just what's in their mind;
'E knows when they are takin' on an' when they've fell be'ind.

'E knows each talkin' corp'ral that leads a squad astray;
'E feels 'is innards 'eavin', 'is bowels givin' way;
'E sees the blue-white faces all tryin 'ard to grin,
An 'e stands an' waits an' suffers till it's time to cap 'em in.

An' now the hugly bullets come peckin' through the dust,
An' no one wants to face 'em, but every beggar must;
So, like a man in irons, which isn't glad to go,
They moves 'em off by companies uncommon stiff an' slow.

Of all 'is five years' schoolin' they don't remember much
Excep' the not retreatin', the step an' keepin' touch.
It looks like teachin' wasted when they duck an' spread an 'op –
But if 'e 'adn't learned 'em they'd be all about the shop.

An' now it's "Oo goes backward?" an' now it's "Oo comes on?"
And now it's "Get the doolies," an' now the Captain's gone;

---

4 "Lance": promoted to Lance Corporal or junior non-commissioned officer.

An' now it's bloody murder, but all the while they 'ear
'Is voice, the same as barrick-drill, a-shepherdin' the rear.

'E's just as sick as they are, 'is 'eart is like to split,
But 'e works 'em, works 'em, works 'em till he feels them take the bit;
The rest is 'oldin' steady till the watchful bugles play,
An 'e lifts 'em, lifts 'em, lifts 'em through the charge that wins the day!

The 'eathen in 'is blindness bows down to wood an' stone –
'E don't obey no orders unless they is 'is own.
The 'eathen in 'is blindness must end where 'e began
But the backbone of the Army is the Non-commissioned Man!

Keep away from dirtiness – keep away from mess,
Don't get into doin' things rather-more-or-less!
Let's ha' done with abby-nay, kul, and hazar-ho;
Mind you keep your rifle an' yourself jus' so!

The British army has a long tradition of producing the finest non-commissioned officers in the world (examples of these ranks are lance corporals, corporals, sergeants, colour-sergeants, and sergeants major). In civilian terms non-commissioned officers function as first-line supervisors and are part of the 'blue collar' work force. They often come from working-class backgrounds and are not as highly educated as their commissioned officer counterparts. In modern films British non-commissioned officers are typecast as large, brave and stalwart men of few words, who set an example by their complete disregard for the dangers of combat.

'The 'eathen' is Kipling's tribute to British non-commissioned officers, who are rightly regarded as the finest in the world. The 'eathen himself is a metaphor for an untrained raw recruit who brings his sloppy civilian habits and behaviour into the army. The army and its sergeants then bend and break the heathen recruit, transforming him into a disciplined fighting man.

Poetry and the Profession of Arms

All along of abby-nay, kul, an' hazar-ho,
Mind you keep your rifle an' yourself jus' so!

These particular words are Hindustani terms assimilated into the regimental vocabulary reflecting the slip-shod and undisciplined habits of primitive tribesmen. Soldiers stationed in distant lands often pick up the words of the local peoples. These tend to be directive or exclamatory terms. The American soldiers in Vietnam, for example, commonly used Vietnamese words such as *đại úy* (lieutenant) and *để đi một* (move out). 'The 'eathen' reminds recruits to discard their sloppy civilian habits as quickly as possible and care for their rifle and kit like soldiers.

> But day by day they kicks 'im, which 'elps 'im on a bit,
> Till 'e finds 'isself one mornin' with a full an' proper kit.

The nature of basic training is the daily repetition of tasks, which are closely supervised by sergeants. And somewhere along in the process, much to his own surprise, a recruit finds that he has mastered the basics of soldiering.

> Of all 'is five years' schoolin' they don't remember much.
> Excep' the not retreatin', the step an' keepin' touch.

The chaotic and dangerous nature of combat is such that new soldiers sometimes forget what they have learned in training. The battlefield is not a place for deliberate and complex thinking; rather it is the domain of immediacy and action. In order to overcome the confusion of the heat of battle, modern battle drills seek to instil instinctive behaviours that become second nature in combat.

> 'E's just as sick as they are, 'is 'eart is like to split,
> But 'e works 'em, works 'em, works 'em till he feels them take the bit;
> The rest is 'oldin' steady till the watchful bugles play,
> An 'e lifts 'em, lifts 'em, lifts 'em through the charge that wins the day!

The affection with which sergeants care for their men can be an obstacle to success in combat. Sergeants realize that, at all costs, the mission comes first at the expense of the lives of the men they have trained, and leaders must distance themselves from personal relationships in the heat of combat. Moreover, it is the sergeant's job to inspire soldiers and lift their spirits in order to defeat their enemies.

> The 'eathen in 'is blindness must end where 'e began.
> But the backbone of the Army is the Non-commissioned Man!

Kipling's choice of the phrase 'the backbone of the army' reflects the long-held idea that non-commissioned officers are the stiff spine around which the rest of the army is built. He notes that the incoming flow of new recruits is an endless stream with no beginning and no end, but throughout this process it is the non-commissioned officer who keeps the army together.

***

The Shut-Eye Sentry

A poem about learning the relationship between enlisted men and the officer corps, published in *The Seven Seas and Further Barrack Room Ballads* in 1896. The voice is that of a senior sergeant.

Sez the Junior Orderly Sergeant
To the Senior Orderly Man:
"Our Orderly Orf'cer's *hokee-mut*,[1]
You 'elp 'im all you can.
For the wine was old and the night is cold,
An' the best we may go wrong,
So, 'fore 'e gits to the sentry-box,
You pass the word along".

So it was "Rounds! What Rounds?" at two of a frosty night,
'E's 'oldin' on by the sergeant's sash, but, sentry, shut your eye.
An' it was "Pass! All's well! Oh, ain't 'e drippin' tight!
'E'll need an affidavit pretty badly by-an'-by."

The moon was white on the barricks,
The road was white an' wide,
An' the Orderly Orf'cer took it all,
An' the ten-foot ditch beside.
An' the corporal pulled an' the sergeant pushed,
An' the three they danced along,
But I'd shut my eyes in the sentry-box,
So I didn't see nothin' wrong.

Though it was "Rounds! What Rounds?" O corporal, 'old 'im up!
'E's usin' 'is cap as it shouldn't be used, but, sentry, shut your eye.
An' it was "Pass! All's well! Ho, shun the foamin' cup!
'E'll need," etc.

'Twas after four in the mornin';
We 'ad to stop the fun,
An' we sent 'im 'ome on a bullock-cart,
With 'is belt an' stock undone;
But we sluiced 'im down an' we washed 'im out,
An' a first-class job we made,
When we saved 'im, smart as a bombardier,
For six-o'clock parade.

It 'ad been "Rounds! What Rounds? Oh, shove 'im straight again!
'E's usin' 'is sword for a bicycle, but, sentry, shut your eye."

---

[1] *hokee-mut*: Very drunk

An' it was "Pass! All's well! 'E's called me 'Darlin' Jane!'
'E'll need," etc.

The drill was long an' 'eavy,
The sky was 'ot an' blue,
An' 'is eye was wild an' 'is 'air was wet,
But 'is sergeant pulled 'im through.
Our men was good old trusties –
They'd done it on their 'ead;
But you ought to 'ave 'eard 'em markin' time
To 'ide the things 'e said!

For it was "Right flank – wheel!" for "'Alt, an' stand at ease!"
An' "Left extend!" for "Centre close!" O marker, shut your eye!
An' it was, "'Ere, sir, 'ere! before the Colonel sees!"
So he needed affidavits pretty badly by-an'-by.

There was two-an'-thirty sergeants,
There was corp'rals forty-one,
There was just nine 'undred rank an' file
To swear to a touch o' sun.
There was me 'e'd kissed in the sentry-box,
As I 'ave not told in my song,
But I took my oath, which were Bible truth,
I 'adn't seen nothin' wrong.

There's them that's 'ot an' 'aughty,
There's them that's cold an' 'ard,
But there comes a night when the best gets tight,
And then turns out the Guard.
I've seen them 'ide their liquor
In every kind o' way,
But most depends on makin' friends
With Privit Thomas A.!

When it is "Rounds! What Rounds? 'E's breathin' through 'is nose.
'E's reelin', rollin', roarin' tight, but, sentry, shut your eye."
An' it is "Pass! All's well!" An' that's the way it goes:
We'll 'elp 'im for 'is mother, an' 'e'll 'elp us by-an'-by!

In the British Army an 'Orderly Orf'cer' is appointed for a twenty-four
hour period. His job is to supervise the garrison guard as well as other tasks
such as checking the mess hall, conducting guard mount, and inspecting the
guard posts on a rotational schedule called 'rounds'. The 'Orderly Orf'cer' is

normally a lieutenant or junior officer, who is often inexperienced in the ways of the army.

Poetry and the Profession of Arms

> "Our Orderly Orf'cer's *hokee-mut*,
> You 'elp 'im all you can."
> For the wine was old and the night is cold,
> An' the best we may go wrong,

While drunkenness on duty is a rarity in today's army, it is common for sergeants and soldiers to look after their junior officers. It is a given that an informal responsibility of a platoon sergeant is to train his platoon commander (who is a newly commissioned lieutenant) in the ways of the real army. It is also not uncommon for the enlisted ranks to assist favoured lieutenants who err – sometimes to the extent of covering up their mistakes. This is especially true when the error is due to inexperience rather than incompetence or malicious intent.

> But most depends on makin' friends,
> With Privit Thomas A.!

While officers are not 'friends' (as we understand that term) with the enlisted ranks, a certain affection and respect between officers and men is necessary for a unit to reach its full military effectiveness. The line between friendship and respect is a thin one and not easily discovered. Experienced officers understand this, but it must be learned the hard way by young officers.

> An' it is "Pass! All's well!" An' that's the way it goes:
> We'll 'elp 'im for 'is mother, an' 'e'll 'elp us by-an'-by!

In the end the respect and affection between the officer corps and the enlisted ranks is a two-way street. Acts of kindness based on respect are remembered and returned with interest. It is to the advantage of the soldier to occasionally 'look the other way' in the hopes that a lesson learned by a fledgling lieutenant will be returned in kind at a later date.

Chapter 2

Thomas Atkins Goes To War

Introduction

Kipling himself, at this time in his early life, was an intensely patriotic man who held his fellow Britons – many of whom were what we might call today 'sunshine patriots' – in great scorn. He was contemptuous of those who loudly and publicly supported war, while at the same time failed to commit themselves and their families to the effort. The theme of this chapter is deployment and what happens after soldiers are trained and sent into combat. It focuses on the experiences of soldiers going off to war, as well as the effects on those left behind.

Kipling also recognized that those left behind – wives and children – formed an important part of the story and the national narrative. It is true that most of the junior officers and men in Victoria's army were bachelors, but it is also true that many of the senior officers and sergeants were married. These regimental wives and families were relatively few in number and often travelled with the regiment to distant stations.

However, the creation of a formal reserve structure of militia and volunteer battalions linked to army regiments under the Childers Reforms of 1881 led to a situation where many of Britain's citizen-soldiers were married. More often than not these reservists were older and had substantial responsibilities in their civilian professions. Until the Boer War these men were not mobilized and paid lip service to the thought of being called to the colours. No institutional support systems for families existed, nor were the regimental depots prepared

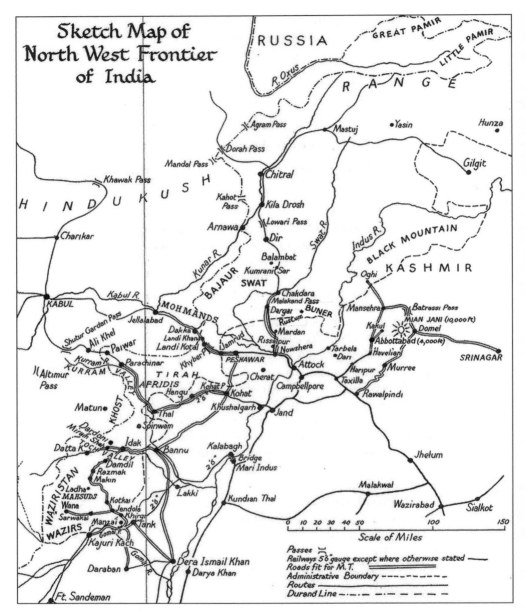

Sketch map, North West Frontier. Readers will note the city of Peshawar in the centre, which sits at the eastern end of the Khyber Pass. Of interest are the names and locations of many of the tribal entities which appear throughout Kipling's verses. Map courtesy of the Gill family.

to assist families in need. Throughout his life Kipling vigorously campaigned to raise public awareness of the plights of deployed soldiers and the families they left behind.

Kipling also addressed the issue of whether married men in combat arms regiments were less bold than single men on the battlefield. He felt that mature men with family responsibilities were less prone to take risks and this hurt the collective well-being of line battalions in combat. The poems I have selected for this chapter are 'The Young British Soldier', 'The Absent-Minded Beggar', 'Troopin'', and 'The Married Man'. Other similar poems which may be found on the Kipling Society's superb website and which I recommend to the reader are 'Gentleman-Rankers' and '"Birds of Prey" March'.

The Young British Soldier

This well-known poem was first published in *Departmental Ditties, Barrack-Room Ballads and Other Verses* in 1890, but was remarked on and quoted extensively later in the twenty-first century when NATO forces deployed to Afghanistan. The voice is that of a senior non-commissioned officer observing what happens when a recruit goes to war and giving him advice.

When the 'arf-made recruity goes out to the East
'E acts like a babe an' 'e drinks like a beast,
An' 'e wonders because 'e is frequent deceased
   Ere 'e's fit for to serve as a soldier.
     Serve, serve, serve as a soldier,
     Serve, serve, serve as a soldier,
     Serve, serve, serve as a soldier,
       So-oldier *OF* the Queen!
Now all you recruities what's drafted to-day,
You shut up your rag-box an' 'ark to my lay,
An' I'll sing you a soldier as far as I may:
   A soldier what's fit for a soldier.
     Fit, fit, fit for a soldier...
First mind you steer clear o' the grog-sellers' huts,
For they sell you Fixed Bay'nets that rots out your guts –
Ay, drink that 'ud eat the live steel from your butts –
   An' it's bad for the young British soldier.
     Bad, bad, bad for the soldier...
When the cholera comes – as it will past a doubt –
Keep out of the wet and don't go on the shout,
For the sickness gets in as the liquor dies out,
   An' it crumples the young British soldier.
     Crum-, crum-, crumples the soldier...

But the worst o' your foes is the sun over'ead:
You *must* wear your 'elmet for all that is said:
If 'e finds you uncovered 'e'll knock you down dead,
    An' you'll die like a fool of a soldier.
       Fool, fool, fool of a soldier...
If you're cast for fatigue by a sergeant unkind,
Don't grouse like a woman nor crack on nor blind;
Be handy and civil, and then you will find
    That it's beer for the young British soldier.
       Beer, beer, beer for the soldier...
Now, if you must marry, take care she is old –
A troop-sergeant's widow's the nicest I'm told,
For beauty won't help if your rations is cold,
    Nor love ain't enough for a soldier.
       'Nough, 'nough, 'nough for a soldier...
If the wife should go wrong with a comrade, be loath
To shoot when you catch 'em – you'll swing, on my oath! –
Make 'im take 'er and keep 'er: that's Hell for them both,
    An' you're shut o' the curse of a soldier.
       Curse, curse, curse of a soldier...
When first under fire an' you're wishful to duck,
Don't look nor take 'eed at the man that is struck,
Be thankful you're livin', and trust to your luck
    And march to your front like a soldier.
       Front, front, front like a soldier...
When 'arf of your bullets fly wide in the ditch,
Don't call your Martini[1] a cross-eyed old bitch;
She's human as you are – you treat her as sich,
    An' she'll fight for the young British soldier.
       Fight, fight, fight for the soldier...
When shakin' their bustles like ladies so fine,
The guns o' the enemy wheel into line,
Shoot low at the limbers an' don't mind the shine,
    For noise never startles the soldier.
       Start-, start-, startles the soldier...
If your officer's dead and the sergeants look white,
Remember it's ruin to run from a fight:
So take open order, lie down, and sit tight,
    And wait for supports like a soldier.
       Wait, wait, wait like a soldier...
When you're wounded and left on Afghanistan's plains,

---

[1] The Martini-Henry rifle was a breech-loaded rifle sighted to 1,800 yards but rarely used at that extreme range. Production began in 1871 and the Martini (in several variants and marks) was the British Army's standard infantry weapon into the twentieth century.

And the women come out to cut up what remains,
Jest roll to your rifle and blow out your brains
    An' go to your Gawd like a soldier.
      Go, go, go like a soldier,
      Go, go, go like a soldier,
      Go, go, go like a soldier,
        So-oldier *of* the Queen!

There is considerable humour and tongue-in-cheek irony in this particular poem about what is important and what is not important for soldiers to remember when sent to war. There is 'a boatload' of advice built on the bedrock of experience in 'The Young British Soldier' about imbibing strong drink, sickness in camp, proper dress in the field, performing unpleasant duties, getting married, what it's like to come under fire, and finally what to do when under fire.

Poetry and the Profession of Arms

    When the 'arf-made recruity goes out to the East
    'E acts like a babe an' 'e drinks like a beast,
    An' 'e wonders because 'e is frequent deceased

Kipling's turn of the phrase speaks to a moment of pause when a young soldier reflects on why so many of his comrades are dead. In the film *Forrest Gump*, Lieutenant Dan's advice to Forrest and Bubba (newly in country in Vietnam) is "Don't do anything stupid that will get yourself killed." In fact, experienced soldiers know that many men become casualties not because the enemy was better than them, but because they made simple and easily preventable mistakes.

    If your officer's dead and the sergeants look white,
    Remember it's ruin to run from a fight:
    So take open order, lie down, and sit tight,
      And wait for supports like a soldier.

Discipline wins battles and saves lives. When things are the darkest and the enemy is upon you, disciplined fighting soldiers bear down and focus on the battle at hand.

    When you're wounded and left on Afghanistan's plains,
    And the women come out to cut up what remains,
    Jest roll to your rifle and blow out your brains
      An' go to your Gawd like a soldier.

This is the most frequently quoted and widely known stanza of 'The Young British Soldier'. More than a few of George Armstrong Custer's men at the Battle of the Little Big Horn did, in fact, save the last bullet for themselves rather than be taken alive by the American Indians. Modern sensibilities demand that wounded soldiers are not left behind on the battlefield, and both the British and American armies today go to extreme lengths to evacuate wounded.

***

The Absent-Minded Beggar

Kipling wrote this poem to raise money for the families of reservists sent to the Boer War (1899–1902), and it was first published in the *Daily Mail* on 31 October 1899. Over £300,000 was raised. The voice is Kipling's own.

> When you've shouted "Rule Britannia", when you've sung "God save the Queen",
>> When you've finished killing Kruger[1] with your mouth,
> Will you kindly drop a shilling in my little tambourine
>> For a gentleman in khaki going South?
> He's an absent-minded beggar, and his weaknesses are great –
>> But we and Paul must take him as we find him –
> He is out on active service, wiping something of a slate –
>> And he's left a lot of little things behind him!
> Duke's son – cook's son – son of a hundred kings –
>> (Fifty thousand horse and foot going to Table Bay!)[2]
> Each of 'em doing his country's work
>> (and who's to look after his things?)
> Pass the hat for your credit's sake,
>>> and pay – pay – pay!
> There are girls he married secret, asking no permission to,
>> For he knew he wouldn't get it if he did.
> There is gas and coals and vittles, and the house-rent falling due,
>> And it's more than rather likely there's a kid.
> There are girls he walked with casual. They'll be sorry now he's gone,
>> For an absent-minded beggar they will find him,
> But it ain't the time for sermons with the winter coming on.
>> We must help the girl that Tommy's left behind him!

---

[1] Paul Kruger (1825–1904): President of the South African Republic during the Second Anglo-Boer War and well-known world figure. His nickname was *Omm Paul* (Uncle Paul).

[2] Table Bay: the harbour at Capetown which was the port of debarkation for British Army units deploying to South Africa.

Cook's son – Duke's son – son of a belted Earl –
   Son of Lambeth publican – it's all the same today!
Each of them doing the country's work
    (and who's to look after the girl?)
Pass the hat for your credit's sake,
        and pay – pay – pay!
They are families by thousands, far too proud to beg or speak,
   And they'll put their sticks and bedding up the spout,
And they'll live on half o' nothing, paid 'em punctual once a week,
   'Cause the man that earns the wage is ordered out.
He's an absent-minded beggar, but he heard his country call,
   And his reg'ment didn't need to send to find him!
He chucked his job and joint it – so the job before us all
   Is to help the home that Tommy's left behind him!
Duke's job – cook's job – gardener, baronet, groom,
   Mews or palace or paper-shop, there's someone gone away!
Each of 'em doing his country's work
    (and who's to look after the room?)
Pass the hat and for your credit's sake,
        and pay – pay – pay!
Let us manage so as later, we can look him in the face,
   And tell him – what he'd very much prefer –
That, while he saved the Empire, his employer saved his place,
   And his mates (that's you and me) looked out for her.
He's an absent-minded beggar and he may forget it all,
   But we do not want his kiddies to remind him
That we sent 'em to the workhouse while their daddy hammered
Paul,
   So we'll help the homes that Tommy left behind him!
Cook's home – Duke's home – home of millionaire,
   (Fifty thousand horse and foot going to Table Bay!)
Each of 'em doing his country's work
    (and what have you got to spare?)
Pass the hat for your credit's sake
       and pay – pay – pay!

Secretary of State for War Edward Cardwell orchestrated an important series
of army reforms which were designed to standardize the army and, more
importantly, create a reserve force of trained soldiers similar to the Germans.
Notably, Cardwell pushed the Army Enlistment Act of 1870 (commonly
known as the Short Service Act) through parliament. This reduced the term
of enlistment from twelve years to six years, after which a man had the option
of continuing regular service or serving in the reserves for the remainder of

the enlistment period of twelve years. The Short Service Act created a trained body of reservists that Britain could call on in a period of emergency.

The Childers Reforms of 1881, orchestrated by Secretary of State for War Hugh Childers, established a formal system of reserve battalions, which were linked directly to the county-based regular army regiments. In theory each infantry regiment had two regular battalions and two militia battalions (except in Ireland where each regiment had three militia battalions). In the rifle regiments the reservist battalions were called volunteer battalions. In practice there were discrepancies as some regiments only had a single battalion. Responsibility for training the militia and reserves then fell to the regimental depot.

The manpower needed for the Second Anglo-Boer War drained the pool of battalions available for deployment to South Africa and the War Office asked the soldiers of the volunteer units to answer the call to the colours. Thousands responded and the volunteer and yeomanry battalions formed Volunteer Active Service Companies that joined their regiments in South Africa. This was Britain's first overseas deployment of its reserve forces. Under Secretary of State for War Richard Haldane's reforms, the Territorial and Reserve Forces Act of 1907 converted the volunteer and yeomanry units into the modern Territorial Force, while the militia was disbanded to form the Special Reserve of the regular army.

Kipling recognized that patriotic civilians volunteering for duty overseas were most often married professionals with responsibilities for families and full-time jobs. Sadly, army pay was far less than civilian pay, thereby imposing an immediate hardship on the families left behind in Britain. Moreover, no legislation guaranteeing the veteran his old job when he returned yet existed. He also recognized that British society was generally unaware of the plight of the families and he also saw the supreme irony of flag-waving 'sunshine patriots' who were keen to send off the army when they themselves didn't have to go.

Kipling recognized that the army was a great leveller of the static socio-economic classes that were a signature of life in Britain. And he also thought that many of the working-class families would do without rather than ask for charity. Finally, the phrase 'the absent-minded beggar' conveys an affectionate regard for a reservist, who volunteered to serve, but perhaps didn't stop to consider the consequences or the effect of his patriotism on his family.

Poetry and the Profession of Arms

> When you've shouted "Rule Britannia," when you've sung "God save the Queen,"
> When you've finished killing Kruger with your mouth,
> Will you kindly drop a shilling in my little tambourine
> For a gentleman in khaki going South?

Many soldiers will see the irony of the 'sunshine patriot' who demonstrates publicly and vocally in support of the nation's wars. Kipling uses guilt and embarrassment to remind Britain of society's obligation to the families of those deployed to South Africa.

> Cook's son – Duke's son – son of a belted Earl –
> Son of Lambeth publican – it's all the same today!

Military service is the supreme leveller and breaker of the class barriers that characterize society. Moreover, service in a combat zone imposes further imperatives that force soldiers together regardless of their backgrounds, education, or place in society. In the end, wherever a soldier began in civilian life, they and their families now carry the dignity and elevation of a position deserving of the recognition of society.

> That, while he saved the Empire, his employer saved his place,
>   And his mates (that's you and me) looked out for her.
> He's an absent-minded beggar and he may forget it all,
>   But we do not want his kiddies to remind him
> That we sent 'em to the workhouse while their daddy hammered Paul,

Reservists called to the colours and sent to a combat war for an extended deployment have more on their minds than the simple dangers and exigencies of combat. They worry about whether they will have a job when they return and they worry about their families.

***

Troopin'

(Our Army in the East)

Kipling published this poem about returning home from an overseas posting in the *Scots Observer* on 17 May 1890. It was collected in *Departmental Ditties*. The voice is that of a six-year recruit whose enlistment has expired.

> Troopin', troopin', troopin' to the sea:
> 'Ere's September come again – the six-year men are free.
> O leave the dead be'ind us, for they cannot come away
> To where the ship's a-coalin' up that takes us 'ome to-day.
>   We're goin' 'ome, we're goin' 'ome,
>   Our ship is at the shore,
>   An' you must pack your 'aversack,
>   For we won't come back no more.

> Ho, don't you grieve for me,
>   My lovely Mary-Ann,
> For I'll marry you yit on a fourp'ny bit
>   As a time-expired man.

The *Malabar*'s in 'arbour with the ~*Jumner*~[1] at 'er tail,
An' the time-expired's waitin' of 'is orders for to sail.
Ho! the weary waitin' when on Khyber 'ills we lay,
But the time-expired's waitin' of 'is orders 'ome to-day.

They'll turn us out at Portsmouth wharf in cold an' wet an' rain,
All wearin' Injian cotton kit, but we will not complain;
They'll kill us of pneumonia – for that's their little way –
But damn the chills and fever, men, we're goin' 'ome to-day!

Troopin', troopin', winter's round again!
See the new draf's pourin' in for the old campaign;
Ho, you poor recruities, but you've got to earn your pay –
What's the last from Lunnon,[2] lads? We're goin' there to-day.

Troopin', troopin', give another cheer –
'Ere's to English women an' a quart of English beer.
The Colonel an' the regiment an' all who've got to stay,
Gawd's mercy strike 'em gentle – Whoop! we're goin' 'ome to-day.
>   We're goin' 'ome, we're goin' 'ome,
>   Our ship is at the shore,
>   An' you must pack your 'aversack,
>   For we won't come back no more.
>   Ho, don't you grieve for me,
>   My lovely Mary-Ann,
>   For I'll marry you yit on a fourp'ny bit
>   As a time-expired man.

Unlike extended modern wars such as the First and Second World Wars, wherein soldiers went to war and did not return until the war was finished, soldiers in Kipling's time had a defined termination date for their enlistment. Cardwell's Short Service Act of 1870 established the initial term of enlistment at six years. Men sent overseas to routine garrison assignments in the empire knew this and could count on going home. However, soldiers sent on the Queen's expeditionary and punitive campaigns were there from start to finish (the Boer War fell into this category).

---

[1] Jumner: HMS *Jumna*, a troopship making scheduled runs to India, named after a river in India.
[2] Lunnon: Slang pronunciation of London.

The movement of large groups of replacements were known as drafts and these were carried out in the days of sailing ships according to the most advantageous seasonal winds. The rhythm of these drafts continued into the age of steam when the wind became irrelevant to shipping. In Kipling's time the Royal Navy ran the troopships, which were therefore all designated HMS *So-and-So*. There were five Indian troopships (*Malabar, Jumna, Crocodile, Serapis*, and *Euphrates*), and they ran scheduled trooping trips to India – basically Portsmouth to Bombay and back – during the trooping season, September to April. They took just over four weeks each way: one of the five was always in refit, so the service was maintained by the other four, leaving Portsmouth at roughly three-week intervals. They all called at Malta, Port Said and Suez: some called additionally at Queenstown (the name then for Cobh, the port of Cork), and/or Gibraltar and/or Aden. Each ship did two or three complete trips each season.

Poetry and the Profession of Arms

> The *Malabar*'s in 'arbour with the ~*Jumner*~ at 'er tail,
> An' the time-expired's waitin' of 'is orders for to sail.

Personnel in combat zones and on overseas postings today know when they are going home. Many will keep 'short-timer's' calendars on which they block out or cross off with a large X the days that pass by.

> Troopin', troopin', winter's round again!
> See the new draf's pourin' in for the old campaign;
> Ho, you poor recruities, but you've got to earn your pay –
> What's the last from Lunnon, lads? We're goin' there to-day.

The incoming drafts and replacements invariably meet the outgoing soldiers, and it is not uncommon for the men going home to joke and remind the newly arrived that 'we are going home and you are not.' They point out that winter is coming – no small event in the Khyber Hills or in the mountains of the frontier.

> Ho, don't you grieve for me,
>   My lovely Mary-Ann,
> For I'll marry you yit on a fourp'ny bit
>   As a time-expired man.

Soldiers deployed overseas dream of home and they make plans for the future. A combat unit such as an infantry platoon is a very small world and conversation often drifts to what they will do when they finally get home. By the end of the deployment everybody knows what their comrades plan to do when they get off the 'freedom bird' at RAF Brize Norton or Pope Air Force Base. For some it may involve going back to school or eating a favourite meal, but for many it involves a sweetheart and getting married.

***

The Married Man

Reservist of the Line[1]

This poem was probably written in 1901, but was published as one of sixteen 'Service Songs' at the close of *The Five Nations* in 1905. The voice is that of an experienced regular soldier who has served in combat with the recalled reservists in the Boer War.

> The bachelor 'e fights for one
>> As joyful as can be;
> But the married man don't call it fun,
>> Because 'e fights for three –
> For 'Im an' 'Er an' It
>> (An' Two an' One make Three)
> 'E wants to finish 'is little bit,
>> An' e' wants to go 'ome to 'is tea!
>
> The bachelor pokes up 'is 'ead
>> To see if you are gone;
> But the married man lies down instead,
>> An' waits till the sights come on,
> For 'im an' 'Er an' a hit
>> (Direct or recochee)
> 'E wants to finish 'is little bit,
>> An' 'e wants to go 'ome to 'is tea.
>
> The bachelor will miss you clear
>> To fight another day;
> But the married man, 'e says "No fear!"
>> 'E wants you out of the way
> Of 'Im an' 'Er an' It
>> (An' 'is road to 'is farm or the sea),
> 'E wants to finish 'is little bit,
>> An' 'e wants to go 'ome to 'is tea.

---

[1] Of the Line: refers to infantry regiments of the line other than guards. Kipling makes a distinction between those in the line who engage in close combat with the enemy and those in support positions behind the line.

The bachelor 'e fights 'is fight
    An' streches out an' snores;
But the married man sits up all night –
    For 'e don't like out-o'-doors.
'E'll strain an' listen an' peer
    An' give the first alarm –
For the sake o' the breathin' 'e's used to 'ear,
    An' the 'ead on the thick of 'is arm.

The bachelor may risk 'is 'ide
    To 'elp you when you're downed;
But the married man will wait beside
    Till the ambulance comes round.
'E'll take your 'ome address
    An' all you've time to say,
Or if 'e sees there's 'ope, 'e'll press
    Your art'ry 'alf the day –

For 'Im an' 'Er an' It
    (An' One from Three leaves Two),
For 'e knows you wanted to finish your bit,
    An' 'e knows 'oo's wantin' you.
Yes, 'Im an' 'Er an' It
    (Our 'only One in Three),
We're all of us anxious to finish our bit,
    An' we want to get 'ome to our tea!

Yes, It an' 'Er an' 'Im,
    Which often makes me think
The married man must sink or swim
    An' – 'e can't afford to sink!
Oh, 'Im an' It an' 'Er
    Since Adam an' Eve began!
So I'd rather fight with the bache*ler*
    An' be nursed by the married man!

Men who took advantage of the six-year enlistment went into the reserve forces with the understanding that, if mobilized or called to the colours, they would immediately leave their jobs, homes, and families and return to service. Those who were trained as infantry, cavalry, or artillerymen could expect to find themselves in close combat with the enemy and thus at great risk. During the Boer War all reservists were recalled to the colours.

Poetry and the Profession of Arms

> The bachelor 'e fights for one
>> As joyful as can be;
> But the married man don't call it fun,
>> Because 'e fights for three –

Does a single soldier fight harder and with less regard for his own safety than a married soldier? This poem states explicitly that this is a battlefield truth. Serving professionals today may have formed opinions about this based on anecdotal personal observations, but the author knows of no serious studies which may support this view or its opposites. The received wisdom in Kipling's day was strongly supportive of this theme.

> The bachelor may risk 'is 'ide
>> To 'elp you when you're downed;
> But the married man will wait beside
>> Till the ambulance comes round.

Will a married man be more cautious? One thing that is true today is that commanders and leaders will sometimes consider a soldier's marital status when assigning dangerous or potentially hazardous duties. Moreover, in garrison single soldiers are far more likely to be assigned duties on Christmas Day!

> Oh, 'Im an' It an' 'Er
>> Since Adam an' Eve began!
> So I'd rather fight with the bachel*er*
>> An' be nursed by the married man!

Kipling believed that the army needed its reservists, but he thought they belonged in the service support branches (such as field hospitals) and not in front-line units. While many reservists serve in line units today, in many modern armies the bulk of the reservists are to be found in the rear areas in service support units. Importantly, the issue today is not their courage, or their marital status, but the level of training and physical endurance required of line combat units.

Chapter 3

War Experienced – India and Burma

Introduction

Many readers will immediately associate Rudyard Kipling with India and Burma because of such classic verses as 'Gunga Din' and stories like *The Jungle Book*. Kipling was born in Bombay in 1865 and was left in England with the Holloway family in Southsea from 1871 to 1877. He returned to India for six months and then spent an unhappy three-year stint being educated in England. Kipling then lived in British India (the Raj) from autumn 1882 until 1889, giving him eleven years all told in India. During his time in India, Britain launched at least fifteen expeditionary campaigns in what are now Afghanistan, Burma, India, and Pakistan, as well as fighting the Second Afghan War and the Third Burma War. It is beyond doubt that growing up in his formative years amid such military activity affected Kipling's worldview.

This chapter highlights the uniqueness of the Afghanistan–Northwest Frontier–Burma theatre of operations. These areas in Kipling's time were inhabited by tribal groups led by chieftains and we would call them today 'ungoverned spaces' because of an absence of security provided by centralized government. The adversaries the army faced used irregular tactics, often employing ambushes or sniping. Such tactics come unexpectedly out of the blue, surprising those affected. In such a tactical environment leaders, officers and non-commissioned officers (and today frequently radiomen as well), are the primary targets for the enemy. The poems I have selected for this chapter are 'Arithmetic on the Frontier', '"Bobs"', 'Gunga Din', 'The Grave of the

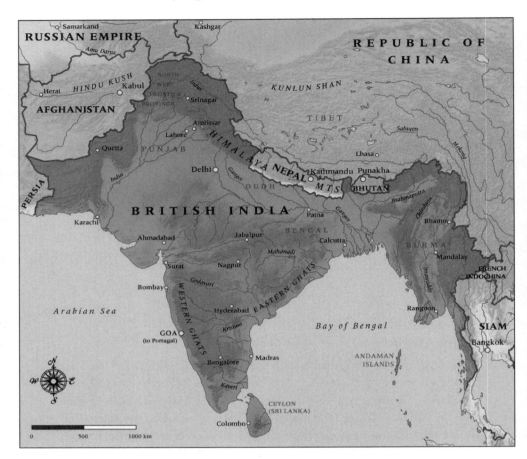

British India. This depicts the entirety of what Victorian-era Englishmen knew as 'India'. This huge area encompassed some 5,000 kilometres east to west and 4,000 kilometres north to south and held a 'vast and various kinds of man'. Map courtesy of the New Zealand government.

Hundred Head', 'The Ballad of Boh Da Thone', and 'Route Marchin''. Other similar poems which may be found on the Kipling Society's superb website and which I recommend to the reader are 'Cholera Camp', 'Ford O' Kabul River', and 'Oonts'.

Arithmetic on the Frontier

This poem was published in the first edition of *Departmental Ditties and Other Verses* in June 1886. The voice is Kipling's, reflecting on how cheaply a life can be taken on the frontier.

A great and glorious thing it is
    To learn, for seven years or so,

The Lord knows what of that and this,
    Ere reckoned fit to face the foe –
The flying bullet down the Pass,
That whistles clear: "All flesh is grass."

Three hundred pounds per annum spent
    On making brain and body meeter[1]
For all the murderous intent
    Comprised in "villanous saltpetre!"
And after – ask the Yusufzaies[2]
What comes of all our 'ologies.[3]

A scrimmage in a Border Station –
    A canter down some dark defile –
Two thousand pounds of education
    Drops to a ten-rupee *jezail*[4] –
The Crammer's boast,[5] the Squadron's pride,
Shot like a rabbit in a ride!

No proposition Euclid wrote,
    No formulae the text-books know,
Will turn the bullet from your coat,
    Or ward the tulwar's[6] downward blow
Strike hard who cares – shoot straight who can –
The odds are on the cheaper man.

One sword-knot stolen from the camp
    Will pay for all the school expenses
Of any Kurrum Valley scamp
    Who knows no word of moods and tenses,
But, being blessed with perfect sight,
Picks off our messmates left and right.

With home-bred hordes the hillsides teem,
    The troopships bring us one by one,
At vast expense of time and steam,

---

[1] The comparative of 'meet' meaning fit for a purpose, or more suitable.
[2] Yusufzaies: A tribe on the Northwest Frontier.
[3] 'ologies: Western sciences ending in '-ology', for example, Biology.
[4] A ten-rupee *jezail*: a jezail is an long-barrelled Afghan flintlock rifle which was inexpensive and crude in comparison to British arms.
[5] Crammers: Young men seeking admission to Sandhurst or university often hired 'crammers' or personal tutors who would help prepare them for the rigorous entrance exams. This was not cheap. Kipling's son, John, attended a crammers course in Bournemouth in the early summer of 1914.
[6] Tulwar: An Indian sabre.

> To slay Afridis[7] where they run.
> The "captives of our bow and spear"
> Are cheap, alas! as we are dear.

Most British officers in Kipling's time came from the classically educated upper classes of British society. Upon hearing of his public school friend Lieutenant Dury's death in Burma, Kipling remarked, '£1,800 worth of education gone to smash'. Similarly today the officer corps of modern armies is composed of highly educated men and women. Most have university degrees when commissioned and this is typically followed up by a year or so of military training before they join a battalion. The personal and institutional investment in human capital is significant, yet the uncertainties and randomness of combat dictate that some die before seeing an adequate 'return on investment' (if you will permit me to use that phrase).

Poetry and the Profession of Arms

> Three hundred pounds per annum spent
>   On making brain and body meeter
> For all the murderous intent
>   Comprised in "villanous saltpetre!"
> And after – ask the Yusufzaies
> What comes of all our 'ologies.

Kipling notes that a very expensive western education focusing on sciences and maths may not be as useful in combat as the mastery of weapons and gunpowder (saltpetre being a primary ingredient in gunpowder).

> A scrimmage in a Border Station –
>   A canter down some dark defile –
> Two thousand pounds of education
>   Drops to a ten-rupee *jezail* –
> The Crammer's boast, the Squadron's pride,
> Shot like a rabbit in a ride!

Death can come unexpectedly and quickly in combat. The nation's 'best and brightest' men and women, in whom hundreds of thousands of pounds or dollars have been invested, can die in an instant like a rabbit driven out of its cover. Unfortunately, officers are 'high-value targets' because their loss has an obvious and immediate impact on the unit and its effectiveness.

---

[7] Afridis: Another tribe on the North-West Frontier.

Strike hard who cares – shoot straight who can –
The odds are on the cheaper man.

Kipling notes that battlefield skills and survival sometimes rest on hard-won experience and understanding of terrain and the enemy rather than on an expensive Western education.

***

"Bobs"
(Field Marshal Lord Roberts of Kandahar)

"'Bobs'" was first published in the *Pall Mall Gazette* in December 1893 and collected in the Bombay edition of *The Seven Seas* in 1913. Field Marshal Lord Roberts died in France in 1914. The voice is that of an experienced soldier who served under Roberts.

There's a little red-faced man,
    Which is Bobs,
Rides the tallest 'orse 'e can –
    Our Bobs.
If it bucks or kicks or rears,
'E can sit for twenty years
With a smile round both 'is ears –
    Can't yer, Bobs?

Then 'ere's to Bobs Bahadur – little Bobs, Bobs, Bobs!
'E's our pukka Kandaharder –
    Fightin' Bobs, Bobs, Bobs!
'E's the Dook of *Aggy Chel;*[1]
'E's the man that done us well,
An' we'll follow 'im to 'ell –
    Won't we, Bobs?

If a limber's slipped a trace,
    'Ook on Bobs.
If a marker's lost 'is place,
    Dress by Bobs.
For 'e's eyes all up 'is coat,
An' a bugle in 'is throat,
An' you will not play the goat
    Under Bobs.

---

[1] Dook of *Aggy Chel*: An advocate of 'Get ahead!'

'E's a little down on drink
    Chaplain Bobs;
But it keeps us outer Clink –
    Don't it, Bobs?
So we will not complain
Tho' 'e's water on the brain,
If 'e leads us straight again –
    Blue-light Bobs.[2]

If you stood 'im on 'is head,
    Father Bobs,
You could spill a quart of lead
    Outer Bobs.
'E's been at it thirty years,
An-amassin' souveneers
In the way o' slugs an' spears –
    Ain't yer Bobs?

What 'e does not know o' war,
    Gen'ral Bobs,
You can arst the shop next door –
    Can't they, Bobs?
Oh, 'e's little but he's wise;
'E's terror for 'is size,
An' – *'e – does – not – advertise –*[3]
    Do yer, Bobs?

Now they've made a bloomin 'Lord'
    Outer Bobs,
Which was but 'is fair reward –
    Weren't it, Bobs?:
So 'e'll wear a coronet
Where 'is 'elmet used to set;
But we know you won't forget –
    Will yer, Bobs?

Then 'ere's to Bobs Bahadur – little Bobs, Bobs, Bobs,
Pocket-Wellin'ton 'an *arder*[4]
    Fightin' Bobs, Bobs, Bobs!

---

[2] Blue light: temperance.

[3] Britain had an 'advertising general' in the person of Sir Garnet Wolseley in the 1870s and 80s who relentlessly self-publicized his own efforts in positive terms. The expression 'It's all Sir Garnet' meant that everything was going to plan.

[4] *Arder*: And a half. Meaning half again as good as Lord Wellington.

This ain't no bloomin' ode,
But you've 'elped the soldier's load,
An' for benefits bestowed,
    Bless yer, Bobs!

Field Marshal Sir Frederick Sleigh Roberts, 1st Lord of Kandahar, VC, KG, KP, GCB, OM (1832–1914) was Britain's preeminent soldier during the reign of Queen Victoria. Roberts was born in India and after Eton and Sandhurst joined the East India Company Army (soon to become the Indian Army). He won the Victoria Cross for gallantry during the Indian Mutiny in 1858. He fought in Abyssinia (modern Ethiopia) and Afghanistan. Roberts led the relief force from Kabul to Kandahar in 1880, for which he received a baronetcy. He served in Ireland and in the Second Anglo–Boer War, where he put the British campaign on the path to victory, for which he was elevated to Earl Roberts of Kandahar. In retirement Roberts became an advocate of national military preparedness. He died in October 1914 of pneumonia while visiting the Indian Corps on the Western Front in France.

Although Roberts was a smallish man he was a fearless fighter, frequently wounded, and a man of constant action. As the poem describes, Roberts was beloved, admired, and respected by the men serving in the army. The verse highlights timeless leadership traits and characteristics by which men are effectively led into combat and danger. Broadly speaking there are many similarities between Roberts, Robert E. Lee, and Erwin Rommel in their use of leadership skills. In Clausewitzian terms they were natural soldiers of genius and all possessed *coup d'oeil* (the ability to see the battlefield 'at a glance' intuitively and immediately understanding its dynamics). All three generals were beloved by their soldiers, who would do anything asked of them.

Poetry and the Profession of Arms

If it bucks or kicks or rears,
'E can sit for twenty years
With a smile round both 'is ears –

Soldiers respect and are attracted to positive personalities who make light of difficulties.

If a limber's slipped a trace,
    'Ook on Bobs.
If a marker's lost 'is place,
    Dress by Bobs.

Soldiers greatly admire officers who lead by example, not only in overcoming danger in combat, but also in everyday working or fatigue situations. Erwin Rommel was known to jump in and fix flat tyres with his driver and help push vehicles out of the mud. Robert E. Lee was famous for sharing the hardships of campaigning with his men by living in a small tent, eating the same rations, and constantly being with the army.

> 'E's been at it thirty years,
> An-amassin' souveneers
> In the way o' slugs an' spears –

It goes without saying that soldiers admire bravery and that much respect is earned by being wounded in action, which is proof positive that one has 'seen the elephant.'

> Oh, 'e's little but he's wise;
> 'E's terror for 'is size,
> An' – *'e – does – not – advertise –*

The qualities of modesty and humility are tremendously valuable in practising the Profession of Arms. Soldiers are especially sensitive to leaders who take the credit for themselves, or who unnecessarily glorify their own achievements.

***

Gunga Din

'Gunga Din' is Rudyard Kipling's most beloved and well-known military poem. First published in the *New York Tribune* on 22 May 1890, 'Gunga Din' found its way into the 1892 updated edition of *Barrack-Room Ballads and Other Verses*. The voice is that of a British regular who has been badly wounded in action.

> You may talk o' gin and beer
> When you're quartered safe out 'ere,
> An' you're sent to penny-fights an' Aldershot[1] it;
> But when it comes to slaughter
> You will do your work on water,
> An' you'll lick the bloomin' boots of 'im that's got it.
> Now in Injia's sunny clime,
> Where I used to spend my time

---

[1] Aldershot is a British Army training base west of London.

A-servin' of 'Er Majesty the Queen,
Of all them blackfaced crew
The finest man I knew
Was our regimental bhisti,[2] Gunga Din,
    He was "Din! Din! Din!
  "You limpin' lump o' brick-dust, Gunga Din!
  "Hi! Slippy *hitherao*[3]
    "Water, get it! *Panee lao,*[4]
"You squidgy-nosed old idol, Gunga Din."

The uniform 'e wore
Was nothin' much before,
An' rather less than 'arf o' that be'ind,
For a piece o' twisty rag
An' a goatskin water-bag[5]
Was all the field-equipment 'e could find.
When the sweatin' troop-train lay
In a sidin' through the day,
Where the 'eat would make your bloomin' eyebrows crawl,
We shouted "Harry By!"[6]
Till our throats were bricky-dry,
Then we wopped 'im 'cause 'e couldn't serve us all.
    It was "Din! Din! Din!
"You 'eathen, where the mischief 'ave you been?
    "You put some *juldee*[7] in it
    Or I'll *marrow*[8] you this minute
"If you don't fill up my helmet, Gunga Din!"

'E would dot an' carry one
Till the longest day was done;
An' 'e didn't seem to know the use o' fear.
If we charged or broke or cut,
You could bet your bloomin' nut,
'E'd be waitin' fifty paces right flank rear.
With 'is mussick on 'is back,
'E would skip with our attack,
An' watch us till the bugles made 'Retire,'

---

[2] Bhisti: Native water carrier.
[3] *Hitherao*: 'ither aw' – Hindi for 'Come here!'
[4] *Panee lao*: Bring water swiftly.
[5] Goatskin water-bag: a water skin made of pigskin would offend Muslims and one made of cow or calf skin would offend Hindus, thus goatskin allowed all to drink.
[6] Harry By: Oh brother.
[7] *Juldee*: be quick.
[8] *Marrow*: hit you.

An' for all 'is dirty 'ide
'E was white, clear white, inside
When 'e went to tend the wounded under fire!
    It was "Din! Din! Din!'
  With the bullets kickin' dust-spots on the green.
    When the cartridges ran out,
    You could hear the front-ranks shout,
  "Hi! ammunition-mules an' Gunga Din!"

I shan't forgit the night
When I dropped be'ind the fight
With a bullet where my belt-plate should 'a been.
I was chokin' mad with thirst,
An' the man that spied me first
Was our good old grinnin', gruntin' Gunga Din.
'E lifted up my 'ead,
An' he plugged me where I bled,
An' 'e guv me 'arf-a-pint o' water green.
It was crawlin' and it stunk,
But of all the drinks I've drunk,
I'm gratefullest to one from Gunga Din.
    It was "Din! Din! Din!
  "'Ere's a beggar with a bullet through 'is spleen;
  "'E's chawin' up the ground,
    "'An' 'e's kickin' all around:
  "For Gawd's sake git the water, Gunga Din!"

'E carried me away
To where a dooli[9] lay,
An' a bullet come an' drilled the beggar clean.
'E put me safe inside,
An' just before 'e died,
"I 'ope you liked your drink," sez Gunga Din.
So I'll meet 'im later on
At the place where 'e is gone –
Where it's always double drill and no canteen.
'E'll be squattin' on the coals
Givin' drink to poor damned souls,
An' I'll get a swig in hell from Gunga Din!
    Yes, Din! Din! Din!
  You Lazarushian-leather[10] Gunga Din!

---

[9] Dooli: planquin (a large covered box-like litter for one passenger on horizontal poles).

[10] Lazarushian-leather: a word apparently coined by Kipling – a dark and dried leather.

> Though I've belted you and flayed you,
>   By the livin' Gawd that made you,
>   You're a better man than I am, Gunga Din!

In the nineteenth century the British Army and its Indian Army counterpart was composed mostly of combat arms soldiers and many essential services were hired out to local civilians and the families which accompanied the army. Although it was common to find sergeant's wives mending uniforms or tending to the sick, such necessary functions as logistics and transportation were hired as needed for particular campaigns. At the tactical level water boys accompanied infantry regiments when they were transported by troop train as well as into combat.

Western armies today are largely self-contained in terms of logistics and combat support; however, when deployed for long periods to combat zones requiring semi-permanent garrisons and forward operating bases, many functions are contracted out. Indeed, one of the defining features of service in Afghanistan and Iraq in this century is the presence and support of contractors. The contractors sometimes even outnumber the soldiers and they provide mess and billeting facilities, as well as the transportation and storage of supplies, and the maintenance and repair of equipment. Contractors are a signature of our armies and in this regard we are not as far today from 'Gunga Din' as we might think.

The affection and respect that the teller of the story has for the dignity, sense of duty, and bravery of a native water carrier is self-evident from reading the verse. However, it would appear that this eye-opening respect was only won at the cost of the life of a native water carrier. In truth, combat arms soldiers in all armies tend to underappreciate the combat support and combat service support elements of the force until they actually need their help.

Perhaps the most recognizable counterpart situation to 'Gunga Din' today is that of the local translator. Western armies do not have linguistic depth in their conventional forces and the local translator is 'joined-at-the-hip' to leaders of every rank in combat zones today. Over time most come to admire the dignity and work ethic of their translator and many form life-long bonds of friendship.

Poetry and the Profession of Arms

> We shouted "Harry By!"
> Till our throats were bricky-dry,
> Then we wopped 'im 'cause 'e couldn't serve us all.

Members of the combat arms might reflect on developing a sense of humility and appreciation for those who support them.

> An' for all 'is dirty 'ide
> 'E was white, clear white, inside
> When 'e went to tend the wounded under fire!

Kipling is often taken to task for his racial phrasing and his belief in Anglo-Saxon ethnic superiority. 'Gunga Din' is representative of that tendency. The idea that a native would sacrifice his life for the comfort of a wounded British soldier obviously surprised the teller of the story. In fact it is not uncommon for Western soldiers to prejudge local people as less sophisticated socially and under-developed morally in comparison to their own sensibilities and values. It is only through close association in periods of intense stress that Westerners might break the self-imposed prejudices about non-Western people.

> 'E put me safe inside,
> An' just before 'e died,
> "I 'ope you liked your drink," sez Gunga Din.

The dedication and sense of duty displayed by contractors, translators, and local hires is often over looked by those busy with the business of fighting.

> Though I've belted you and flayed you,
> By the livin' Gawd that made you,
> You're a better man than I am, Gunga Din!

How often, in retrospect, do we acknowledge our debt to another while failing to do so in the present?

***

The Grave of the Hundred Head

This poem was published in *The Week's News* and the *Civil and Military Gazette* in January 1888. It was collected in 1890 in *Departmental Ditties and other Verses*. The voice is Kipling as an observer and re-teller of the tale.

> *There's a widow in sleepy Chester*
> *Who weeps for her only son;*
> *There's a grave on the Pabeng River,*[1]

---

[1] Pabeng River: a river in Burma.

A grave that the Burmans shun;
And there's Subadar Prag Tewarri[2]
Who tells how the work was done.

A Snider[3] squibbed in the jungle,
　　Somebody laughed and fled,
And the men of the First Shikaris[4]
　　Picked up their Subaltern[5] dead,
With a big blue mark in his forehead
　　And the back blown out of his head.

Subadar Prag Tewarri,
　　Jemadar Hira Lal,[6]
Took command of the party,
　　Twenty rifles in all,
Marched them down to the river
　　As the day was beginning to fall.

They buried the boy by the river,
　　A blanket over his face –
They wept for their dead Lieutenant,
　　The men of an alien race –
They made a *samadh*[7] in his honor,
　　A mark for his resting-place.

For they swore by the Holy Water,
　　They swore by the salt they ate,
That the soul of Lieutenant Eshmitt Sahib[8]
　　Should go to his God in state,
With fifty file of Burmans
　　To open him Heaven's gate.

The men of the First Shikaris
　　Marched till the break of day,
Till they came to the rebel village,
　　The village of Pabengmay –

---

[2] Subadar: the senior native officer in a Sepoy company in the Indian Army. These officers held a Viceroy's commission, which gave them authority over Indian troops only.

[3] Snider: a British Army rifle which was replaced by the Martini. In this case one captured by the Burmans.

[4] First Shikaris: An imaginary Indian Army regiment which appears in several of Kipling's stories.

[5] Subaltern: an older word for lieutenant or platoon leader.

[6] Jemadar: the second ranking native officer in a Sepoy company.

[7] *Samadh*: a memorial.

[8] Eshmitt Sahib: Indian pronunciation of Mr Smith.

A *jingal*[9] covered the clearing,
    Calthrops[10] hampered the way.

Subadar Prag Tewarri,
    Bidding them load with ball,
Halted a dozen rifles
    Under the village wall;
Sent out a flanking-party
    With Jemadar Hira Lal.

The men of the First Shikaris
    Shouted and smote and slew,
Turning the grinning *jingal*
    On to the howling crew.
The Jemadar's flanking-party
    Butchered the folk who flew.

Long was the morn of slaughter,
    Long was the list of slain,
Five score heads were taken,
    Five score heads and twain;[11]
And the men of the First Shikaris
    Went back to their grave again,

Each man bearing a basket
    Red as his palms that day,
Red as the blazing village –
    The village of Pabengmay,
And the *"drip-drip-drip"* from the baskets
    Reddened the grass by the way.

They made a pile of their trophies
    High as a tall man's chin,
Head upon head distorted,
    Set in a sightless grin,
Anger and pain and terror
    Stamped on the smoke-scorched skin.

---

[9] *Jingal*: a native cannon with its mouth cast as a tiger.
[10] Calthrops: an anti-cavalry device made of steel and shaped like children's jacks so that a sharp spike is always pointing up.
[11] 102.

Subadar Prag Tewarri
   Put the head of the Boh[12]
On the top of the mound of triumph,
   The head of his son below –
With the sword and the peacock-banner[13]
   That the world might behold and know.

Thus the *samadh* was perfect,
   Thus was the lesson plain
Of the wrath of the First Shikaris –
   The price of a white man slain;
And the men of the First Shikaris
   Went back into camp again.

Then a silence came to the river,
   A hush fell over the shore,
And Bohs that were brave departed,
   And Sniders squibbed no more;
For the Burmans said
   That a white man's head
Must be paid for with heads five-score.

There's a widow in sleepy Chester
   Who weeps for her only son;
There's a grave on the Pabeng River,
   A grave that the Burmans shun;
And there's Subadar Prag Tewarri
   Who tells how the work was done.

The Third Burma War lasted from 1885 to 1887. The Burma Wars pitted the conventional forces of the Indian Army against irregular forces led by tribal leaders. Although combat in these wars was episodic and of short duration, the engagements were almost always costly in blood.

   The subject of punitive expeditions and punitive operations was a consistent aspect of Victorian military policy. Farwell lists only four distinctly named punitive expeditions, but we should keep in mind that 'sending a message' to the locals was always a part of nineteenth-century British military practices. During the suppression of the Sepoy Rebellion, for example, ring leaders were strapped to the muzzles of cannon and blown apart in public squares. This was an acceptable practice in Kipling's time. Moreover, the idea was reflected in such works as Antoine-Henri Jomini's *The Art of War*, which included punitive

---

[12] Boh: a tribal chieftain of a band of Dacoits (bandits).
[13] Peacock banner: a flag sacred in Burma.

wars in the list of the types of war. Colonel C.E. Callwell's 1896 classic *Small Wars* also included the idea of punitive campaigning, but Callwell cautioned that punitive operations using overly heavy-handed methods were counterproductive because they tended to anger the population and unify opposition.

The relationship between British officers and their native counterparts is a recurrent theme in Kipling's verse. This relationship is a two-way street and is based on respect and trust. On contemporary battlefields, such as in Afghanistan, Iraq, and Syria, small numbers of Western officers and non-commissioned officers are assigned to lead, advise, and train indigenous forces. The relationships that evolve are accelerated by danger and close bonds develop quickly. This is particularly true of the inevitable translator who accompanies the unit.

Poetry and the Profession of Arms

> Subadar Prag Tewarri,
> Jemadar Hira Lal,
> Took command of the party,
> Twenty rifles in all,
> Marched them down to the river.
> As the day was beginning to fall.

Key leaders on the battlefield are targeted by the enemy in the hopes that their death will paralyse the unit. Western professional armies have great depth in this regard and in almost all cases today the affected unit will push on regardless of the loss of a leader. In Kipling's imaginary regiment, the First Shikaris, Subadar Prag Tewarri and Jemadar Hira Lal, although they were natives, were long-service professional non-commissioned soldiers, who were determined to carry on and punish the perpetrators.

*****

The Ballad of Bo Da Thone

1888

Burma War, 1883–1885

First published in *Barrack-Room Ballads and other Verses* in 1889. The voice is Kipling as a humorous story teller.

> *This is the ballad of Boh Da Thone,*
> *Erst a Pretender to Theebaw's Thone,*[1]
> *Who harried the district of Alalone:*

---

[1] Thibaw Min: the last king of the dynasty ruling Burma.

How he met with his fate and the V.P.P.[2]
At the hand of Harendra Mukerji,
Senior Gomashta, G.B.T.[3]

Boh Da Thone was a warrior bold:
His sword and his rifle were bossed with gold,

And the Peacock Banner his henchmen bore
Was stiff with bullion, but stiffer with gore.

He shot at the strong and he slashed at the weak
From the Salween scrub to the Chindwin teak:

He crucified noble, he scarified mean,
He filled old ladies with kerosene:

While over the water the papers cried,
"The patriot fights for his countryside!"

But little they cared for the Native Press,
The worn white soldiers in Khaki dress,

Who tramped through the jungle and camped in the byre,
Who died in the swamp and were tombed in the mire,

Who gave up their lives, at the Queen's Command,
For the Pride of their Race and the Peace of the Land.

Now, first of the foemen of Boh Da Thone
Was Captain O'Neil of the Black Tyrone,[4]

And his was a Company, seventy strong,
Who hustled that dissolute Chief along.

There were lads from Galway and Louth and Meath
Who went to their death with a joke in their teeth,

And worshipped with fluency, fervour, and zeal
The mud on the boot-heels of "Crook" O'Neil.

But ever a blight on their labours lay,
And ever their quarry would vanish away,

---

[2] V.P.P.: Value Payable Parcels Post, collect on delivery.
[3] *Senior Gomashta, G.B.T.*: Senior Clerk of the Government Bullock Train.
[4] The Black Tyrone: an imaginary Irish regiment which appears in some of Kipling's stories.

Till the sun-dried boys of the Black Tyrone
Took a brotherly interest in Boh Da Thone:

And, sooth, if pursuit in possession ends,
The Boh and his trackers were best of friends.

The word of a scout – a march by night –
A rush through the mist – a scattering fight –

A volley from cover – a corpse in the clearing –
The glimpse of a loin-cloth and heavy jade earring –

The flare of a village – the tally of slain –
And... the Boh was abroad on the raid again!

They cursed their luck, as the Irish will,
They gave him credit for cunning and skill,

They buried their dead, they bolted their beef,
And started anew on the track of the thief

Till, in place of the "Kalends of Greece",[5] men said,
"When Crook and his darlings come back with the head."

They had hunted the Boh from the hills to the plain –
He doubled and broke for the hills again:

They had crippled his power for rapine and raid,
They had routed him out of his pet stockade,

And at last, they came, when the Daystar[6] tired,
To a camp deserted – a village fired.

A black cross blistered the morning-gold,
And the body upon it was stark and cold.

The wind of the dawn went merrily past,
The high grass bowed her plumes to the blast.

And out of the grass, on a sudden, broke
A spirtle of fire, a whorl of smoke –

---

[5] Kalends of Greece: Calends are the first day of a Roman month; there are no Kalends of Greece. Kipling means an impossibility.

[6] Venus, the Morning-Star, the last star to fade in the dawn.

And Captain O'Neil of the Black Tyrone
Was blessed with a slug in the ulnar-bone –
The gift of his enemy Boh Da Thone.

(Now a slug that is hammered from telegraph-wire
Is a thorn in the flesh and a rankling fire.)

The shot-wound festered – as shot-wounds may
In a steaming barrack at Mandalay.

The left arm throbbed, and the Captain swore,
"I'd like to be after the Boh once more!"

The fever held him – the Captain said,
"I'd give a hundred to look at his head!"

The Hospital punkahs creaked and whirred,
But Babu Harendra (Gomashta) heard.

He thought of the cane-brake, green and dank,
That girdled his home by the Dacca tank.

He thought of his wife and his High School son,
He thought – but abandoned the thought – of a gun.

His sleep was broken by visions dread
Of a shining Boh with a silver head.
He kept his counsel and went his way,
And swindled the cartmen of half their pay.

And the months went on, as the worst must do,
And the Boh returned to the raid anew.

But the Captain had quitted the long-drawn strife,
And in far Simoorie had taken a wife;

And she was a damsel of delicate mould,
With hair like the sunshine and heart of gold,

And little she knew the arms that embraced
Had cloven a man from the brow to the waist:

And little she knew that the loving lips
Had ordered a quivering life's eclipse,

Or the eye that lit at her lightest breath
Had glared unawed in the Gates of Death.

(For these be matters a man would hide,
As a general rule, from an innocent Bride.)

And little the Captain thought of the past,
And, of all men, Babu Harendra last.

But slow, in the sludge of the Kathun road,
The Government Bullock Train toted its load.

Speckless and spotless and shining with ghi,[7]
In the rearmost cart sat the Babu-jee.

And ever a phantom before him fled
Of a scowling Boh with a silver head.

Then the lead-cart stuck, though the coolies slaved,
And the cartmen flogged and the escort raved;

And out of the jungle, with yells and squeals,
Pranced Boh Da Thone, and his gang at his heels!

Then belching blunderbuss answered back
The Snider's snarl and the carbine's crack,

And the blithe revolver began to sing
To the blade that twanged on the locking-ring,

And the brown flesh blued where the bay'net kissed,
As the steel shot back with a wrench and a twist,

And the great white oxen with onyx eyes
Watched the souls of the dead arise,

And over the smoke of the fusillade
The Peacock Banner staggered and swayed.

Oh, gayest of scrimmages man may see
Is a well-worked rush on the G.B.T.!

The Babu shook at the horrible sight,
And girded his ponderous loins for flight,

---

[7] Ghee: clarified butter used in the Indian kitchen.

But Fate had ordained that the Boh should start
On a lone-hand raid of the rearmost cart,

And out of that cart, with a bellow of woe,
The Babu fell – flat on the top of the Boh!

For years had Harendra served the State,
To the growth of his purse and the girth of his *pêt*[8]

There were twenty stone,[9] as the tally-man knows,
On the broad of the chest of this best of Bohs.

And twenty stone from a height discharged
Are bad for a Boh with a spleen enlarged.

Oh, short was the struggle – severe was the shock –
He dropped like a bullock – he lay like a block;

And the Babu above him, convulsed with fear,
Heard the labouring life-breath hissed out in his ear.

And thus in a fashion undignified
The princely pest of the Chindwin died.

Turn now to Simoorie where, lapped in his ease,
The Captain is petting the Bride on his knees,

Where the whit of the bullet, the wounded man's scream
Are mixed as the mist of some devilish dream –

Forgotten, forgotten the sweat of the shambles
Where the hill-daisy blooms and the gray monkey gambols,

From the sword-belt set free and released from the steel,
The Peace of the Lord is on Captain O'Neil.

Up the hill to Simoorie – most patient of drudges –
The bags on his shoulder, the mail-runner trudges.

"For Captain O'Neil, Sahib. One hundred and ten
Rupees to collect on delivery." ... Then

---

[8] *pêt*: stomach.
[9] Twenty stone: 127 kilograms.

(Their breakfast was stopped while the screw-jack and hammer
Tore waxcloth, split teak-wood, and chipped out the dammer;)[10]

Open-eyed, open-mouthed, on the napery's snow,
With a crash and a thud, rolled – the Head of the Boh!

And gummed to the scalp was a letter which ran: –
"IN FIELDING FORCE SERVICE.
"Encampment,
"10th Jan.

"Dear Sir, – I have honour to send, *as you said,*
"For final approval (see under) Boh's Head;

"Was took by myself in most bloody affair.
By High Education brought pressure to bear.

"Now violate Liberty, time being bad,
To mail V.P.P. (rupees hundred) Please add

"Whatever Your Honour can pass. Price of Blood
Much cheap at one hundred, and children want food;

"So trusting Your Honour will somewhat retain
True love and affection for Govt. Bullock Train,

"And show awful kindness to satisfy me,
I am,
Graceful Master,
Your
H. MUKERJI."

As the rabbit is drawn to the rattlesnake's power,
As the smoker's eye fills at the opium hour,

As a horse reaches up to the manger above,
As the waiting ear yearns for the whisper of love,

From the arms of the Bride, iron-visaged and slow,
The Captain bent down to the Head of the Boh.

And e'en as he looked on the Thing where It lay
'Twixt the winking new spoons and the napkins' array,

---

[10] dammer: sealing wax.

The freed mind fled back to the long-ago days –
The hand-to-hand scuffle – the smoke and the blaze –

The forced march at night and the quick rush at dawn –
The banjo at twilight, the burial 'ere morn –

The stench of the marshes – the raw, piercing smell
When the overhand stabbing-cut silenced the yell –

The oaths of his Irish that surged when they stood
Where the black crosses hung o'er the Kuttamow flood.

As a derelict ship drifts away with the tide
The Captain went out on the Past from his Bride,

Back, back, through the springs to the chill of the year,
When he hunted the Boh from Maloon to Tsaleer.

As the shape of a corpse dimmers up through deep water,
In his eye lit the passionless passion of slaughter,

And men who had fought with O'Neil for the life
Had gazed on his face with less dread than his wife.

For she who had held him so long could not hold him –
Though a four-month Eternity should have controlled him –

But watched the twin Terror – the head turned to head –
The scowling, scarred Black, and the flushed savage Red –

The spirit that changed from her knowing and flew to
Some grim hidden Past she had never a clue to.

But It knew as It grinned, for he touched it unfearing,
And muttered aloud, "So you kept that jade earring!"

Then nodded, and kindly, as friend nods to friend,
"Old man, you fought well, but you lost in the end."

The visions departed, and Shame followed Passion: –
"He took what I said in this horrible fashion,

"I'll write to Harendra!" With language unsainted
The Captain came back to the Bride… who had fainted.

And this is a fiction? No. Go to Simoorie
And look at their baby, a twelve-month old Houri,

A pert little, Irish-eyed Kathleen Mavournin –
She's always about on the Mall of a mornin' –

And you'll see, if her right shoulder-strap is displaced,
This: *Gules* upon *argent*, a Boh's Head, *erased!*[11]

Kipling's defined time period locates this poem in the two-year period immediately before the Third Burma War (1885–1887). The frontier between British India and what is now modern Myanmar was what we know today as 'ungoverned space'. The army patrolled the region cautiously but continuously, and incidents of banditry were common.

This is a rollicking tongue-in-cheek ballad that speaks to several serious themes in fighting 'Small Wars' against irregular enemies. In such wars conventional forces find it difficult to pin down insurgents and guerrillas and bring them to battle. They are elusive and have the ability to slip away when the situation turns against them. The verse speaks to a situation which will be familiar to modern practitioners of the art of war – the willingness of regulars to go out day after day and, in the end, to be frustrated by casualties or the failure to kill or capture insurgent leaders. Kipling also speaks to the fact that long after the Irish return home, the fight continues and the locals are left with problems to deal with. It is often pointed out to British and American soldiers in Afghanistan and Iraq that 'at the end of a year… *you* get to go home.'

Poetry and the Profession of Arms

And e'en as he looked on the Thing where It lay
'Twixt the winking new spoons and the napkins' array,

The freed mind fled back to the long-ago days –
The hand-to-hand scuffle - the smoke and the blaze –

The forced march at night and the quick rush at dawn -
The banjo at twilight, the burial ere morn –

The stench of the marshes - the raw, piercing smell
When the overhand stabbing-cut silenced the yell –

---

[11] A play on English heraldry. Red on Silver. Erased: On a shield an animal's head with a jagged edge, having been torn off the body.

Mental flashbacks to combat are not uncommon for veterans of hard-fought battles. We call this post-traumatic stress disorder (PTSD) today and objects, sounds, or smells can immediately trigger a vivid return to the battlefield.

> As a derelict ship drifts away with the tide
> The Captain went out on the Past from his Bride,

Soldiers talk of a 'thousand-yard stare' and for those affected by PTSD a lapse into the past happens occasionally. A war follows you home whether you want it to or not.

***

Route Marchin'

First published in *Barrack Room Ballads* in 1892. The voice is that of a British regular soldier assigned to a regiment in India.

> We're marchin' on relief over Injia's sunny plains,
> A little front o' Christmas-time an' just be'ind the Rains;
> Ho! get away you bullock-man, you've 'eard the bugle blowed,
> There's a regiment a-comin' down the Grand Trunk Road;[1]
>> With its best foot first
>> And the road a-sliding past,
>> An' every bloomin' campin'-ground exactly like the last;
>> While the Big Drum says,
>> With 'is *"rowdy-dowdy-dow!"* –
>> *"Kiko kissywarsti* don't you *hamsher argy jow?"*[2]

> Oh, there's them Injian temples to admire when you see,
> There's the peacock round the corner an' the monkey up the tree,
> An' there's that rummy silver grass a-wavin' in the wind,
> An' the old Grand Trunk a-trailin' like a rifle-sling be'ind.
>> While it's best foot first,...

> At half-past five's Revelly, an' our tents they down must come,
> Like a lot of button mushrooms when you pick 'em up at 'ome.
> But it's over in a minute, an' at six the column starts,

---

[1] The Grand Trunk Road: a 1,500 mile road from Calcutta to Peshawar built by the Mughal Dynasty in the 1600s. It has been called 'the backbone of India.'

[2] *"Kiko kissywarsti* don't you *hamsher argy jow?"*: Kipling's own footnote explains this as Tommy Atkins' pronunciation of Hindi meaning 'Why don't you get on?'

While the women and the kiddies sit an' shiver in the carts.[3]
    An' it's best foot first,...

Oh, then it's open order, an' we lights our pipes an' sings,
An' we talks about our rations an' a lot of other things,
An' we thinks o' friends in England, an' we wonders what they're at,
An' 'ow they would admire for to hear us sling the *bat*[4]
    An' it's best foot first,...

It's none so bad o' Sunday, when you're lyin' at your ease,
To watch the kites a-wheelin' round them feather-'eaded trees,
For although there ain't no women, yet there ain't no barrick-
yards,
So the orficers goes shootin' an' the men they plays at cards.
    Till it's best foot first,...

So 'ark an' 'eed, you rookies, which is always grumblin' sore,
There's worser things than marchin' from Umballa to Cawnpore;
An' if your 'eels are blistered an' they feels to 'urt like 'ell,
You drop some tallow in your socks an' that will make 'em well.
    For it's best foot first,...

We're marchin' on relief over Injia's coral strand,
Eight 'undred fightin' Englishmen, the Colonel, and the Band;[5]
Ho! get away you bullock-man, you've 'eard the bugle blowed,
There's a regiment a-comin' down the Grand Trunk Road;
    With its best foot first
    And the road a-sliding past,
    An' every bloomin' campin'-ground exactly like the last;
    While the Big Drum says,
    With 'is "*rowdy-dowdy-dow!*"
    "*Kiko kissywarsti* don't you *hamsher argy jow?*"

Under the reforms of the 1880s the British Army developed a rotational
scheme of bringing fresh battalions from the United Kingdom to replace the
garrisons of the empire. Regiments sent to India marched from their ports of
debarkation to their new garrisons. In fact most of a soldier's experience in the

---

[3] The families of non-commissioned officers travelled with British and Indian Army regiments in the
nineteenth century.
[4] *Bat*: a slang term for language. Kipling noted that Tommy fancied himself 'a profound Orientalist
and a fluent speaker of Hindustani.' But, 'As a matter of fact, he depends largely on sign-language.'
[5] The fighting strength of a British infantry regiment was about a thousand men but they generally
had about eight hundred on hand.

overseas empire did not involve actual fighting, but subjected him instead to the tyranny of garrison life.

Poetry and the Profession of Arms

> We're marchin' on relief over Injia's sunny plains,
> A little front o' Christmas-time an' just be'ind the Rains;
> Ho! get away you bullock-man, you've 'eard the bugle blowed,
> There's a regiment a-comin' down the Grand Trunk Road;
>> With its best foot first
>> And the road a-sliding past,
>> An' every bloomin' campin'-ground exactly like the last;

In this poem Kipling speaks to the terrible boredom and repetitive nature of peacetime soldiering. In spite of this soldiers must 'put their best foot forward' and Kipling's use of this repeated refrain drums home this point.

> So 'ark an' 'eed, you rookies, which is always grumblin' sore,
> There's worser things than marchin' from Umballa to Cawnpore;

Veterans remind the 'newbies' to appreciate the fact that in peacetime they are not on campaign and not in mortal danger from combat. Soldiers must learn to overcome boredom and to take the good with the bad.

Chapter 4

War Experienced – The Transvaal and the Boers

Introduction

The Second Anglo-Boer War (1899–1901) was a transformative event for the British military system. It began as a conventional war against the two Boer republics, the Transvaal and the Orange Free State, and it evolved in three stages. The war began in October 1899 when the Boers responded to a British ultimatum by crossing the border into Cape Colony and Natal. Out of a regular army of about a quarter of a million men spread across the globe, Britain had about 15,000 soldiers in South Africa, but an expeditionary force of some 47,000 men under General Sir Redvers Buller was inbound to the colony. The Boers had the initiative, encircling Ladysmith in Natal, and Kimberley and Mafeking in the Northern Cape Colony, thereby putting the British on the defensive. Early attempts to relieve the towns failed disastrously when the British commander, Major General Sir Paul Methuen, attempted to take strongly held hilltops with direct frontal assaults. His assaults at the Modder River were carelessly executed and characterized by no reconnaissance, ineffective artillery support, and bad tactics.

By early December Buller arrived and led an operational offensive on three axes of advance to relieve the besieged towns. Between 10–17 December 1899, the three British forces were again badly defeated: Buller at Colenso, Methuen at Magersfontein, and General William Gatacre at Stormberg. The British press immediately named this 'Black Week' and it shocked a British public

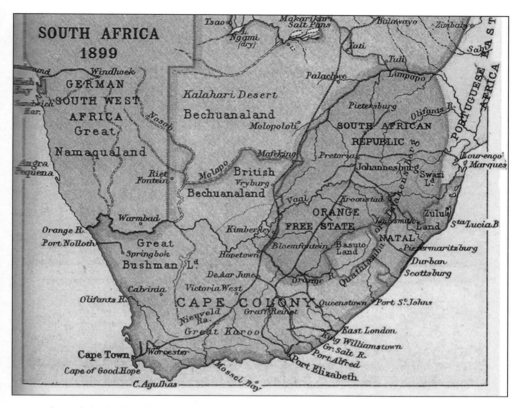

Second Anglo-Boer War. The relatively large size of the two Boer republics is apparent on this map of the political boundaries as they appeared in 1899. Readers might also note how isolated the Boers were from outside assistance. Map courtesy of the Canadian War Museum.

long used to victories in the Queen's small wars. Another defeat at Spion Kop six weeks later added to the despair.

The War Office acted quickly, by sending General Sir Frederick Roberts to replace Buller, which was somewhat of a surprise to the Establishment, since Roberts was an Indian Army officer. The WO assigned General Herbert H. Kitchener, who had recently conquered the Sudan, as Roberts' second-in-command. Roberts arrived in Capetown on 10 January 1900. Joining Methuen on the Modder River, Roberts reenergized the campaign and relieved Kimberley. On 27 February he outflanked and captured Boer General Piet Cronjé and 4,000 Boers at the Battle of Paardeberg. Roberts swept through the veldt, but quickly realized that his infantry was penalized in the open plains. He collected up all the horses he could find and ordered each infantry battalion to form a company of mounted infantry. This gave the army the mobility enjoyed by the enemy. Over the following year Roberts fired five generals, six brigadiers, and two dozen regimental commanders, replacing them with younger, trusted men. On 17 May Mafeking was relieved, an event which generated huge public celebrations in Britain, as well as turning author and future founder of the Boy Scouts, Robert Baden-Powell, into an overnight celebrity.

On 5 June Roberts took Pretoria and Boer president Paul Kruger fled to Europe; however, many Boers refused to surrender and began a campaign of guerrilla warfare. Queen Victoria died on 22 January 1901, ending a reign of eighty-one years and seven months. Unable to suppress the Boer commandos (who were employing guerrilla tactics), Roberts and Kitchener launched a counter-guerrilla campaign based on relocation and sweeping the veldt clear of the Boer units. They forcibly removed the civilian Boer population to concentration camps, burned their farms, and killed or seized all the livestock. Then they constructed blockhouse and barbed-wire lines, which divided the Boer republics into sectors. Kitchener formed highly mobile combined arms columns and placed them under the command of young and aggressive commanders. The columns proceeded to sweep and destroy the weakened commandos by pushing them against the blockhouse lines.

The last of the Boers surrendered in May 1902, ending an unexpectedly long and expensive war. In the end Britain and the empire sent almost half a million men to the theatre, forcing the newly created volunteer system into action. The imprisonment and deaths of large numbers of Boer non-combatants held by the British in concentration camps became a *cause célèbre*, resulting in extremely bad publicity as well as parliamentary commissions investigating the war.

Kipling went down to Cape Colony during the war and saw how unprepared the British Army was and he formed opinions about the conduct of the war. The Boer War provided Kipling with grist for his mill and his verses about the war were published as *The Five Nations* in 1903. *The Five Nations* centred on the war fought by Britain and its white colonies, Australia, New Zealand, Canada, and the Cape Colony. The poems I have selected for this chapter are 'Two Kopjes', 'Boots', 'Stellenbosch', and 'Mounted Infantry'. Other similar poems, which may be found on the Kipling Society's website and which I recommend to the reader, are 'Bridge-Guard in the Karroo', 'Columns', 'The Parting of the Columns', and '"Wilful-Missing"'.

Two Kopjes

(Made Yeomanry[1] toward End of Boer War)

Part of Kipling's collection of sixteen 'Service Songs' published in *The Five Nations* in 1903. The voice is that of an experienced soldier hardened by war expressing a cautionary warning about the enemy's use of the ground.

---

[1] Yeomanry. Mounted infantry or cavalry.

Only two African kopjes,[2]
Only the cart-tracks that wind
Empty and open between 'em,
Only the Transvaal behind;
Only an Aldershot column[3]
Marching to conquer the land...
Only a sudden and solemn
Visit, unarmed, to the Rand.

Then scorn not the African kopje,
The kopje that smiles in the heat,
The wholly unoccupied kopje,
The home of Cornelius and Piet.[4]
You can never be sure of your kopje,
But of this be you blooming well sure,
A kopje is always a kopje,
And a Boojer[5] is always a Boer!

Only two African kopjes,
Only the vultures above,
Only baboons – at the bottom,
Only some buck on the move;
Only a Kensington draper
Only pretending to scout...
Only bad news for the paper,
Only another knock-out.

Then mock not the African kopje,
And rub not your flank on its side,
The silent and simmering kopje,
The kopje beloved by the guide.
You can never be, etc.

Only two African kopjes,
Only the dust of their wheels,
Only a bolted commando,
Only our guns at their heels...
Only a little barb-wire,
Only a natural fort,
Only "by sections retire,"
Only "regret to report!"

---

2 Kopje. A South African word for a small hill generally surrounded by flat areas.
3 Derived from a formation taught in the Aldershot training camp in the UK.
4 Common Boer forenames taken by Tommy as nicknames for their Boer adversaries.
5 Boojer: A slang term for a Boer derived from the Dutch 'burgher' or citizen.

Then mock not the African kopje,
Especially when it is twins,
One sharp and one table-topped kopje
For that's where the trouble begins.
You never can be, etc.

Only two African kopjes
Baited the same as before –
Only we've had it so often,
Only we're taking no more...
Only a wave to our troopers,
Only our flanks swinging past,
Only a dozen voorloopers,[6]
Only we've learned it at last!

Then mock not the African kopje,
But take off your hat to the same,
The patient, impartial old kopje,
The kopje that taught us the game!
For all that we knew in the Columns,
And all they've forgot on the Staff,
We learned at the Fight o' Two Kopjes,
Which lasted two years an' a half.

O mock not the African kopje,
Not even when peace has been signed –
The kopje that isn't a kopje –
The kopje that copies its kind.
You can never be sure of your kopje,
But of this be you blooming well sure,
That a kopje is always a kopje,
And a Boojer is always a Boer!

In the Victorian and Edwardian eras the yeomanry regiments of the British army were part of the organized reserves and later formed part of the Territorial system. The yeomanry regiments were county-based and composed of volunteer cavalry. Naturally, most yeomanry regiments originated in the fox-hunting counties of Britain and many of the officers and men were landed gentry. During the Second Boer War many British infantry regiments were given horses in order to counter the superior mobility of the mounted Boer guerrillas.

---

[6] A Boer term for riders leading a team of horses or oxen, men on horseback.

The poem speaks to the nature of warfare, terrain appreciation, and understanding the capabilities of the enemy. Inexperienced troops often disregard at their peril terrain which favours the enemy, and the tactics and techniques learned in training are no substitute for experience.

Poetry and the Profession of Arms

> You can never be sure of your kopje,
> But of this be you blooming well sure,
> A kopje is always a kopje,
> And a Boojer is always a Boer!

There is a bit of sarcasm in this bit of advice for the uninitiated and that is that an empty, and apparently unoccupied hill may look like just an unoccupied hill. However, soldiers must always regard any high ground as key terrain and, potentially, a fighting or ambush position for the enemy. And, while one might not know exactly whether the hill is occupied or unoccupied, one can always count on the Boers to act aggressively.

> Only a Kensington draper
> Only pretending to scout...
> Only bad news for the paper,
> Only another knock-out.

Many of the men serving in the war were volunteers or members of the militia and had little actual experience. While most were eager and keen to do the right thing, occasionally a dilettante would perform a critical duty, such as scouting, in a careless way. The result led to defeat and the loss of life.

> Then mock not the African kopje,
> Especially when it is twins,
> One sharp and one table-topped kopje
> For that's where the trouble begins.
>
> Only two African kopjes
> Baited the same as before –
> Only we've had it so often,
> Only we're taking no more.

The Boers were known for their carefully laid ambushes and skilful use of terrain. Born on the veldt and into a self-reliant community of horsemen, the Boer commandos were able to use their understanding of their home ground to advantage. British soldiers, thrust into this unfamiliar tactical environment, had a steep learning curve to overcome in order to defeat the Boers and survive the war.

> For all that we knew in the Columns,
> And all they've forgot on the Staff,
> We learned at the Fight o' Two Kopjes,
> Which lasted two years an' a half.

The distrust that the experienced field soldier has for conventional solutions to tactical problems, as well as his contempt for the staff, appears in this verse. There is no substitute for experience hard won in battle and the length of time that it takes to understand the tactical environment.

***

Boots

This poem was also published in 1903 in *The Five Nations*. The voice is that of an infantryman caught up in the interminable hunt for the Boers on the veldt.

> We're foot–slog–slog–slog–sloggin' over Africa –
> Foot–foot–foot–foot–sloggin' over Africa –
> (Boots–boots–boots–boots–movin' up and down again!)
>   There's no discharge in the war!
>
> Seven–six–eleven–five–nine-an'–twenty mile to-day –
> Four–eleven–seventeen–thirty-two the day before –
> (Boots–boots–boots–boots–movin' up and down again!)
>   There's no discharge in the war!
>
> Don't–don't–don't–don't–look at what's in front of you.
> (Boots–boots–boots–boots–movin' up an' down again);
> Men–men–men–men–men go mad with watchin' 'em,
>   An' there's no discharge in the war!
>
> Try–try–try–try–to think o' something different –
> Oh–my–God–keep–me from goin' lunatic!
> (Boots–boots–boots–boots–movin' up an' down again!)
>   There's no discharge in the war!
>
> Count–count–count–count–the bullets in the bandoliers.
> If–your–eyes–drop–they will get atop o' you!
> (Boots–boots–boots–boots–movin' up and down again) –
>   There's no discharge in the war!

We–can–stick–out–'unger, thirst, an' weariness,
But–not–not–not–not the chronic sight of 'em –
Boots–boots–boots–boots–movin' up an' down again,
   An' there's no discharge in the war!

'Taint–so–bad–by–day because o' company,
But night–brings–long–strings–o' forty thousand million
Boots–boots–boots–boots–movin' up an' down again.
   There's no discharge in the war!

I–'ave–marched–six–weeks in 'Ell an' certify
It–is–not–fire–devils, dark, or anything,
But boots–boots–boots–boots–movin' up an' down again,
   An' there's no discharge in the war!

'Boots' is one of Kipling's most well-known poems and it expresses the almost unendurable difficulty of line infantry marching endlessly in pursuit of a far more mobile enemy. Repetition and boredom accompany foot marches that seem to lead nowhere – not even to an engagement or battle. The endless monotony of marching is broken only by the creativity of a soldier to do something like counting the bullets in the bandoliers of the man marching to his front.

***

Stellenbosch[1]

The poem was written in 1901 when these events were fresh in Kipling's mind, but not published until the revised 1919 edition of *The Five Nations*. Stellenbosch was a town in Cape Colony to which the army sent the commanders it had relieved for incompetence. It became a verb: 'to be Stellenbosched' meant to be relieved or disgraced and sent to the rear.

The General 'eard the firin' on the flank,
  An' 'e sent a mounted man to bring 'im back
The silly, pushin' person's name an' rank
  'Oo'd dared to answer Brother Boer's attack:
For there might 'ave been a serious engagement,
  An' 'e might 'ave wasted 'alf a dozen men;
So 'e ordered 'im to stop 'is operations round the kopjes,
  An' 'e told 'im off before the Staff at ten!

---

[1] The army had a base camp and a remount station at Stellenbosch, which was well outside the area of combat operations.

And it all goes into laundry,
But it never comes out in the wash,[2]
'Ow we're sugared about by the old men
('Eavy-sterned amateur old men!)
That 'amper an' 'inder an' scold men
For fear o' Stellenbosch!

The General 'ad "produced a great effect,"
    The General 'ad the country cleared – almost;
The General "'ad no reason to expect,"
    And the Boers 'ad us bloomin' well on toast!
For we might 'ave crossed the drift before the twilight,
    Instead o' sitting down an' takin' root;
But we was not allowed, so the Boojers scooped the crowd,
    To the last survivin' bandolier an' boot.

The General saw the farm'ouse in 'is rear,
    With its stoep so nicely shaded from the sun;
Sez 'e, "I'll pitch my tabernacle 'ere,"
    An' 'e kept us muckin' round till 'e 'ad done.
For 'e might 'ave caught the confluent pneumonia
    From sleepin' in his gaiters in a dew;
So 'e took a book an' dozed while the other columns closed,
    And De Wet's commando[3] out an' trickled through!

The General saw the mountain-range ahead,
    With their 'elios showin' saucy on the 'eight,[4]
So 'e 'eld us to the level ground instead,
    An' telegraphed the Boojers wouldn't fight.
For 'e might 'ave gone an' sprayed 'em with a pompom,[5]
    Or 'e might 'ave slung a squadron out to see –
But 'e wasn't takin' chances in them 'igh an' 'ostile kranzes[6] –
    He was markin' time to earn a K.C.B.[7]

The General got 'is decorations thick
    (The men that backed 'is lies could not complain),

---

[2] An old English saying that has come to mean a cover up or something that has been lost or hidden.

[3] General Christiaan De Wet was a famous Boer commando leader who was well-known for his elusive tactics and ability to slip his men through the lines of columns and blockhouses.

[4] 'elios. Heliographs were a line-of-sight signalling device which reflected the sun on an angled mirror. Tactically the heliograph stations were set up on high hills.

[5] PomPom. A quick-firing one-pounder (37mm) gun which when fired made a distinctive automatic pom-pom-pom report.

[6] Kranze – a Boer word for steep craggy hill.

[7] K.C.B. Knight Commander of the Bath, a British honour.

The Staff 'ad D.S.O.'s till we was sick,[8]
    An' the soldier – 'ad the work to do again!
For 'e might 'ave known the District was an 'otbed,
    Instead of 'andin' over, upside-down,
To a man 'oo 'ad to fight 'alf a year to put it right,
    While the General sat an' slandered 'im in town!

    An' it all went into the laundry,
    But it never came out in the wash.
    We were sugared about by the old men
    (Panicky, perishin' old men)
    That 'amper an' 'inder an' scold men
    For fear o' Stellenbosch!

The first commander to be relieved and sent to Stellenbosch was Colonel George Gough, commander of the 9th Lancers, who had led a disastrous reconnaissance of Boer positions along the Orange River in late November 1899. According to Thomas Packenham, 'Gough himself took the disgrace hard. He blew his brains out with his pistol.' Packenham also noted that Gough was 'first in a long line of COs to be Stellenbosched.'

The poem speaks to the contempt which experienced field soldiers feel toward commanders who hesitate to make sound decisions because they fear criticism that might lead to their relief from command. They are also contemptuous of senior officers who garner medals and honours without facing danger themselves, or not even producing victories. In our contemporary world we sometimes see commanders choosing the safe course of action rather than accept risk. We also see the 'zero defects' mentality, by which risk-averse commanders seek the assurance of knowing that each and every thing that could go wrong is checked and rechecked to avoid failure.

Poetry and the Profession of Arms

    The General 'eard the firin' on the flank,
        An' 'e sent a mounted man to bring 'im back
    The silly, pushin' person's name an' rank
        'Oo'd dared to answer Brother Boer's attack:

Cautious or incompetent leaders sometimes react badly to the initiative of their subordinates. These types of leaders refuse to decentralize responsibility and establish a restrictive command climate in which subordinates must ask permission to act.

---

[8] DSO. Distinguished Service Order, a high British medal.

> For there might 'ave been a serious engagement,
>> An' 'e might 'ave wasted 'alf a dozen men;
> So 'e ordered 'im to stop 'is operations round the kopjes,
>> An' 'e told 'im off before the Staff at ten!

Fear of one's subordinates doing the wrong thing, such as losing men carelessly or getting caught up in a serious fight, caused the commander to stifle the subordinate. Making things all the worse was the scolding of the subordinate at the evening staff briefing.

> The General saw the farm'ouse in 'is rear,
>> With its stoep so nicely shaded from the sun;
> Sez 'e, "I'll pitch my tabernacle 'ere,"
>> An' 'e kept us muckin' round till 'e 'ad done.

Senior officers who fail to share the hardships of their men by establishing comfortable and cushy field headquarters immediately incur the anger of the men on the sharp end of the spear. Nothing angers front-line soldiers as much as finding out that those in the 'rear' are enjoying overly comfortable living conditions.

> The General got 'is decorations thick
>> (The men that backed 'is lies could not complain),
> The Staff 'ad D.S.O.'s till we was sick,
>> An' the soldier – 'ad the work to do again!

Occasionally senior officers and staff are decorated inappropriately. Moreover, occasionally, the narrative recommendations required for such an award are inflated by subordinates currying favour with their seniors. Nothing infuriates soldiers on the front line like observing those in the 'rear' being decorated.

> An' it all went into the laundry,
> But it never came out in the wash.

In both stanzas that lead with this phrase, which has come to mean a cover-up, the notion of eager young professionals held back by cautious, incompetent, anxious, and tired old men is evident. In today's forces criticism of senior commanders rarely results in relief or disgrace. In Kipling's time some incompetents were allowed to remain in the field, but today this is rarely the case. This is partly a function of modern training and education, as well as a reflection of the selection processes by which officers are chosen for higher command.

***

Mounted Infantry

Kipling originally published this poem in 1901 in the *New York Tribune* and it wound up in *The Five Nations* in 1903. The voice is that of an experienced soldier struck by the ironies of his current situation, but who is extremely proud of his accomplishments.

I wish my mother could see me now, with a fence-post under my arm,[1]
And a knife and a spoon in my putties that I found on a Boer farm,
Atop of a sore-backed Argentine, with a thirst that you couldn't buy.
   I used to be in the Yorkshires once[2]
   (Sussex, Lincolns, and Rifles once),
   Hampshires, Glosters, and Scottish once! (ad lib.)
      But now I am M. I.

That is what we are known as – that is the name you must call
If you want officers' servants, pickets an' 'orseguards an' all –
Details for burin'-parties, company-cooks or supply –
Turn out the chronic Ikonas![3] Roll up the – M. I.!

My 'ands are spotty with veldt-sores, my shirt is a button an' frill,
An' the things I've used my bay'nit for would made a tinker ill![4]
An' I don't know whose dam' column I'm in, nor where we're trekkin' nor why.
   I've trekked from the Vaal to the Orange once –
   From the Vaal to the greasy Pongolo once –
   (Or else it was called the Zambesi once) –
      For now I am M. I.!

That is what we are known as – we are the push you require
For outposts all night under freezin', an' rearguard all day under fire.
Anything 'ot or unwholesome? Anything dusty or dry?
Borrow a bunch of Ikonas! Trot out the – M. I.!

---

[1] There are two views on this phrase. On the treeless veldt soldiers found and carried wooden fence posts to burn as firewood; alternatively, the British strung thousands of miles of barbed-wire between their blockhouses which also required fence posts.
[2] These are famous infantry regiments of the British Army.
[3] Ikona. An Afrikander word for 'kitchen kafir' used by Tommy as an imperative 'No, you don't!' or 'There ain't none!' In this context an affectionate nickname for the men scraped up at the bottom of the manpower barrel to serve as MI.
[4] Bayonet

Our Sergeant-Major's a subaltern, our Captain's a Fusilier –
Our Adjutant's "late of Somebody's 'Orse," an' a Melbourne auctioneer;
But you couldn't spot us at 'arf a mile from the crackest caval-ry.
>   They used to talk about Lancers once,
>   Hussars, Dragoons, an' Lancers once,
>   'Elmets, pistols, and carbines once,
>   But now we are M. I.!

That is what we are known as – we are the orphans they blame
For beggin' the loan of an 'ead-stall an' makin' a mount to the same.
Can't even look at their 'orslines but someone goes bellerin' "Hi!
"'Ere comes a burglin' Ikona! Footsack you – M. I.!"[5]

We are trekkin' our twenty miles a day an' bein' loved by the Dutch,
But we don't hold on by the mane no more, nor lose our stirrups – much;
An' we scout with a senior man in charge where the 'oly white flags fly.
>   We used to think they were friendly once,
>   Didn't take any precautions once
>   (Once, my ducky, an' only once!)
>   But now we are M. I.!

That is what we are known as – we are the beggars that got
Three days "to learn equitation," an' six month o' blumin' well trot!
Cow-guns, an' cattle, an' convoys – an' Mister De Wet on the fly –
We are the rolling Ikonas! We are the M. I.!

The new fat regiments come from home, imaginin' vain V.C.'s[6]
(The same as your talky-fighty men which are often Number Threes),[7]
But our words o' command are "Scatter" an' "Close" an' "Let your wounded lie."
>   We used to rescue 'em noble once, –

---

[5] Footsack. Anglicised Boer imperative *voertsak* meaning 'Go Away!' Commonly used to drive away dogs.

[6] VC. The Victoria Cross, the highest British honour for valour in battle.

[7] When fighting dismounted the number 3 man held the reins of four horses while the number 1, 2, and 4 men engaged the enemy with rifle fire. The horses and, thus the number 3 man, were generally under cover.

Givin' the range as we raised 'em once –
Gettin 'em killed as we saved 'em once –
     But now we are M. I.!

That is what we are known as – we are the lanterns you view
After a fight round the kopjes, lookin' the men that we knew;
Whistlin' an' callin' together, 'altin' to catch the reply: –
"'Elp me! O 'elp me, Ikonas! This way, the – M. I.!"

I wish my mother could see me now, a-gathering news on my own,
When I ride like a General up to the scrub and ride back like Tod
Sloan,[8]
Remarkable close to my 'orse's neck to let the shots go by.
     We used to fancy it risky once
     (Called it a reconnaissance once),
     Under the charge of the orf'cer once,
          But now we are M. I.!

That is what we are known as – that is the song you must say
When you want men to be Mausered at one and a penny a day;[9]
We are no five-bob Colonials – we are the 'ome-made supply,[10]
Ask for the London Ikonas! Ring up the – M.I.!

I wish myself could talk to myself as I left 'im a year ago;
I could tell 'im a lot that would save 'im a lot on the things that 'e
ought to know!
When I think o' that ignorant barrack-bird, it almost makes me cry.
     I used to belong in an Army once
     (Gawd! what a rum little Army once),
     Red little, dead little Army once![11]
          But now I am M. I.!

This is what we are known as – we are the men that have been
Over a year at the business, smelt it an' felt it an' seen.
We 'ave got 'old of the needful – *you* will be told by and by;
Wait till you've 'eard Ikonas, spoke to the old M.I.!

---

[8] Tod Sloan was a well-known jockey who invented a famous horseracing technique called the 'monkey-ride'.

[9] Mausered at one and a penny a day. The Boers were armed with German Mauser rifles. In this context to be shot at by rifle fire for a wage of one bob (a slang term for one shilling or 1/20 of a British Pound) and one penny a day.

[10] A source of complaint for British soldiers was the much lower daily pay they received than their counterparts from the white colonies, who were known as 'five-bob colonials.'

[11] Kipling takes a swing at the red coats formerly worn by British soldiers, which made them highly visible targets. MI, of course, wore the newly issued khaki.

Mount – march Ikonas! Stand to your 'orses again!
Mop off the frost on the saddles, mop up the miles on the plain.
Out go the stars in the dawnin', up goes our dust to the sky,
Walk – trot, Ikonas! Trek jou,[12] the old M. I.

The empire had dispatched five divisions to defeat the Boers, including an entire cavalry division commanded by Lieutenant General Sir John French. This proved to be an effective mix when confronting the regular Boer army in conventional battles. However, as the war entered the guerrilla phase the greater mobility of the mounted Boer commandos created a dilemma for British commanders in South Africa. Making things worse in the late spring of 1900, French's cavalry division had suffered over 1,500 casualties. General Roberts determined that a solution might be found by converting infantry regiments into mounted infantry (MI) columns. Finding adequate numbers of horses was an immediate problem because Roberts wanted 15,000 MI ready to go as spring faded into summer. This was not a new idea, as the army had been experimenting with MI since the 1880s in India and Africa. When enough horses could not be found at the Stellenbosch remount station, Britain imported large numbers of horses from Argentina. Twenty-eight MI battalions were raised from the regular infantry regiments sent to South Africa.

Training men, who had no experience with horses or riding, proved to be the hardest part of raising MI battalions, which were composed of four companies. The earliest efforts focused on selecting men with appropriate backgrounds; however, as the demand increased city dwellers who normally walked to work in an industrial factory were enlisted as well. Despite this, the MI columns of Roberts' army did surprisingly well in action.

Today it is common for commanders in combat and operational areas to find themselves with forces that are not exactly tailored to the tactical needs of the situation. Commanders frequently find themselves with too many with one skill and not enough of another. In 1944, General Dwight Eisenhower found himself with too many anti-aircraft gunners and too many Afro-American truck drivers, and not enough infantrymen. Ack-Ack men and the truck drivers soon found themselves in infantry platoons. It is not uncommon for artillerymen, air defence gunners, and chemical specialists to find their skills redundant in the lower end of the range of active military operations today. Frequently these groups, as well as many others, find themselves re-roled (re-tasked) to guard perimeters, run checkpoints and convoys, and to plus-up active patrols. Soldiers thus re-roled find themselves learning on-the-job (OTJ) and often emerge very proud of having successfully overcome the

---

12 *Trek jou*. Boer imperative for 'Get Ahead!'

odds of their experience. New Zealanders thus re-roled will tell you proudly they 'got made infantry!'

Poetry and the Profession of Arms

> That is what we are known as – we are the push you require
> For outposts all night under freezin', an' rearguard all day under fire.
> Anything 'ot or unwholesome? Anything dusty or dry?
> Borrow a bunch of Ikonas! Trot out the – M. I.!

Tongue-in-cheek sarcasm is overlaid on the sense of pride that field soldiers feel about their lot in life. Nobody enjoys hot climates or being under fire. However, stoic endurance of hardship and the associated risk of being killed in the field are often a source of pride because soldiers know that the war cannot be fought and won without them. They are also somewhat contemptuous of those in uniform who are not serving in such arduous circumstances.

> The new fat regiments come from home, imaginin' vain V.C.'s
> (The same as your talky-fighty men which are often Number Threes),
> But our words o' command are "Scatter" an' "Close" an' "Let your
> wounded lie".

Experienced field soldiers look askance at the new men fresh from home, and especially look down their noses at the men consciously seeking medals and glory. Field soldiers are also leery of the loudmouth braggart who fails to live up to his boasts in combat. These extravagant and larger-than-life personalities often endanger their comrades and are sometimes marginalized in jobs where they cannot jeopardise their mates.

> I wish my mother could see me now, a-gathering news on my own,
> When I ride like a General up to the scrub and ride back like Tod Sloan,
> Remarkable close to my 'orse's neck to let the shots go by.

The experience of being surprised on a reconnaissance as one casually approaches a dangerous piece of terrain is reversed by a frantic retreat to safety. In context, looking like a general in the casual approach is followed by beating a frantic retreat hunkered down and gripping the horse's mane to lower the silhouette.

> I wish myself could talk to myself as I left 'im a year ago;
> I could tell 'im a lot that would save 'im a lot on the things that 'e
> ought to know!
> When I think o' that ignorant barrack-bird, it almost makes me cry.

The regret about 'not knowing what you don't know' is a common after the fact phenomenon for those engaged in life-threatening situations. This is often accompanied by reflecting on the lives which might have been saved, or the energy which need not have been expended. This experience is not limited to field soldiers.

Chapter 5

Friends and Enemies Respected

Introduction

Rudyard Kipling lived in an imperial world characterized by an elevated and ethnocentric sense of the superiority of the Anglo-Saxon people. This sense of superiority extended to many fields beyond military and naval endeavours, including culture in general, government, trade, and religion. With that said, Kipling was a great admirer of people who demonstrated such virtues as honour, courage, self-reliance, and pluck. His life in India exposed him to the idea of 'martial races' and he was deeply respectful of cultures that produced capable and tough fighting men.

Kipling's understanding of the 'martial races', which he believed naturally bred fighting men, is an elemental theme in poems such as 'The Irish Guards' and 'Fuzzy Wuzzy'. These poems also reflect Kipling's deep sense of obligatory duty and his admiration of shared sacrifice. In 'The Irish Guards' his echoing refrain 'Ireland no more' called the Irish to make similar efforts during the First World War. It should not surprise us that the poem was published during the worst days of the war, just a few weeks before Haig's famous 'backs to the wall' order in April 1918. For Kipling the call to duty to defeat the German enemy was a compelling responsibility for the civilized world.

Are some races and cultures born to fight? Are the Irish or the Sudanese natural soldiers, or are they the product of a system that thrives in the trial of combat? Rudyard Kipling's sense of history and his easy linking of historical events with the present day (as it was in his time) is showcased in these verses

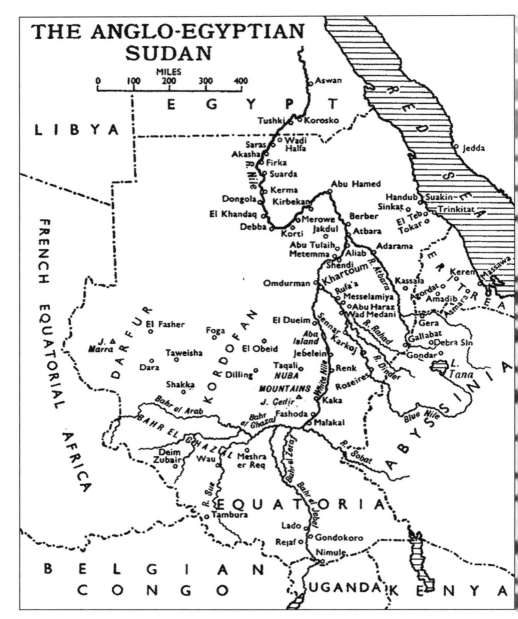

The Anglo–Egyptian Sudan. Britain came to occupy the Sudan as an outcome of protecting Egypt from the depredations of the tribal inhabitants of its southern neighbour. The port of Suakin appears on the Red Sea. Map courtesy of the University of Texas at Austin.

and the answer to these questions is self-evident. The poems I have selected for this chapter are 'The Irish Guards', '"Fuzzy Wuzzy"', 'Piet', and 'The Ballad of East and West'. Other similar poems, which may be found on the Kipling Society's website and which I recommend to the reader, are 'A British-Roman Song', 'Pharaoh and the Sergeant', and 'The Voortrekker'.

The Irish Guards

1918

First published on 18 March 1918 as a special programme for a concert to aid the Irish Guards regimental fund. One hundred copies, signed by Kipling and embossed with the regimental crest, were sold at the concert to raise money for regimental families and wounded veterans. The voice is that of a distinguished historian commenting on the virtues and obligations of a fighting race in the midst of the current war.

> We're not so old in the Army list,
>   But we're not so young at our trade,
> For we had the honour at Fontenoy,
>   Of meeting the Guards' Brigade.
> 'Twas Lally, Dillon, Buckley, Clare,
>   And Lee that led us then,
> And after a hundred and seventy years,
>   We're fighting for France again.
>   Old Days! The wild geese are flighting
>   Head to the storm as they faced it before!
>   For where there are Irish there's bound to be fighting,
>   And when there's no fighting, it's Ireland no more
>   Ireland no more!
>
> The fashion's all for khaki now,
>   But once through France we went
> Full-dressed in scarlet Army cloth,
>   The English left at Ghent.
> They're fighting on our side to-day
>   But, before they changed their clothes,
> The half of Europe knew our fame,
>   As all of Ireland knows!
>   Old Days! The wild geese are flying
>   Head to the storm as they faced it before!
>   For where there are Irish there's memory undying,
>   And when we forget, it is Ireland no more!
>   Ireland no more!

From Barry Wood to Gouzeaucourt,
    From Boyne to Pilkem Ridge,
The ancient days come back no more
    Than water under the bridge.
But the bridge it stands and the water runs
    As red as yesterday,
And the Irish move to the sound of the guns
    Like salmon to the sea.
        Old Days! The wild geese are ranging,
            Head to the storm as they faced it before!
        For where there are Irish their hearts are unchanging,
            And when they are changed, it is Ireland no more!
                Ireland no more!

We're not so old in the Army list but,
    But we're not so new in the ring.
For we carried our packs with Marshal Saxe
    When Louis was our King.
But Douglas Haig's our marshal now,
    And we're King George's men
After one hundred and seventy years
    We're fighting for France again.
        Ah, France! And did we stand by you
            Then life was made splendid with gifts, and rewards?
        Ah, France! And will we deny you
            In the hour of your agony, Mother of Swords?[1]
        Old Days! The wild geese are flighting,
            Head to the storm as they faced it before,
        For where there are Irish, there's loving and fighting,
            And when we stop either, It's Ireland no more!
                Ireland no more!

The Irish Guards were formed on 1 April 1900 by order of Queen Victoria to commemorate the many courageous acts performed by Irish soldiers in the Second Anglo-Boer War. The regiment joined the foot guards in the Guards Brigade and its motto of *'Quis Separabit'* or *'Who shall separate us?'* is taken from the Order of Saint Patrick (an order of chivalry founded by King George II). The regiment celebrates Saint Patrick's Day with the presentation of fresh shamrocks to its members. The regiment's first colonel-in-chief was Field Marshal Lord Roberts of Kandahar.

---

[1] Mother of Swords. Kipling's phrase pays tribute to the glorious military heritage of France.

In the seniority of British army regiments the Irish Guards was a young regiment with only the Welsh Guards (formed in February 1915) behind it in the order of precedence of foot guards. The officers of the Irish Guards were listed in the Army Lists (a document started in 1702, which lists the seniority of officers) upon its formation.

Kipling wrote 'The Irish Guards' in the spring of 1918 to raise money for the Irish Guards' War Fund and he had already agreed to write the post-war regimental history. His reasons for doing so were beyond simple sentiment. In August 1914, Kipling used his influence with Lord Roberts to obtain a commission in the 2nd Battalion, Irish Guards for his only son, John Kipling, who had been rejected for service because of poor eyesight. Lieutenant Kipling's battalion deployed to France in August 1915 and he was killed at the Battle of Loos.

Poetry and the Profession of Arms

> Old Days! The wild geese are flighting
>> Head to the storm as they faced it before!
> For where there are Irish there's bound to be fighting,
>> And when there's no fighting, it's Ireland no more
>>> Ireland no more!

The story of the Wild Geese begins with the Jacobite Rebellion in Ireland, in which supporters of James II fought against the Williamites (the Protestant supporters of William of Orange). The rebellion culminated with the Battle of the Boyne in 1690, which the Catholic forces lost, and which assured Protestant ascendency in Ireland for the next 200 years. The rebellion concluded in 1691 with Treaty of Limerick. The treaty contained military articles which allowed the defeated Jacobite soldiers to depart Ireland safely with their arms and regimental colours. About 14,000 of these soldiers left the country in what has come to be called the 'Flight of the Wild Geese'. Many settled in Catholic France, where they were joined by a five-regiment Irish Brigade, which was already fighting against the Dutch for Louis XV. Akin to the patterns of migratory geese, the homeless Irish became travelling mercenaries bound to kings by financial rewards.

> For we had the honour at Fontenoy,
>> Of meeting the Guards' Brigade.
> 'Twas Lally, Dillon, Buckley, Clare,
>> And Lee that led us then,
> And after a hundred and seventy years,
>> We're fighting for France again.

In the War of Austrian Succession, one of the series of Anglo-French wars that raged in the eighteenth century, Britain sent an army to the Continent that included a Guards Brigade (composed of Grenadier, Coldstream, and Scots Guards). In May 1745 the French Army, led by French Marshal Maurice de Saxe, met the Anglo-Dutch army at Fontenoy (in modern Belgium). Marshal Saxe's army included an Irish Brigade of six Wild Geese regiments. Arthur Dillon commanded one of these regiments, as did Gerald Lally. Bulkeley, Clare, and Lee were also colonels in the Irish Brigade. At the Battle of Fontenoy Saxe placed the Irish Brigade in reserve behind the Wood of Barry, where it made a gallant stand, but it was drawn into the fighting in doomed counter-attacks, most notably by Dillon's regiment.

> The fashion's all for khaki now,
>   But once through France we went
> Full-dressed in scarlet Army cloth,
>   The English left at Ghent
>
> From Barry Wood to Gouzeaucourt,
>   From Boyne to Pilkem Ridge,
> The ancient days come back no more
>   Than water under the bridge.
> But the bridge it stands and the water runs
>   As red as yesterday,
> And the Irish move to the sound of the guns
>   Like salmon to the sea.

After the battle of Fontenoy the defeated British retreated from Ghent abandoning their stores and scarlet uniforms, which the Irish then wore as replacements for their own tattered garments. In the twentieth century in France during the First World War, under the command of General Douglas Haig's British Expeditionary Force, the khaki-uniformed Irish Guards fought at Gouzeaucourt after the blood-letting on the Somme and later on Pilkem Ridge near Ypres.

> Ah, France! And did we stand by you
>   Then life was made splendid with gifts, and rewards?
> Ah, France! And will we deny you
>   In the hour of your agony, Mother of Swords?

The spring of 1918 was a dismal period for the allies in the First World War. Russia had collapsed and signed the Treaty of Brest-Litovsk, giving Germany the ability to shift massive forces to the Western Front. The American Army had not yet arrived in force, nor was it ready for trench warfare. Heroic France had endured massive casualties, parts of its army had mutinied in 1917, and it teetered on the brink of collapse. In Kipling's view France had paid dearly for holding back the Germans, and the allies had an obligation to come to her aid in her hour of need.

***

"Fuzzy-Wuzzy"[1]

Soudan Expeditionary Force, Early Campaign

Published in *The Scots Observer* on 15 March 1890 and then included in *Departmental Ditties, Barrack Room Ballads and Other Verses* that same year. The voice is that of a veteran of the expeditionary campaign in the Sudan against the Mahdi in 1884–85 paying tribute to his enemy.

We've fought with many men acrost the seas,
 An' some of 'em was brave an' some was not:
The Paythan an' the Zulu an' Burmese;
 But the Fuzzy was the finest o' the lot.
We never got a ha'porth's change of 'im:
 'E squatted in the scrub an' 'ocked our 'orses,
'E cut our sentries up at Suakim,
 An' 'e played the cat an' banjo with our forces.
  So 'ere's *to* you, Fuzzy-Wuzzy, at your 'ome in the Soudan;
  You're a pore benighted 'eathen but a first-class fightin' man;
  We gives you your certificate, an' if you want it signed
  We'll come an' 'ave a romp with you whenever you're inclined.

We took our chanst among the Khyber 'ills,
 The Boers knocked us silly at a mile,
The Burman give us Irriwaddy chills,
 An' a Zulu impi dished us up in style:
But all we ever got from such as they
 Was pop to what the Fuzzy made us swaller;
We 'eld our bloomin' own, the papers say,
 But man for man the Fuzzy knocked us 'oller.
  Then 'ere's *to* you, Fuzzy-Wuzzy, an' the missis and the kid;
  Our orders was to break you, an' of course we went an' did.
  We sloshed you with Martinis, an' it wasn't 'ardly fair;
  But for all the odds agin' you, Fuzzy-Wuz, you broke the square.

---

[1] Black Sudanese with wild, frizzy hair (often bleached with lime to a dirty hay colour).

'E 'asn't got no papers of 'is own,
    'E 'asn't got no medals nor rewards,
So we must certify the skill 'e's shown
    In usin' of 'is long two-'anded swords:
When 'e's 'oppin' in an' out among the bush
    With 'is coffin-'eaded shield an' shovel-spear,
An 'appy day with Fuzzy on the rush
    Will last an 'ealthy Tommy for a year.
        So 'ere's *to* you, Fuzzy-Wuzzy, an' your friends which are
    no more,
        If we 'adn't lost some messmates we would 'elp you to deplore;
But give an' take's the gospel, an' we'll call the bargain fair,
        For if you 'ave lost more than us, you crumpled up the square!

'E rushes at the smoke when we let drive,
    An', before we know, 'e's 'ackin' at our 'ead;
'E's all 'ot sand an' ginger when alive,
    An' 'e's generally shammin' when 'e's dead.
'E's a daisy, 'e's a ducky, 'e's a lamb!
    'E's a injia-rubber idiot on the spree,
'E's the on'y thing that doesn't give a damn
    For a Regiment o' British Infantree!
        So 'ere's *to* you, Fuzzy-Wuzzy, at your 'ome in the Soudan;
        You're a pore benighted 'eathen but a first-class fightin' man;
        An' 'ere's *to* you, Fuzzy-Wuzzy, with your 'ayrick 'ead of 'air –
        You big black boundin' beggar – for you broke a British square!

Britain's troubles with the Fuzzies derived from a pre-existing conflict between the Ottoman Egyptian administration in the Sudan and a charismatic Sudanese leader called the Mahdi (Muhammad Ahmad). The annihilation of William Hicks' Egyptian Army by the Mahdi in 1883, with an army composed of Arab tribesmen and black Sudanese (whose wild, frizzy hair, often bleached with lime to a dirty hay colour), led to the appellation Fuzzy-Wuzzy. A further expedition by Valentine Baker seized the port of Suakin. Baker's army, likewise, was an Egyptian army led by British officers; it was badly handled by raiding Fuzzies, and catastrophically defeated at El Teb by the Dervishes of Osman Dinga.

A third expeditionary force, led by Gerald Graham, advanced from Suakin in 1884 to punish the Dervishes. At the battle of Tamai on 13 March 1884, a charge by the Black Watch left a corner of Graham's square open to attack from another direction. Osman's frizzy-haired Beja tribesman briefly broke into the square before the British formation was restored. To the present day the Black Watch are sensitive to the accusation 'broken square'.

Poetry and the Profession of Arms

> 'E 'asn't got no papers of 'is own,
>   'E 'asn't got no medals nor rewards,
> So we must certify the skill 'e's shown
>   In usin' of 'is long two-'anded swords:
> So 'ere's *to* you, Fuzzy-Wuzzy, an' your friends which are no more,
>   If we 'adn't lost some messmates we would 'elp you to deplore;
> But give an' take's the gospel, an' we'll call the bargain fair.
> For if you 'ave lost more than us, you crumpled up the square!

Kipling notes that the Fuzzies are a 'come as you are' unconventional army that neither pays nor respects its soldiers. He pays tribute to the courage and pluck of the Fuzzies by emphasising in each stanza (four times altogether), 'So 'here's *to* you, Fuzzy-Wuzzy...' The public recognition by British fighting men of the bravery of the enemy fighting men is honour enough in Kipling's eyes.

> 'E's the on'y thing that doesn't give a damn
> For a Regiment o' British Infantree!
>   So 'ere's *to* you, Fuzzy-Wuzzy, at your 'ome in the Soudan;
>   You're a pore benighted 'eathen but a first-class fightin' man;
> An' 'ere's *to* you, Fuzzy-Wuzzy, with your 'ayrick 'ead of 'air –
> You big black boundin' beggar – for you broke a British square!

Neither Napoleon's guards nor Russian veterans in the Crimea could break a British square, yet through incredible bravery the Fuzzies managed to accomplish this near-impossible feat. On behalf of the British Army Kipling acknowledges Fuzzy-Wuzzy as a first-class fighting man. Soldiers often bestow an informal nickname on their enemy and, oddly, sometimes these are terms of affection and honour (examples include Johnny Turk and Fritz). At the other end are derisory nicknames (such as Haji, Nip, or the Hun).

***

Piet

Regular of the Line

Written in 1901, this poem closed the sixteen 'Service Songs' in *The Five Nations*. The voice is that of a British soldier paying tribute to his Boer enemy while reflecting on his fighting ability.

> I do not love my Empire's foes,
>   Nor call 'em angels; still,

What is the sense of 'atin' those
    'Oom you are paid to kill?
So, barrin' all that foreign lot
    Which only joined for spite,
Myself, I'd just as soon as not
    Respect the man I fight.
        Ah there, Piet!—'is trousies to 'is knees,[1]
        'Is coat-tails lyin' level in the bullet-sprinkled breeze;
        'E does not lose 'is rifle an' 'e does not lose 'is seat,
        I've known a lot o' people ride a dam' sight worse than Piet.

I've 'eard 'im cryin' from the ground
    Like Abel's blood of old,
An' skirmished out to look, an' found
    The beggar nearly cold.
I've waited on till 'e was dead
    (which couldn't 'elp 'im much),
But many grateful things 'e 's said
    To me for doin' such.
        Ah there, Piet! whose time 'as come to die,
        'Is carcase past rebellion, but 'is eyes inquirin' why.
        Though dressed in stolen uniform with badge o' rank
complete,
        I've known a lot o' fellers go a dam' sight worse than Piet.

An' when there wasn't aught to do
    But camp and cattle-guards,
I've fought with 'im the 'ole day through
    At fifteen 'undred yards;
Long afternoons o' lyin' still,
    An' 'earin' as you lay
The bullets swish from 'ill to 'ill
    Like scythes among the 'ay.
        Ah there, Piet! – be'ind 'is stony kop.
        With 'is Boer bread an' biltong, an' 'is flask of awful Dop;[2]
        'Is Mauser for amusement an' 'is pony for retreat,
        I've known a lot o' fellers shoot a dam' sight worse than Piet.

He's shoved 'is rifle 'neath my nose
    Before I'd time to think,
An' borrowed all my Sunday clo'es

---

[1] Piet (Tommy's affectionate nickname for his Boer adversary) wore baggy civilian trousers without military puttees.
[2] Biltong: dried meat jerky; Dop: slang for an alcoholic drink.

An' sent me 'ome in pink;[3]
An' I 'ave crept (Lord, 'ow I've crept!)
  On 'ands an' knees I've gone,
And spoored and floored and caught and kept
  An' sent him to Ceylon![4]
    Ah there, Piet!—you've sold me many a pup,
    When week on week alternate it was you an' me "'ands up!"
    But though I never made you walk man-naked in the 'eat,
    I've known a lot of fellows stalk a dam' sight worse than Piet.

From Plewman's to Marabastad,
  From Ookiep to De Aar,
Me an' my trusty friend 'ave 'ad,
  As you might say, a war;
But seein' what both parties done
  Before 'e owned defeat,
I ain't more proud of 'avin' won,
  Than I am pleased with Piet.
    Ah there, Piet! – picked up be'ind the drive!
    The wonder wasn't 'ow 'e fought, but 'ow 'e kep' alive,
    With nothin' in 'is belly, on 'is back, or to 'is feet –
    I've known a lot o' men behave a dam' sight worse than Piet.

No more I'll 'ear 'is rifle crack
  Along the block'ouse fence –
The beggar's on the peaceful tack,
  Regardless of expense;
For countin' what 'e eats an' draws,
  An' gifts an' loans as well,
'E's gettin' 'alf the Earth, because
  'E didn't give us 'Ell!
    Ah there, Piet! with your brand-new English plough,
    Your gratis tents an' cattle, an' your most ungrateful frow,[5]
    You've made the British taxpayer rebuild your country seat –
    I've known some pet battalions charge a dam' sight less than
Piet.

After the defeat of the Boer regular armies the Boer generals turned to
guerrilla warfare in order to continue resistance to Britain's occupation

---

[3] The isolated Boers confiscated the uniforms of captured British soldiers leaving them naked (or pink).

[4] Captured Boer prisoners were sent to prisoner of war camps on the island of Ceylon which ensured their cooperation since escape was nearly impossible.

[5] Frow: Wife in Dutch is vrouw (and Frau in German).

of the Boer republics. The subsequent forced removal of the Boer civilian population to concentration camps then cut the commandos' primary source of supplies and isolated them from both internal and external aid. In order to keep fighting the Boers captured from the British and used many of the accoutrements of war (rifles, ammunition, horses, and uniforms). Famously, captured British soldiers were forced to give their uniforms and boots to the Boers, thus leaving them naked on the veldt. The poem reflects the endurance and hardihood of the Boers in the field, who managed to keep fighting without logistical support. The use of humour and a light-hearted tone is evident in 'Piet', which is a tribute to the fighting qualities of the Boer commandos.

The Treaty of Vereeniging, negotiated between 15 and 31 May 1902, ended the long war and transformed the two Boer republics into British colonies. The cost had been high: British casualties numbered almost 98,000 men, of whom 20,870 were killed or died of disease. Boer casualties included some 10,000 killed and wounded, and over 20,000 civilians who died in the concentration camps. Under the treaty Britain made £3 million available to the Boers to cover the costs of resettlement, and another £3 million was made available in interest-free loans. Some 30,000 Boer farms had been burned out and the livestock killed or seized. In addition to the cash reparations Boer landowners were provided with farm implements (such as English ploughs), animals (cattle, sheep, and draught horses), and seeds to rebuild their farms.

Poetry and the Profession of Arms

> So, barrin' all that foreign lot
>> Which only joined for spite,
> Myself, I'd just as soon as not
>> Respect the man I fight.

The great German field marshal Erwin Rommel characterized the war in North Africa as a *krieg ohne hass* (war without hate). Rommel's term evoked the sentiment that soldiers on opposing sides are just doing their job and killing each other was simply their stock and trade rather than the product of hatred. This light-hearted view of one's enemies reflected Tommy's affection and admiration for the Boers. Moreover, war on the veldt, as in the open deserts of North Africa, was essentially a 'clean war', devoid of such modern concerns as collateral damage. Modern soldiers are trained to view their enemy in this way.

> For countin' what 'e eats an' draws,
>> An' gifts an' loans as well,
> 'E's gettin' 'alf the Earth, because
>> 'E didn't give us 'Ell!

For the most part the Boers fought an honourable war and, for that, Kipling's imaginary veteran grants 'Piet' his fair due of the post-war reparations. Despite the brutal civilian relocations, and an occasional atrocity such as that of Breaker Morant, the military engagements and campaigns were something of a gentleman's war, observing the conventions of European combat. Today our contemporary rules of engagement are an attempt to interject an element of humanity into an otherwise inhumane environment. Unfortunately, the irregular enemies we confront on today's battlefields are almost never adherents to international humanitarian conventions.

> Ah there, Piet! with your brand-new English plough,
> Your gratis tents an' cattle, an' your most ungrateful frow,
> You've made the British taxpayer rebuild your country seat –
> I've known some pet battalions charge a dam' sight less than Piet.

Kipling's finely attuned sense of irony is evident here as he comments on the reparations and direct assistance Britain made available to the Boers under the terms of the Treaty of Vereeniging.

***

The Ballad of East and West

Published in the *Pioneer* on 2 December 1889 and in several magazines thereafter. It found its way into *Barrack-Room Ballads and Other Verses*. The voice is that of a storyteller relating a tale of great feats of daring and of the honours accorded to chivalrous and worthy enemies.

> Oh, East is East, and West is West, and never the twain shall meet,
> Till Earth and Sky stand presently at God's great Judgment Seat;
> But there is neither East nor West, Border, nor Breed, nor Birth,
> When two strong men stand face to face,
> tho' they come from the ends of the earth!
>
> Kamal is out with twenty men to raise the Border-side,
> And he has lifted the Colonel's mare that is the Colonel's pride:
> He has lifted her out of the stable-door between the dawn and the day,
> And turned the calkins[1] upon her feet, and ridden her far away.

---

[1] Calkins. Horseshoes: reversing the horseshoes was an old trick employed by the brigands on the frontier.

Then up and spoke the Colonel's son that led a troop of the Guides:[2]
"Is there never a man of all my men can say where Kamal hides?"
Then up and spoke Mahommed Khan, the son of the Ressaldar:[3]
"If ye know the track of the morning-mist, ye know where his pickets are.
At dusk he harries the Abazai – at dawn he is into Bonair,[4]
But he must go by Fort Bukloh to his own place to fare,
So if ye gallop to Fort Bukloh as fast as a bird can fly,
By the favour of God ye may cut him off ere he win to the Tongue of Jagai.
But if he be past the Tongue of Jagai, right swiftly turn ye then,
For the length and the breadth of that grisly plain is sown with Kamal's men.
There is rock to the left, and rock to the right, and low lean thorn between,
And ye may hear a breech-bolt snick where never a man is seen."
The Colonel's son has taken a horse, and a raw rough dun was he,
With the mouth of a bell and the heart of Hell
and the head of the gallows-tree.
The Colonel's son to the Fort has won, they bid him stay to eat –
Who rides at the tail of a Border thief, he sits not long at his meat.
He's up and away from Fort Bukloh as fast as he can fly,
Till he was aware of his father's mare in the gut of the Tongue of Jagai,[5]
Till he was aware of his father's mare with Kamal upon her back,
And when he could spy the white of her eye, he made the pistol crack.
He has fired once, he has fired twice, but the whistling ball went wide.
"Ye shoot like a soldier," Kamal said. "Show now if ye can ride."
It's up and over the Tongue of Jagai, as blown dustdevils go,
The dun he fled like a stag of ten, but the mare like a barren doe.
The dun he leaned against the bit and slugged his head above,
But the red mare played with the snaffle-bars, as a maiden plays with a glove.
There was rock to the left and rock to the right, and low lean thorn between,
And thrice he heard a breech-bolt snick tho' never a man was seen.

---

[2] The Queen's Own Corps of Guides, raised in 1846 and stationed in Mardan, was one of the most famous corps in the Indian Army.

[3] Ressaldar. A native captain in an Indian Army cavalry regiment.

[4] Abazai and Bonair. Frontier districts in the Punjab about forty miles apart.

[5] Tongue of Jagai. The scene of the battle described in Kipling's story *The Drums of the Fore and Aft* (Wee Willie Winkie).

They have ridden the low moon out of the sky, their hoofs drum up the dawn,
The dun he went like a wounded bull, but the mare like a new-roused fawn.
The dun he fell at a water-course – in a woeful heap fell he,
And Kamal has turned the red mare back, and pulled the rider free.
He has knocked the pistol out of his hand – small room was there to strive,
"'Twas only by favour of mine," quoth he, "ye rode so long alive:
There was not a rock for twenty mile, there was not a clump of tree,
But covered a man of my own men with his rifle cocked on his knee.
If I had raised my bridle-hand, as I have held it low,
The little jackals that flee so fast were feasting all in a row:
If I had bowed my head on my breast, as I have held it high,
The kite that whistles above us now were gorged till she could not fly."
Lightly answered the Colonel's son: "Do good to bird and beast,
But count who come for the broken meats before thou makest a feast.
If there should follow a thousand swords to carry my bones away,
Belike the price of a jackal's meal were more than a thief could pay.
They will feed their horse on the standing crop,
their men on the garnered grain,
The thatch of the byres will serve their fires when all the cattle are slain.
But if thou thinkest the price be fair, – thy brethren wait to sup,
The hound is kin to the jackal-spawn, – howl, dog, and call them up!
And if thou thinkest the price be high, in steer and gear and stack,
Give me my father's mare again, and I'll fight my own way back!"
Kamal has gripped him by the hand and set him upon his feet.
"No talk shall be of dogs," said he, "when wolf and gray wolf meet.
May I eat dirt if thou hast hurt of me in deed or breath;
What dam of lances brought thee forth to jest at the dawn with Death?"
Lightly answered the Colonel's son: "I hold by the blood of my clan:
Take up the mare for my father's gift – by God, she has carried a man!"
The red mare ran to the Colonel's son, and nuzzled against his breast;
"We be two strong men," said Kamal then, "but she loveth the younger best.
So she shall go with a lifter's dower, my turquoise-studded rein,
My broidered saddle and saddle-cloth, and silver stirrups twain."
The Colonel's son a pistol drew and held it muzzle-end,
"Ye have taken the one from a foe," said he;
"will ye take the mate from a friend?"
"A gift for a gift," said Kamal straight; "a limb for the risk of a limb.

Thy father has sent his son to me, I'll send my son to him!"
With that he whistled his only son, that dropped from a mountain-
crest –
He trod the ling like a buck in spring, and he looked like a lance
in rest.
"Now here is thy master," Kamal said, "who leads a troop of the
Guides,
And thou must ride at his left side as shield on shoulder rides.
Till Death or I cut loose the tie, at camp and board and bed,
Thy life is his – thy fate it is to guard him with thy head.
So, thou must eat the White Queen's meat, and all her foes are thine,
And thou must harry thy father's hold for the peace of the Border-
line,
And thou must make a trooper tough and hack thy way to power –
Belike they will raise thee to Ressaldar when I am hanged in
Peshawur."

They have looked each other between the eyes, and there they
found no fault,
They have taken the Oath of the Brother-in-Blood on leavened
bread and salt:
They have taken the Oath of the Brother-in-Blood on fire and
fresh-cut sod,
On the hilt and the haft of the Khyber knife, and the Wondrous
Names of God.
The Colonel's son he rides the mare and Kamal's boy the dun,
And two have come back to Fort Bukloh where there went forth
but one.
And when they drew to the Quarter-Guard, full twenty swords
flew clear –
There was not a man but carried his feud with the blood of the
mountaineer.
"Ha' done! ha' done!" said the Colonel's son.
"Put up the steel at your sides!
Last night ye had struck at a Border thief –
to-night 'tis a man of the Guides!"

Oh, East is East, and West is West, and never the twain shall meet,
Till Earth and Sky stand presently at God's great Judgment Seat;
But there is neither East nor West, Border, nor Breed, nor Birth,
When two strong men stand face to face,
tho' they come from the ends of the earth!

This ballad is typical of the kinds of tales that Kipling, the great storyteller, heard and brought back from the sub-continent to England for the enjoyment of a 'shuttered people'. Kipling does not break up the tale into manageable stanzas and it is a longish read. In this story a young English officer pursues an Afghan horse thief into enemy-held tribal country and certain death. However, when the officer's horse collapses from exhaustion the officer's heroism and sense of duty is recognized by the Afghan tribal chieftain, who sends his own son back with the officer to join the corps of guides. This ballad is a poem of fancy rather than a poem of fact, and its style and flow are different from the verses previously presented. In form the poem takes a binary approach as Kipling shifts between a third person narrative and direct dialogue between participants.

The Queen's Own Corps of Guides, raised in 1846 by Sir Harry Lumsden, was created to protect the North-West Frontier of India. Originally it was a highly mobile force of one cavalry troop and two infantry companies, but by 1900 the corps had grown to over 1,400 men. Twenty-seven of its officers were British, as was its colonel, and the remaining officers were native Indians. Britain recruited from among the martial races in order to provide the corps with men who knew the local terrain and inhabitants. Alone among the regiments of the Indian Army the corps had permission to recruit men from any regiment. As such the corps had, among others, Pathans, Sikhs, Punjab Muslims, Dogras, Gurkhas, and Afridis.

Poetry and the Profession of Arms

> Oh, East is East, and West is West, and never the twain shall meet,
> Till Earth and Sky stand presently at God's great Judgment Seat;
> But there is neither East nor West, Border, nor Breed, nor Birth,
> When two strong men stand face to face,
> tho' they come from the ends of the earth!

One of Kipling's most well-known verses, the opening couplet is sometimes misquoted today to support the contemporary 'clash of civilizations' debate. This is an improper use of Kipling's idea, which is that strong and brave men are produced by all cultures and races. Soldiers and civilians must look beyond identities and reflect on the military qualities and attributes of their enemies.

During some of the darkest days of the Second World War Winston Churchill delivered a speech in the House of Commons praising German Field Marshal Erwin Rommel. Churchill noted, to the chagrin of some members, "We have a very daring and skilful opponent against us, and, may I say across the havoc of war, a great general." Churchill's sentiments reflected his life-long regard for the profession of arms and reflected his enduring respect for its practitioners.

> So if ye gallop to Fort Bukloh as fast as a bird can fly,
> By the favour of God ye may cut him off ere he win to the Tongue
> of Jagai.
> But if he be past the Tongue of Jagai, right swiftly turn ye then,
> For the length and the breadth of that grisly plain is sown with
> Kamal's men.

The Tongue of Jagai in our terms might be referred to as a 'chokepoint' and, in the verse, the last opportunity to cut off the thief before he reaches the safety of his own territory. Beyond this point is 'Indian country' within which death lurks behind every scrub bush and atop every piece of high ground.

Chapter 6

Other Arms and Services Respected

Introduction

Kipling was quite aware of the nature of public acclaim and its effect on the public consciousness in creating famous identities both personal and institutional. He was also very aware of the opposite effect and the dilemma of the unsung hero. In these verses he comments on the contributions of the less well known arms and ships whose quiet contributions were so vital to victory on land and sea. Kipling often took it upon himself to give credit to and bring respect to the unsung heroes of the empire.

In the same way that Kipling admired the martial qualities of Britain's friends and enemies, he also expressed deep admiration for particular arms of the Queen's fighting services. The poems selected for this chapter represent the British Army's field artillery and engineers, the Royal Marines, and the Royal Navy. These poems comment on the enduring nature of combined arms on land, the importance and cost of sea power, and the unique character of marines who possess attributes of both land and sea services.

Many of Kipling's poems contain biblical references and allegorical connections. These poems are no exception and a nineteenth-century English reader would have had a basic understanding of many of Kipling's references. The poems I have selected for this chapter are 'Ubique', 'Sappers', 'Song of the Dead II', 'Mine Sweepers', and 'Soldier an' Sailor Too'. Other similar poems, which may be found on the Kipling Society's superb website and which I recommend to the reader, are 'Screw-Guns', 'The Jacket', 'Cruisers', 'Destroyers', '"Tin Fish"', and '"The Trade"'.

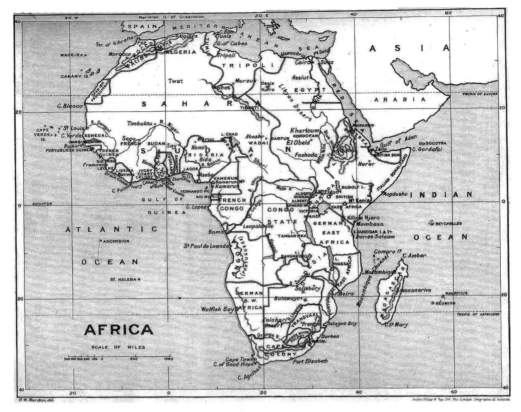

Africa, early to mid-1890s. This map shows Africa after the Berlin Congress of 1884–85 and before the Second Anglo-Boer War in 1899. The congress famously launched the 'Scramble for Africa'. Map courtesy of the University of Texas at Austin.

Ubique[1]

Royal Artillery

One of sixteen 'Service Songs', which close *The Five Nations* (1903). The voice is that of a 'gunner' (an artilleryman) who explains the omnipresence and importance of the artillery.

> There is a word you often see, pronounce it as you may –
> "You bike," "you bykwee," "ubbikwee" – alludin' to R. A.
> It serves 'Orse, Field, an' Garrison as motto for a crest;[2]
> An' when you've found out all it means I'll tell you 'alf the rest.

---

[1] *Ubique* is Latin for 'everywhere' and, after 1833, the word became the motto of the Royal Artillery.

[2] In 1899 a Royal Warrant established the Garrison Artillery in line with Continental practices to denote fixed fortress and coastal artillery. The remaining artillery units were designated as Royal Field Artillery (RFA) or Royal Horse Artillery (RHA).

Ubique means the long-range Krupp be'ind the long-range 'ill –
Ubique means you'll pick it up an', while you do, stand still.
Ubique means you've caught the flash an' timed it by the sound.[3]
Ubique means five gunners' 'ash before you've loosed a round.

Ubique means Blue Fuse, an' make the 'ole to sink the trail.[4]
Ubique means stand up an' take the Mauser's 'alf-mile 'ail.
Ubique means the crazy team not God nor man can 'old.
Ubique means that 'orse's scream which turns your innards cold!

Ubique means "Bank, 'Olborn, Bank – a penny all the way" –[5]
The soothin', jingle-bump-an'-clank from day to peaceful day.
Ubique means "They've caught De Wet,[6] an' now we shan't be long."
Ubique means "I much regret, the beggar's goin' strong!"

Ubique means the tearin' drift where, breach-block jammed
with mud,
The khaki muzzles duck an' lift across the khaki flood.
Ubique means the dancing plain that changes rocks to Boers.
Ubique means mirage again an' shellin' all outdoors.

Ubique means "Entrain at once for Grootdefeatfontein."[7]
Ubique means "Off-load your guns" – at midnight in the rain!
Ubique means "More mounted men. Return all guns to store."
Ubique means the R.A.M.R. Infantillery Corps.[8]

Ubique means that warnin' grunt the perished linesman[9] knows,
When o'er 'is strung an' sufferin' front the shrapnel sprays 'is foes;
An' as their firin' dies away the 'usky whisper runs
From lips that 'aven't drunk all day: "The Guns! Thank Gawd,
the Guns!"

---

[3] It is possible to observe the flash of a cannon being fired and then time the report to estimate the distance from you to the gun. This is called 'flash-to-bang' (based on the speed of sound at sea level being 330 metres a second). Simply count the number of seconds and multiply it by 330 to arrive at a distance in metres.

[4] Blue Fuse. A time fuse marked with a blue band. Most of the artillery's basic load was composed of shrapnel which would detonate at a time determined by the setting of the fuse.

[5] During the Second Anglo-Boer War, many artillery horses had drawn London Omnibuses. As a joke columns would greet artillery on the march with the cries of London 'bus conductors.

[6] Christiaan de Wet. One a number of exceptionally talented Boer generals who consistently evaded capture.

[7] Grootdefeatfontein. A made-up name parodying Afrikaans towns such as Bloemfontein and conveying yet another defeat that the artillery has to pull out of the fire.

[8] R.A.M.R. Infantillery Corps. Royal Artillery Mounted Rifles, nicknamed the Infantillery Corps.

[9] Linesman. An infantryman.

> Extreme, depressed, point-blank or short, end-first or any'ow,
> From Colesberg Kop to Quagga's Poort – from Ninety-Nine till
> now –
> By what I've 'eard the others tell an' I in spots 'ave seen,
> There's nothin' this side 'Eaven or 'Ell Ubique doesn't mean!

There are three classic combat arms – infantry, cavalry, and artillery. Of these infantry and cavalry are manoeuvre arms of decision and artillery plays a supporting role for both. In Kipling's time artillery fought in a direct fire role; that is to say the gunners could see their targets. The field artillery pieces of the day could effectively engage targets at 5–7,000 meters with an elevation of the tube of about 16 degrees and the variety of munitions was limited to case shot, shrapnel, and high-explosive shells. Artillery in the British Army was decentralized and artillery batteries (4–6 guns) were attached to brigades and battalions. Coordination between the manoeuvre arms and the artillery was usually in the form of direct conversation between infantry and cavalry brigade and artillery battery commanders. The factors of relatively short range, low mobility, and lack of centralized gunnery procedures dictated that the artillery of the nineteenth century was almost exclusively a defensive weapon and it was generally ineffective when used offensively.

Everything changed during the First World War because of trench warfare. The static conditions negated the power of manoeuvre, leading to an indirect fire revolution. Developments in artillery, mapping, and aerial reconnaissance led to precision registration and firing 'off the map', which led to massing fires of thousands of artillery pieces. After the first few weeks of that war gunners rarely saw their targets. Munitions evolved to include illumination rounds, gas shells, incendiary shells, smoke shells, and concrete-piercing shells and, by 1918, artillery came to be regarded as a combat arm of decisive action. When Kipling published 'Ubique' in 1903 these events lay in the unforeseen future.

Poetry and the Profession of Arms

> Ubique means "More mounted men. Return all guns to store."
> Ubique means the R.A.M.R. Infantillery Corps

As in Kipling's 'Two Kopjes' and 'Mounted Infantry' (see Chapter 4), British artillery in the Second Anglo Boer War became redundant at the end of the conventional war phase. Like the retasked infantry regiments, Royal Artillery batteries put their guns and ammunition caissons into storage and converted to mounted infantry in the fight against the Boer guerrilla commandos. Similarly, in today's campaigns against insurgents and non-state actors, artillery units are used in roles other than firing their cannons. Leaving their guns in the motor pool gunners typically perform missions such as civil affairs, convoy escort, and guarding checkpoints and bases. Occasionally, artillery 'got made infantry' (in the words of a New Zealand artillery major) and actively joined the war, patrolling and conducting infantry missions.

> Ubique means that warnin' grunt the perished linesman knows,
> When o'er 'is strung an' sufferin' front the shrapnel sprays 'is foes;
> An' as their firin' dies away the 'usky whisper runs
> From lips that 'aven't drunk all day: "The Guns! Thank Gawd, the Guns!"

It is hard to overstate the value of indirect fire (including today mortar and rocket fire) to an infantryman exposed to direct and indirect fire. In today's operational world artillery is 'on call' and able to support manoeuvre forces at will and almost instantly. Unlike aerial fire support, artillery fires can be brought in safely and close to friendly positions (in a mission known as 'danger close'). Moreover, the types of available artillery munitions have grown to include precision munitions, improved conventional munitions (bomblets), and scatterable land mines. Nothing pleases a gunner more than answering the call for fire from infantry in contact who are in desperate need of fire support.

***

Sappers[1]

First published in *The Seven Seas* in 1896. The voice is that of a somewhat put upon, but very proud, Engineer (commonly called Sappers).

> When the Waters were dried an' the Earth did appear,
>   ("It's all one," says the Sapper),
> The Lord He created the Engineer,
>   Her Majesty's Royal Engineer,
>   With the rank and pay of a Sapper!
>
> When the Flood come along for an extra monsoon,
> 'Twas Noah constructed the first pontoon
>   To the plans of Her Majesty's, etc.

---

[1] A sap is a trench or tunnel leading toward the enemy. In the age of siege warfare sappers and miners advanced the lines by digging saps forward. In all armies the name Sapper has come to be synonymous with engineers.

But after fatigue in the wet an' the sun,
Old Noah got drunk, which he wouldn't ha' done
    If he'd trained with, etc.

When the Tower o' Babel had mixed up men's *bat*,[2]
Some clever civilian was managing that,
    An' none of, etc.

When the Jews had a fight at the foot of a hill,
Young Joshua ordered the sun to stand still,
    For he was a Captain of Engineers, etc.

When the Children of Israel made bricks without straw,
They were learnin' the regular work of our Corps,
    The work of, etc.

For ever since then, if a war they would wage,
Behold us a-shinin' on history's page –
    First page for, etc.

We lay down their sidings an' help 'em entrain,
An' we sweep up their mess through the bloomin' campaign,
    In the style of, etc.

They send us in front with a fuse an' a mine
To blow up the gates that are rushed by the Line,
    But bent by, etc.

They send us behind with a pick an' a spade,
To dig for the guns of a bullock-brigade
    Which has asked for, etc.

We work under escort in trousers and shirt,
An' the heathen they plug us tail-up in the dirt,
    Annoying, etc.

We blast out the rock an' we shovel the mud,
We make 'em good roads an' – they roll down the *khud*,[3]
    Reporting, etc.

We make 'em their bridges, their wells, an' their huts,
An' the telegraph-wire the enemy cuts,
    An' it's blamed on, etc.

---

[2] *Bat:* Hindi for talk or language.
[3] *Khud* a steep hillside or precipice.

An' when we return, an' from war we would cease,
They grudge us adornin' the billets of peace,
  Which are kept for, etc.

We build 'em nice barracks – they swear they are bad,
That our Colonels are Methodist, married or mad,
  Insultin', etc.

They haven't no manners nor gratitude too,
For the more that we help 'em, the less will they do,
  But mock at, etc.

Now the Line's but a man with a gun in his hand,
An' Cavalry's only what horses can stand,
  When helped by, etc.

Artillery moves by the leave o' the ground,
But *we* are the men that do something all round,
  For *we* are, etc.

I have stated it plain, an' my argument's thus
  ("It's all one," says the Sapper),
There's only one Corps which is perfect – that's us;
  An' they call us Her Majesty's Engineers,
  Her Majesty's Royal Engineers,
  With the rank and pay of a Sapper!

The Corps of Royal Engineers itself is over 900 years old and has earned thirty-six Victoria Crosses. However, until the Crimean War (1855) there was a separate corps called the Royal Sappers and Miners. After the amalgamation of the two corps the rank of sapper was the lowest rank in the engineers, corresponding to private or trooper in the infantry and cavalry respectively. Today the engineers of the world's regular armies construct fortifications and lay minefields in defensive operations and clear minefields and obstacles and build bridges and roads in offensive operations. Additionally today the engineers are responsible for topographic (survey and map making) operations and repairing infrastructure such as railroads and ports.

In the nineteenth century the top academic graduates from the world's military academies were commissioned into the engineers and artillery. In the British Army these included General Charles 'Chinese' Gordon and Field Marshal H.H. Kitchener. Well-known American engineer officers included Generals Robert E. Lee, George McClellan, and Douglas MacArthur. When not at war many of these officers were seconded to civil projects such as the construction of railroads and ports, and topographic surveys of distant lands.

Poetry and the Profession of Arms

> When the Jews had a fight at the foot of a hill,
> Young Joshua ordered the sun to stand still,
>   For he was a Captain of Engineers, etc.
>
> When the Children of Israel made bricks without straw,
> They were learnin' the regular work of our Corps,
>   The work of, etc.

In addition to the Tower of Babel reference, wherein God punished mankind by mixing up their languages, these verses come from the Old Testament. In the Book of Joshua, Joshua performed the impossible feat of holding the sun in the sky to deny nightfall. Later, in the book Exodus, Pharaoh ordered the Children of Israel to make mud bricks. When straw (which provided a reinforcing structure similar to rebar in concrete) was unavailable, the Israelites performed the impossible feat of making bricks without it. Modern army engineers frequently proclaim that no job is too small or too hard to accomplish. Give an engineer a few days and he will perform miraculous feats of the impossible.

> I have stated it plain, an' my argument's thus
>   ("It's all one," says the Sapper),
> There's only one Corps which is perfect – that's us;
>   An' they call us Her Majesty's Engineers,
>   Her Majesty's Royal Engineers,
>   With the rank and pay of a Sapper!

The versatility of army engineers is undeniable. In addition to building things, engineers can also fight as infantry. Engineers can hold ground. During the Battle of the Bulge (also known as the Ardennes Offensive) in December 1944, United States Army engineers fought against Hitler's panzers and held vital crossroads and bridges long enough for the combat arms to restore the lines. In the South Pacific in the Second World War engineers were frequently found fighting in the front lines as well. However, despite the superb record of the army engineers of the world's armies, they are sometimes underappreciated and neglected.

***

Song of the Dead

II

First published in 1893 in the *English Illustrated Magazine* as one of six sub-sectional verses of 'A Song of the English'. It was collected and published in *The Seven Seas* in 1896. The voice is that of a patriotic Briton reflecting on the cost of sea power.

> We have fed our sea for a thousand years
>   And she calls us, still unfed,
> Though there's never a wave of all her waves
>   But marks our English dead:
> We have strawed our best to the weed's unrest,
>   To the shark and the sheering gull.
> If blood be the price of admiralty,
>   Lord God, we ha' paid in full!
>
> There's never a flood goes shoreward now
>   But lifts a keel we manned;
> There's never an ebb goes seaward now
>   But drops our dead on the sand –
> But slinks our dead on the sands forlore,
>   From the Ducies to the Swin.[1]
> If blood be the price of admiralty,
> If blood be the price of admiralty,
>   Lord God, we ha' paid it in!
>
> We must feed our sea for a thousand years,
>   For that is our doom and pride,
> As it was when they sailed with the *Golden Hind*,[2]
>   Or the wreck that struck last tide –
> Or the wreck that lies on the spouting reef
>   Where the ghastly blue-lights flare.[3]
> If blood be the price of admiralty,
> If blood be the price of admiralty,
> If blood be the price of admiralty,
>   Lord God, we ha' bought it fair!

Britain's Royal Navy has always been its premier service and is truly *primus inter pares* (first among equals). It has an unequalled history of tactical victory

---

[1] Ducie Island is near Pitcairn Island, in the central Pacific; the Swin is one of the channels running north-east to south-west in the Thames Estuary, off the Essex coast.

[2] The *Golden Hind* was Sir Francis Drake's ship during his circumnavigation of the globe (1577–80).

[3] A blue flare sent up is a sign of distress at sea.

in combat and a demonstrated tradition of ensuring command of the sea at the strategic level. Its presence and continuing strength has ensured that Britain has not been invaded since the Normans came in 1066, and the Navy has defied the Spanish, the Dutch, the French, and the Germans. The Royal Navy has a tradition of placing its ships alongside those of the enemy and sailing toward the sound of the guns. The brilliance of its captains and admirals aside, the Royal Navy's sailors have always been the best trained fighting seamen in the world.

However, the fighting skills and endurance of the Royal Navy have come at a cost. The 'Price of Admiralty', or the cost of doing business to secure command of the sea, can only be paid in blood. The Royal Navy is not simply ships and equipment, it is a significant investment in human capital. In peace and war naval operations are expensive in the actual fiscal cost of sending men down to the sea in ships, but naval operations are inherently dangerous. The price of casualties in war is self-evident, but in peacetime ships sink and sailors die as well (readers might recall this when reading about the HMS *Birkenhead* and the HMS *Victoria* in 'Soldier an' Sailor Too' – the last poem in this chapter). Kipling reminds his readers that the maintenance of freedom of the seas in what is now called the global commons is a costly endeavour. Today the United States Navy has assumed Britain's role and commands the seas of the world: Americans would do well to reflect on the relevance of Kipling's thoughts about sea power.

***

Mine Sweepers
1914–1918
Sea Warfare

First published in *The Fringes of the Fleet* in 1915, 'Mine Sweepers' was republished with '1914–1918' included in the title in *Twenty Poems from Rudyard Kipling* in 1918. The voice is that of a distanced observer remarking on the constancy, diligence, and effectiveness of this obscure and under-appreciated service.

> Dawn off the Foreland[1] – the young flood making
>   Jumbled and short and steep –
> Black in the hollows and bright where it's breaking –
>   Awkward water to sweep.

---

[1] The easternmost point of Kent and the southern peninsula of the Thames estuary.

"Mines reported in the fairway,
"Warn all traffic and detain.
*"Sent up Unity, Claribel, Assyrian, Stormcock, and Golden
Gain."*[2]

Noon off the Foreland – the first ebb making
    Lumpy and strong in the bight.
Boom after boom, and the golf-hut shaking
    And the jackdaws wild with fright!
"Mines located in the fairway,
"Boats now working up the chain,
*"Sweepers – Unity, Claribel, Assyrian, Stormcock, and Golden
Gain."*

Dusk off the Foreland – the last light going
    And the traffic crowding through,
And five damned trawlers with their syreens[3] blowing
    Heading the whole review!
"Sweep completed in the fairway.
"No more mines remain.
*"Sent back Unity, Claribel, Assyrian, Stormcock, and Golden
Gain."*

Emerging technologies made naval mine warfare possible as a practical tactic in the First World War. It became possible to produce reliable underwater mines by the thousands and both cruisers and submarines were fitted to lay minefields. Ships of that age were extremely vulnerable to damage by hitting a mine and the result was almost always a catastrophic sinking of the vessel. Indeed, the advent of underwater mines irrevocably changed naval operations in the First World War. Ottoman minefields prevented the Royal Navy from breaking through the Dardanelles in 1915, leading to the disastrous Gallipoli campaign. Field Marshal Sir H.H. Kitchener drowned when the cruiser HMS *Hampshire* sank after hitting a mine in 1916. At the conclusion of the Battle of Jutland, British Admiral Sir John Jellicoe refused to pursue the defeated German High Seas Fleet because of the danger of enemy minefields.

Navies were unprepared to combat the presence of underwater mines when Europe went to war in August 1914. The Royal Navy's first minesweepers were civilian fishing trawlers contracted by the Admiralty. The civilian skippers and crews were retained and a few Royal Navy sailors and junior officers were assigned to the vessels. The minesweepers themselves were unarmoured and

---

[2] Early in the First World War Royal Navy minesweepers were simply civilian trawlers brought into service and equipped with cables for minesweeping. These ships retained their civilian names, which were in many cases commonplace and sometimes banal.
[3] *Syreens*: Sirens.

uncompartmented against underwater explosions. The minesweeping gear consisted of steel cables dragged on the aft flanks, which snagged tethered underwater mines. When the mine broke the surface of the water, the Royal Navy sailors onboard would attempt to sink it by perforating the water-tight casing with a well-aimed rifle shot. Of course, occasionally they would hit a detonating 'horn', thereby causing a huge explosion! The work was dangerous in uncontested waters such as the English Channel and downright deadly in contested places such as the Dardanelles, when the vessels were under direct enemy fire.

Because Britain was dependent on imports, clearing the seaways, such as the English Channel, the Thames estuary, the Bristol Channel, and the sea lanes of the Irish Sea, became strategically critical priorities. The *ad hoc* and expedient fleets of civilian trawlers became as vitally important to victory as the Navy's destroyers hunting U-boats in the North Atlantic. However, as Kipling saw, the men and ships dedicated to minesweeping operations never received the acclaim and publicity of Beatty's battlecruisers or Jellicoe's dreadnoughts.

Poetry and the Profession of Arms

"Mines located in the fairway,
   "Boats now working up the chain,
"Sweepers *Unity, Claribel, Assyrian, Stormcock, and Golden
   Gain.*"

The daily grind of routine operations is tedious and such work-a-day activities as minesweeping tend to go unnoticed when compared to the supposed glamour and glory of combat duties. In truth the success of minesweeping is reflected in the fact that all ships get through to port and no ships are sunk or damaged. However, without the consistent efforts of the minesweepers, seaborne commerce into the British Isles in the First World War would have stopped, and with it the vast production of war material the British Army in France required to win the war. Minesweepers continue to be active today in the Persian Gulf and I would be remiss not to mention the under-appreciated efforts of today's brown-water coastal squadrons and the 'gators' or amphibious ships.

"Sweep completed in the fairway.
   "No more mines remain.
"*Sent back Unity, Claribel, Assyrian, Stormcock, and Golden
   Gain.*"

Success achieved and the minesweepers return. No medals are awarded, no newspaper reporter covers the story, and no officer is mentioned in dispatches.

The only reward is knowing that tomorrow the minesweepers must go back out to repeat their performance. Day after day they return to sweep up German mines. This poem reminds the professional that duty well performed, however small or seemingly inconsequential, is duty well performed. Professionals perform their duty regardless of the cost or of a lack of public acclaim – it is what professionals do.

***

Soldier an' Sailor Too

First published in *The Seven Seas* in 1896. The voice is that of an experienced British soldier explaining in very affectionate terms what a Royal Marine is and what a Royal Marine can do.

> As I was spittin' into the Ditch aboard o' the ~*Crocodile*~,[1]
> I seed a man on a man-o'-war got up in the Reg'lars' style.
> 'E was scrapin' the paint from off of 'er plates, an' I sez to 'im,
> "Oo are you?"
> Sez 'e, 'I'm a Jolly – 'Er Majesty's Jolly[2] – soldier an' sailor too!'
> Now 'is work begins by Gawd knows when, and 'is work is never through;
> 'E isn't one o' the reg'lar Line, nor 'e isn't one of the crew.
> 'E's a kind of a giddy harumfrodite[3] – soldier an' sailor too!
>
> An' after I met 'im all over the world, a-doin' all kinds of things,
> Like landin' 'isself with a Gatlin' gun to talk to them 'eathen kings;[4]
> 'E sleeps in an 'ammick instead of a cot, an' 'e drills with the deck on a slew,
> An' 'e sweats like a Jolly – 'Er Majesty's Jolly – soldier an' sailor too!
> For there isn't a job on the top o' the earth the beggar don't know, nor do –
> You can leave 'im at night on a bald man's 'ead, to paddle 'is own canoe –
> 'E's a sort of a bloomin' cosmopolouse[5] – soldier an' sailor too.

---

[1] The *Crocodile* was one of five troopships used by the Royal Navy to transport troops throughout the empire (mostly to India) in the last thirty years of the nineteenth century.

[2] *Her Majesty's Jolly:* nickname for the Royal Marines in the nineteenth century. Derived from handsome, lively, as in 'jolly good'. Today Royal Marine Commandos are called 'Bootnecks'.

[3] Harumfrodite: hermaphrodite, a being having both male and female sexual organs.

[4] Gatling gun: the predecessor to the modern machine gun with revolving barrels.

[5] Cosmopoluse. A made-up word meaning a person familiar with many countries and cultures.

We've fought 'em in trooper, we've fought 'em in dock, and drunk
with 'em in betweens,
When they called us the seasick scull'ry-maids, an' we called 'em the
Ass Marines;[6]
But, when we was down for a double fatigue, from Woolwich to
Bernardmyo,[7]
We sent for the Jollies – 'Er Majesty's Jollies – soldier an' sailor too!
They think for 'emselves, an' they steal for 'emselves, and they never
ask what's to do,
But they're camped an' fed an' they're up an' fed before our bugle's
blew.
Ho! they ain't no limpin' procrastitutes – soldier an' sailor too.

You may say we are fond of an 'arness-cut, or 'ootin' in barrick-yards,
Or startin' a Board School mutiny along o' the Onion Guards;[8]
But once in a while we can finish in style for the ends of the earth
to view,
The same as the Jollies – 'Er Majesty's Jollies – soldier an' sailor too!
They come of our lot, they was brothers to us; they was beggars we'd
met an' knew;
Yes, barrin' an inch in the chest an' the arm, they was doubles o' me
an' you;
For they weren't no special chrysanthemums – soldier an' sailor too!

To take your chance in the thick of a rush, with firing all about,
Is nothing so bad when you've cover to 'and, an' leave an' likin' to
shout;
But to stand an' be still to the ~*Birken'ead*~ drill is a damn tough
bullet to chew,[9]
An' they done it, the Jollies – 'Er Majesty's Jollies – soldier an'
sailor too!
Their work was done when it 'adn't begun; they was younger nor
me an' you;
Their choice it was plain between drownin' in 'eaps an' bein'
mopped by the screw,

---

[6] Ass Marines: Kipling's meaning is uncertain today, but may be linked to the use of donkeys for
transport.
[7] Woolwich, England. Bernardmyo, Burma. Two locations in the empire where soldiers and marines
found themselves stationed together.
[8] The Onion Guards: in 1890 the men of the 2nd Battalion Grenadier Guards, coming off Royal
guard duty and due weekend privileges, refused to leave Wellington Barracks for field training.
In punishment they were sent to garrison Bermuda for a year, earning an embarrassing nickname.
[9] The Birkenhead Drill. In 1852 the HMS *Birkenhead* transport sank off Simon's Bay. According to
Kipling's footnotes, 'the Marines aboard her went down as drawn up on her deck.'

Plate 1   Scotland Forever!   Elizabeth Southerden Thompson

This is the charge of the Royal Scots Greys, which took place on 18 June 1815 during the Battle of Waterloo. Elizabeth Southerden Thompson, Lady Butler, painted it in 1881 and the title reflects the Greys' battle-cry, 'Scotland Forever!' Lady Butler famously positioned herself in front of the charging horses of her husband's regiment during training manoeuvres in order to get the correct perspective of the beginning of a cavalry charge. The painting was exhibited in the Egyptian Hall in Piccadilly in 1881.

Plate 2   The 28th Regiment at Quatre Bras   Elizabeth Southerden Thompson

Lady Butler read an account of the 28th (North Gloucestershire) Regiment of Foot at the Battle of Quatre Bras on 16 June 1815 (immediately before Waterloo). She completed this painting in 1875 showing the regiment formed in a square. As with 'Scotland Forever!', in her thirst for accuracy Lady Butler employed 300 soldiers from the Royal Engineers to form a square and fire their rifles.

Plate 3   The Charge of the Light Brigade   Richard Caton Woodville, Jr.
In this 1894 painting Richard Caton Woodville shows the 17th Lancers at the start of the
infamous charge at Balaclava on 25 October 1854. The central figure in the painting is
Private James Wightman, who was wounded and taken prisoner. Three soldiers from this
regiment received the new Victoria Cross for their heroism during the charge. The regiment's
cap badge had an empty skull with 'Or Glory' emblazoned below as the motto. Naturally
the regiment became known as the Death or Glory Boys.

Plate 4   Balaclava   Elizabeth Southerden Thompson
Although Lady Butler painted this eighteen years before Caton Woodville's famous painting,
it is best to view it after studying Woodville's 'The Charge of the Light Brigade'. Elizabeth
Thompson's 'Balaclava' shows the returning survivors of the Light Brigade making their
way back from the charge and there are both lancers and hussars among the survivors. The
shocked and haunted expression on the face of the central dismounted hussar is most striking.
A mounted lancer carries a wounded comrade as other soldiers attempt to calm the survivors.

Plate 5   The Thin Red Line   Robert Gibb
In his poem 'Tommy' Kipling remarked on the famous stand of the 93rd (Sutherland
Highlanders) Regiment of Foot at the Battle of Balaclava on 25 October 1854. The
Highlanders, commanded by Sir Colin Campbell and outnumbered five to one, withstood a
charge by Russian cavalry. William H. Russell, correspondent from The Times, *observed*
the scene at a considerable distance and reported it appearing as 'a thin red streak tipped
with a line of steel' (later referred to as 'the thin red line'). In his 1881 painting Robert
Gibb shows the Russian cavalry much closer than they actually managed to achieve.

Plate 6   The Colours   Elizabeth Southerden Thompson
In her 1899 painting 'The Colours, The advance of the Scots Guards at the Alma' Lady
Butler depicts Captain Lindsay (later Lord Wantage) of the Scots Fusilier Guards holding
aloft the regimental colour. The scene represents the Scots Guards' counter-attack after the
Russians had broken through the Royal Welsh Fusiliers during the Battle of the Alma on
20 September 1854.

Plate 7   Listed for the Connaught Rangers   Elizabeth Southerden Thompson
Painted by Lady Butler in 1878, the scene is that of two recruits who have enlisted for the
88th (Connaught Rangers) Regiment of Foot. The poverty of nineteenth-century Ireland is
represented by the ruins of a stone cottage and the muddy road meandering through a stark
and treeless landscape. Accompanying the recruiting sergeant is a drummer boy, on whose
drum head the recruits were 'listed' by placing their mark on a contract.

Plate 8   Defence of Rorke's Drift   Alphonse de Neuville
Alphonse de Neuville painted this well-known painting in 1880 based on eyewitness accounts
of the 1879 battle in Natal. Notably Lieutenant John Chard is to the right of the mealy bag
parapet in pale trousers loading a rifle. Lieutenant Gonville Bromhead stands in the centre
pointing to his left, while Private Henry Hook carries Private John Connolly on his back
out of the burning hospital. Private Frederick Hitch, previously wounded in the head, stands
behind Bromhead. These men are four of the eleven officers and soldiers awarded Victoria
Crosses for their actions on 22 January 1879.

Plate 9   The Defence of Rorke's Drift   Elizabeth Southerden Thompson
Lady Butler's representation of the Battle of Rorke's Drift is much less detailed than de
Neuville's and depicts Lieutenant Chard in the centre, pointing with his left arm, standing
next to Lieutenant Bromhead, who is holding a sword. The famous mealy bag parapet is
very visible in this painting. Queen Victoria commissioned this painting and Lady Butler
completed it in 1880.

Plate 10   Saving the Guns at the Battle of Maiwand   Richard Caton Woodville, Jr.
In 1883 Richard Caton Woodville depicted the hasty withdrawal of E Battery, B Brigade,
Royal Horse Artillery at the Battle of Maiwand, Afghanistan, on 27 July 1880. After four
hours of combat the battery limbered up and attempted to withdraw under enemy fire. Its
left flank section was overrun and two guns captured, while the remainder withdrew. The
battery won two Victoria Crosses on this day.

Plate 11   The Last Stand of the 44th Foot   William Barnes Wollen
William Barnes Wollen's 1898 painting depicts the Essex Regiment's retreat from Kabul.
Following a large rebellion the British withdrew from Kabul, Afghanistan, and attempted to
retreat to Jellalabad in the winter of 1842. Pashtun tribesmen surrounded and slaughtered the
column until the last fifty or so men, most of whom were from 44th (East Essex) Foot, were left.
Isolated they fought to the death and only one man, Thomas Souter, survived to tell the tale.

Plate 12   Remnants of an Army   Elizabeth Southerden Thompson
Lady Butler's famously haunting 1879 painting depicts the supposed last survivor from Kabul, an assistant surgeon in the Bengal Army named William Brydon, arriving at the gates of Jellalabad on 13 January 1842. About 16,000 soldiers and camp followers lost their lives during this infamous retreat. The artist depicts a shattered Brydon on an exhausted horse making his way through the dismal landscape towards the safety of the city gates. In fact, other stragglers arrived over the coming weeks and some prisoners were eventually released by the Afghans as well.

Plate 13   Frederick Gustavus Burnaby   James Tissot
In this 1870 portrait of then-Captain Fred Burnaby (3 March 1842–17 January 1885)
French painter James Tissot captured Burnaby in a languid pose while in the uniform
of the Royal Horse Guards. Burnaby was a large man for his times (6ft 4in tall) and
weighed twenty stone. As an officer of the Household Cavalry he was the epitome of a bon
vivant *Victorian soldier. He was fearless, spoke several languages fluently, wrote books,*
went ballooning across the English Channel, and was very popular with the ladies. The
press lionized Burnaby's achievements and his expeditions into Central Asia, but Burnaby
was frustrated by the lack of active service opportunities caused by being stationed with
his regiment in London and he repeatedly volunteered for extra-regimental secondment to
expeditionary operations.

Plate 14   Stand Fast Craigellachie   Elizabeth Southerden Thompson
Lady Butler painted this representation of an 1895 incident involving the 2nd Battalion,
Seaforth Highlanders on the North-West Frontier in 1903. The title is the traditional war
cry of Clan Grant and the central figure is believed to be Lieutenant John Patrick Grant.
The clan burned signal fires on Craig Elachie (the Rock of an Alarm) to raise and gather
the clan for war.

Plate 15   The Storming of Tel el Kebir   Alphonse de Neuville
Alphonse de Neuville's 1883 painting depicts the storming of the Egyptian entrenchments by Highlanders at the Battle of Tel el Kebir on 13 September 1882 during the Anglo-Egyptian War. The troops are the 2nd Battalion, Black Watch Regiment. This particular battalion had been the 73rd (Perthshire) Regiment of Foot, but was amalgamated with the 1st Battalion, 42nd Regiment of Foot under the Childers Reforms of 1881.

Plate 16   Battle of Abu Klea   William Barnes Wollen
William Barnes Wollen painted this representation of the Battle of Abu Klea, 17 January 1885, in 1896. The battle marked the culmination of the failed relief expedition to save General Charles Gordon in the besieged city of Khartoum. The painting captures the moment when the Mahdists surged against the left rear corner of the square. The famous Victorian soldier, Colonel Fred Burnaby, Royal Horse Guard (see plate 13), was killed in hand-to-hand fighting during this battle.

Plate 17   Gordon's Last Stand   George W. Joy
*George W. Joy's 1893 painting shows General Charles Gordon awaiting the Mahdi's
soldiers at Khartoum on 26 January 1885. Gordon is depicted stoically and heroically
awaiting his fate as the Dervishes pause before finally killing him. According to Joy's
autobiography, an eyewitness told him that 'over-awed by the calm dignity of his presence,
they hesitated for a moment to approach nearer'.*

Plate 18   Patient Heroes, A Royal Horse Artillery Gun Team in Action   Elizabeth Southerden Thompson
Lady Butler painted this magnificent study of a gun team in 1882. It is thought to represent the Anglo-Egyptian War of that year, but whether it represents an actual event or a particular gun section is unknown. Like all of Lady Butler's paintings the harnesses, uniforms, and equipment are authentically portrayed. The painting is suggestive of Kipling's poem "'Snarleyow'" in Chapter 8.

Plate 19   Field Marshal Earl Roberts, K.G., V.C.   John Singer Sargent
American artist John Singer Sargent painted this superb portrait of Lord Roberts in 1906.
Lord Roberts is portrayed in the uniform of a British field marshal. Roberts was promoted
to that rank on 25 May 1895, giving him an approximate depicted age in his late sixties.

Plate 20   A 'V.C.' of the Seaforths   Elizabeth Southerden Thompson
This watercolour was painted by Lady Butler in 1916. While she is associated mostly
with nineteenth-century themes, she lived well past the First World War and continued to
paint until she died in 1933. Widespread use of khaki service dress in the Second Afghan
War (1878–80) led to its official adoption in 1885 by the British and Indian armies in
India. The soldier portrayed is likely Corporal Sidney Ware of the 1st Battalion Seaforth
Highlanders, who won the Victoria Cross in Mesopotamia on 6 April 1916 during the failed
relief of Kut al Amara.

So they stood an' was still to the ~*Birken'ead*~ drill, soldier an'
sailor too![10]

We're most of us liars, we're 'arf of us thieves, an' the rest are as
rank as can be,
But once in a while we can finish in style (which I 'ope it won't
'appen to me).
But it makes you think better o' you an' your friends, an' the work
you may 'ave to do,
When you think o' the sinkin' *Victorier*'s Jollies[11] – soldier an'
sailor too!
Now there isn't no room for to say ye don't know – they 'ave
proved it plain and true –
That whether it's Widow, or whether it's ship, *Victorier*'s work is
to do,
An' they done it, the Jollies – 'Er Majesty's Jollies – soldier an'
sailor too!

The Royal Marines were formed officially in 1755 and their motto is *Per Mare, Per Terram* (By Sea, By Land). They are the Royal Navy's infantry force and they trace their origins back to 28 October 1664 when the Duke of York and Albany's Maritime Regiment of Foot was established. Originally the Royal Marines composed small units as a part of ships companies, which gave the fleet capabilities such as putting marksmen in the rigging, amphibious raiding, and maintaining order on the King's ships. In the First World War Royal Marine light infantry battalions were organized in brigades and fought the Turks and Germans on land in the Royal Naval Division. They also provided gun crews for many of the heavy gun turrets of the Grand Fleet's dreadnoughts and battlecruisers. In the Second World War, the Royal Marines evolved into the highly specialized commando force that it remains to this day.

Kipling pays tribute to the 'come-as-you-are' 'we-can-do-anything' nature and capabilities of the Royal Marines. The narrator of these verses is obviously an experienced British soldier who has fought Royal Marines in peacetime pubs, observed them on fatigue duty, and fought by their side in combat. The affection and admiration with which the narrator regards the Royal Marines is based on the shared experience of peacetime regular duties and of his high regard for the resolute discipline and professionalism of the corps.

---

[10] In fact there were only four marines on board as well as 482 soldiers.

[11] *Victorier:* The HMS *Victoria*, flagship of Admiral Tryon, was rammed on fleet exercises in the Mediterranean in 1893 by the HMS *Camperdown*. The *Victoria* went down rapidly, taking 50 per cent of her sailors and marines to the bottom.

Poetry and the Profession of Arms

> An' after I met 'im all over the world, a-doin' all kinds of things,
> Like landin' 'isself with a Gatlin' gun to talk to them 'eathen kings
> For there isn't a job on the top o' the earth the beggar don't know,
> nor do –
>
> You can leave 'im at night on a bald man's 'ead, to paddle 'is own canoe –
> 'E's a sort of a bloomin' cosmopolouse – soldier an' sailor too.

Royal Marines are a one-size-fits-all outfit that can be 'plugged in' to almost any situation. The Marines have a sense of professionalism which is functionally synergistic and combines the finest attributes of the sea and land services.

Chapter 7

Thomas Atkins Comes Home

Introduction

We live in an era of a common understanding about the human cost and consequences involved in surviving the experience of war and returning home. Civilians who have never served are familiar with PTSD (post-traumatic stress disorder), which is often blamed for a variety of post-service personal problems. It is not a new problem, certainly not unique to combat veterans, and afflicts survivors of catastrophes in civilian life who experience similar symptoms. There are other manifestations of this, such as 'shell shock', which appeared as a result of the intensity of artillery bombardment in First World War trench warfare combat. During the Second World War new terms such as 'combat fatigue', coined by experts in the fast-growing field of psychiatry, were used to describe generalized conditions of exhaustion and anxiety.

Today's veterans are blessed, at least in Britain and the United States, with a robust offering of tiered official and private organizations, which serve the needs of those returning from war. In Kipling's time there was no such assistance for reintegrating veterans back into society, and no help whatsoever for psychological injuries. There was a military hospital in Chelsea and a counterpart soldier's home in Washington, DC, but these could only assist a few physically disabled veterans in a very limited and localized way, and Kipling was troubled by this throughout his entire life. Beyond this the British regimental system, moving towards its apogee of effectiveness at this time,

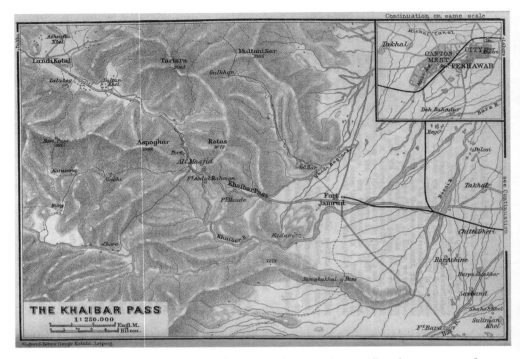

Khyber Pass, 1914. The difficulty of the mountainous terrain, as well as the narrowness of the defiles, is apparent in this map. Readers will note the presences of three British forts in the 'gut of the pass' itself. Map courtesy of the University of Texas at Austin.

provided an unofficial family-like network of active and former members who provided money and services to support the regiment voluntarily.

Beyond traumatic psychological and physical injuries Kipling was very much aware of a more common syndrome that affected veterans of all types – not simply those returning from intense combat. He was very conscious of the fact that veterans were cast adrift, without the intimate support network of the relationships that are developed in all military and naval units. The close association of soldiers in the field, especially in combat or in dangerous training such as parachuting at night or landing on an aircraft carrier's deck, builds a comradeship that is arguably unique in the human condition. Shakespeare wrote of 'We few, we happy few.... we band of brothers,' and similar phrases have been thoroughly used by statesmen and movie producers alike in modern times. This accurately describe the uniqueness of the close relationship between comrades–in–arms. Kipling recognised that to be cut off suddenly from your comrades is a problem that afflicts all veterans.

Kipling also develops the idea of remembrance and reflection by veterans. Some soldiers 'never come home' and remain fixed on a distant time and place where their lives had purpose and life was good. By 'good' we might note that British soldiers' pay went much further in poor underdeveloped colonies, allowing them to live on a scale which was impossible in Britain. Beautiful women and an easier lifestyle were available to Tommy Atkins in colonies such as Burma or India.

Kipling was also a strident advocate of reminding Britons of the obligations owed by the country to its veterans. He was especially conscious of the plight of homeless veterans, as well as the plight of the newly-released men whose six-year enlistment had returned them home unprepared for civilian life. Finally, Kipling recognized that all veterans universally acknowledge that service life broadened their world-view and substantially changed and matured them. The poems I have selected for this chapter are 'The Return', 'Lichtenberg', 'Shillin' a Day', 'Mandalay', 'Back to the Army Again', 'The Last of the Light Brigade', and 'The Veterans'.

The Return

Published in *The Five Nations* in 1903. The voice is that of a returning veteran who reflects on the lessons of war and how service in combat has turned him into a mature 'thinking man'.

> Peace is declared, and I return
> To 'Ackneystadt, but not the same;[1]
> Things 'ave transpired which made me learn
> The size and meanin' of the game.
> I did no more than others did,
> I don't know where the change began;
> I started as an average kid,
> I finished as a thinkin' man.
>
> *If England was what England seems*
> *An' not the England of our dreams,*
> *But only putty, brass, an' paint,*
> *'Ow quick we'd drop 'er! But she ain't!*
>
> Before my gappin' mouth could speak
> I 'eard it in my comrade's tone;
> I saw it on my neighbour's cheek
> Before I felt it flush my own.
> An' last it come to me – not pride,
> Nor yet conceit, but on the 'ole

---

[1] 'Ackneystadt: in Kipling's time Hackney was a poor district in London's East End, and by labelling it as a 'stadt' (a common Dutch/Boer term meaning town, i.e., Marbastadt or Kroonstadt) our soldier shows a dry wit.

(If such a term may be applied),
The makin's of a bloomin' soul.

Rivers at night that cluck an' jeer,
Plains which the moonshine turns to sea,
Mountains that never let you near,
An' stars to all eternity;
An' the quick-breathin' dark that fills
The 'ollows of the wilderness,
When the wind worries through the 'ills –
These may 'ave taught me more or less.

Towns without people, ten times took,
An' ten times left an' burned at last;[2]
An' starvin' dogs that come to look
For owners when a column passed;
An' quiet, 'omesick talks between
Men, met by night, you never knew
Until – 'is face – by shellfire seen –
Once – an' struck off. They taught me, too.

The day's lay-out – the mornin' sun
Beneath your 'at-brim as you sight;
The dinner-'ush from noon till one,
An' the full roar that lasts till night;
An' the pore dead that look so old
An' was so young an hour ago,
An' legs tied down before they're cold –
These are the things which make you know.

Also Time runnin' into years –
A thousand Places left be'ind –
An' Men from both two 'emispheres
Discussin' things of every kind;
So much more near than I 'ad known,
So much more great than I 'ad guessed –
An' me, like all the rest, alone –
But reachin' out to all the rest!

So 'ath it come to me – not pride,
Nor yet conceit, but on the 'ole

---

[2] In the second phase of the Second Anglo-Boer war, Kitchener executed a draconian strategy of population removal to concentration camps during which Boer farms and villages were burned to the ground.

(If such a term may be applied),
The makin's of a bloomin' soul.
But now, discharged, I fall away
To do with little things again....
Gawd, 'oo knows all I cannot say,
Look after me in Thamesfontein![3]

If England was what England seems
An' not the England of our dreams,
But only putty, brass, an' paint,
'Ow quick we'd chuck 'er! But she ain't!

It is a universal truth that combat changes a man or a woman in many ways. The experience of seeing destruction and death first hand, and then having the opportunity to reflect on it, is a profound and life-changing event. No veteran, even if they have not gone to war, returns home the same as when they left. Veterans are wise beyond their years with a self-awareness borne of an appreciation of how quickly life and possessions can be taken away by the exigent circumstances of war.

The Second Anglo–Boer war introduced draconian tactics into the British way of war when the Boer commandos refused to surrender and then took to the veldt as guerrillas. The army turned to a strategy of relocation, which moved the Boer civilian population into concentration camps. Associated with this was the nearly complete destruction of Boer homes, farms, livestock, and crops.

Poetry and the Profession of Arms

I did no more than others did,
I don't know where the change began;
I started as an average kid,
I finished as a thinkin' man.

We often think of veterans as elderly, but they begin as 'kids' and many return to civilian life as twenty-two-year-old combat veterans. Teenage civilians finish school and move on into the profession of arms, making modern combat the province of the 'everyman.' Most veterans recognise that their experiences are not particularly unique but, in the end, somehow their worldview changed along the way, without them realizing what happened. I have met few combat

---

[3] Thamesfontein: another juxtaposition of a Boer place name (i.e. Bloemfontein) imposed on Thames (for Americans, the river which runs through London).

veterans who did not believe that the experience of service had made them a more reflective and introspective human being.

> An' the quick-breathin' dark that fills
> The 'ollows of the wilderness,
> When the wind worries through the 'ills –
> These may 'ave taught me more or less.

Combat is 'bookended' by periods of tactical and operational quietude that is characterised by boredom or training. Often soldiers spend these times in remote outdoor spaces. This gives the combat soldier further opportunity to impose meaning on their experiences.

> Towns without people, ten times took,
> An' ten times left an' burned at last;
> An' starvin' dogs that come to look
> For owners when a column passed;

Contemporary readers have all seen film footage of places like Aleppo and Mosul and have a sense of the devastation of war. However, it is more than simply shattered buildings and rubble; it is often a startlingly empty landscape, which is devoid of almost all life.

> An' quiet, 'omesick talks between
> Men, met by night, you never knew
> Until – 'is face – by shellfire seen –
> Once – an' struck off. They taught me, too.

> Also Time runnin' into years –
> A thousand Places left be'ind –
> An' Men from both two 'emispheres
> Discussin' things of every kind;

Rationalising the experience of war *in situ* comes in many forms. Thinking about war is an inherently individual act, but often soldiers have an opportunity to talk about it with their comrades-in-arms (who shortly before had been strangers). Combat both compresses and extends time in odd ways. Minutes turn to hours and hours go by in what seem like minutes. These personal and collective experiences enable veterans to develop more nuanced understandings about the nature of war and life.

> But now, discharged, I fall away
> To do with little things again....

Gawd, 'oo knows all I cannot say,
Look after me in Thamesfontein!

Discharged soldiers often have a sense that they are no longer doing important work and have returned to a world of mundane and ordinary tasks – in effect self-devaluing their own identity and self-worth. Moreover, a returning veteran's new-found awareness and understanding are not easily translated into concepts and vocabulary that his civilian counterparts will easily comprehend. Many veterans are guarded about exposing their feelings and sometimes the lessons and experiences of war are best kept to oneself.

If England was what England seems
An' not the England of our dreams,
But only putty, brass, an' paint,
'Ow quick we'd chuck 'er! But she ain't!

This might be the punch line, if there is one, and is rather difficult to explain. Kipling's use of italics emphatically makes the point that superficially one's homeland might seem to be a bit of a Potemkin village. However shallow British society and life (in this case) may seem, on reflection, our 'thinking man' the combat veteran realises the value of a free and safe society.

***

Lichtenberg
(New South Wales Contingent)

Published as one of sixteen 'Service Songs' in *The Five Nations* in 1903. The voice is that of an Australian soldier who has flashbacks to an engagement in the Second Anglo–Boer War.

Smells are surer than sounds or sights
    To make your heart-strings crack –
They start those awful voices o' nights
    That whisper, "Old man, come back!"
That must be why the big things pass
    And the little things remain,
Like the smell of the wattle[1] *by Lichtenberg,*[2]
    Riding in, in the rain.

---
[1] Wattle is a thorny acacia plant, which when interwoven may form a fence. It is common to South Africa and to Australia and it has a strong and distinctive fragrance.
[2] Lichtenberg is a small town, built around a market square, in the western Transvaal.

There was some silly fire on the flank
 And the small wet drizzling down –
There were the sold-out shops and the bank
 And the wet, wide-open town;
And we were doing escort-duty
 To somebody's baggage-train,
And I smelt wattle by Lichtenberg –
 Riding in, in the rain.

It was all Australia to me –
 All I had found or missed:
Every face I was crazy to see,
 And every woman I'd kissed
All that I shouldn't ha' done, God knows!
 (As He knows I'll do it again),
That smell of the wattle round Lichtenberg,
 Riding in, in the rain!

And I saw Sydney the same as ever,
 The picnics and brass-bands;
And my little homestead on Hunter River[3]
 And my new vines joining hands.
It all came over me in one act
 Quick as a shot through the brain –
With the smell of the wattle round Lichtenberg,
 Riding in, in the rain.

I have forgotten a hundred fights,
 But one I shall not forget –
With the raindrops bunging up my sights
 And my eyes bunged up with wet;
And through the crack and the stink of the cordite
 (Ah Christ! My country again!)
The smell of the wattle by Lichtenberg,
 Riding in, in the rain!

It is said that Kipling overheard an Australian soldier talking about the smell of wattle around Lichtenberg and expanded the story into the poem. In this poem a flashback is triggered by the smell of wattle, but, as we all know, they may also be triggered by sights, sounds, people, terrain, and many other associations embedded within human memory. The intensity of the

---

[3] The Hunter River is a major river in New South Wales and famous for its vineyards.

experience ranges from a passing thought to a full-blown 'stop-you-in-your-tracks' re-creation of an event.

'Lichtenberg' does not directly come out and state what happened there (presumably an ambush of unsuspecting men on baggage train escort duty), but its remembrance is clearly painful to the soldier. Casualties, accidents and even fratricide in combat are sometimes the result of carelessness and inattention, rather than due to the direct actions of the enemy. Constant and relentless focus is what keeps soldiers alive in combat. Distractions, however minor, are an advantage to the enemy and often become fate's opportunity for unintentional self-destruction by one's own actions.

Poetry and the Profession of Arms

> They start those awful voices o' nights
>   That whisper, "Old man, come back!"
> That must be why the big things pass
>   And the little things remain,

Night and things remembered seem to be an inseparable part of human consciousness and the demons of memory are particularly active after dark. Back home, in the dark solitude of night, our soldier vividly snaps back to one particular battle.

> It was all Australia to me –
>   All I had found or missed:
> Every face I was crazy to see,
>   And every woman I'd kissed

Memory is a double-edged sword, and our soldier remembers that he was reminded of Australia and distracted when riding into an unexpected ambush at Lichtenberg. It is unsaid in the poem, but I suspect that there were consequences for this distraction. Many soldiers are killed or wounded not because the enemy was more effective or better armed, but simply because something distracted them just long enough for them to lose situational awareness. Death arrives unexpectedly, in the blink of an eye, and it thrives on preoccupation and distraction.

***

Shillin' a Day

First published in *Barrack-Room Ballads and Other Verses* in 1892. The voice is that of an older Tommy Atkins who has retired from the army.

My name is O'Kelly, I've heard the Revelly[1]
From Birr to Bareilly, from Leeds to Lahore,
Hong-Kong and Peshawur,
Lucknow and Etawah,
And fifty-five more all endin' in "pore."[2]
Black Death and his quickness, the depth and the thickness,
Of sorrow and sickness I've known on my way,
But I'm old and I'm nervis,
I'm cast from the Service,
And all I deserve is a shillin' a day.[3]

(Chorus) Shillin' a day,
Bloomin' good pay –
Lucky to touch it, a shillin' a day!

Oh, it drives me half crazy to think of the days I
Went slap for the Ghazi, my sword at my side,
When we rode Hell-for-leather
Both squadrons together,
That didn't care whether we lived or we died.
But it's no use despairin', my wife must go charin'
An' me commissairin' the pay-bills to better,
So if me you be'old
In the wet and the cold,
By the Grand Metropold, won't you give me a letter?

(Full chorus) Give 'im a letter –
Can't do no better,
Late Troop-Sergeant-Major an' – runs with a letter!
Think what 'e's been,
Think what 'e's seen,
Think of his pension an' –
GAWD SAVE THE QUEEN.

---

[1] 'Reveille' is a bugle call traditionally used to wake up soldiers.
[2] These are all garrison towns throughout the British Empire.
[3] The government provided Tommy Atkins with a small retirement pension.

Sebastian Junger's insightful book *Tribe, On Homecoming and Belonging* describes the difficulty of leaving one's comrades behind and the intense sense of loss of belonging that occurs as a result. The 1946 American movie, *The Best Years of Our Lives*, written by Robert Sherwood and directed by William Wyler, also speaks to the loss of belonging to a group and having a defined role in the group's operations. The movie is not about PTSD; rather it is about the difficulty of re-establishing one's own identity and the difficulty of explaining what one actually did while serving one's country. A major theme in the movie, as well as in Junger's book, is that the 'best years of our lives' were not in the civilian world, but were instead spent in the company of serving soldiers doing dangerous work under arduous and sometimes almost impossible conditions. The dilemma for returning veterans, well understood by Kipling, Sherwood, Wyler, and Junger, is one of a convergence of reality and memory. There is truth to the adage, 'When an old war horse is put out to pasture, he doesn't think about the pasture… he thinks about war.'

Poetry and the Profession of Arms

> Oh, it drives me half crazy to think of the days I
> Went slap for the Ghazi, my sword at my side,
> When we rode Hell-for-leather
> Both squadrons together,

In a sort of 'reverse PTSD', which discards the trauma and embraces the good times, some veterans nostalgically dwell on the camaraderie, excitement, and shared danger of their wartime service. Bruce Springsteen's song 'Glory Days' speaks to ex-high school sports heroes living on memories of their past glories. Similarly, there are some veterans who spend their later years reminiscing about their wartime exploits, which sometimes become exaggerated in the retelling.

> But it's no use despairin', my wife must go charin'
> An' me commissairin' the pay-bills to better,
> So if me you be'old
> In the wet and the cold,
> By the Grand Metropold, won't you give me a letter?

Living on a military pension alone is almost impossible anywhere, and retired soldiers all have to work at a second career of some sort. In this case a retired sergeant major is forced to deliver letters while his wife is a charwoman. Retirement is humbling experience for many and causes some resentment among those who do not successfully cross the occupational bridge back to civilian life.

In Kipling's time a private soldier's pension was a shilling a day, while a retired troop sergeant major's pension was actually over two shillings a day. In 2017 this equates to about £2,500 per annum (about $3,250).

***

Mandalay

First published in the *Scots Observer* in 1890, the poem made its way into *Barrack-Room Ballads and Other Verses* in 1892. The voice is that of an older Tommy Atkins who has left the army and is living in London.

By the old Moulmein Pagoda,[1] lookin' eastward to the sea,
There's a Burma girl a-settin', and I know she thinks o' me;
For the wind is in the palm-trees, and the temple-bells they say:
"Come you back, you British soldier; come you back to Mandalay!"
    Come you back to Mandalay,
    Where the old Flotilla lay:
    Can't you 'ear their paddles chunkin' from Rangoon to Mandalay?[2]
    On the road to Mandalay,
    Where the flyin'-fishes play,
    An' the dawn comes up like thunder outer China 'crost the Bay!

'Er petticoat was yaller an' 'er little cap was green,
An' 'er name was Supi-yaw-lat – jes' the same as Theebaw's Queen,[3]
An' I seed her first a-smokin' of a whackin' white cheroot,
An' a-wastin' Christian kisses on an 'eathen idol's foot:
    Bloomin' idol made o'mud –
    Wot they called the Great Gawd Budd –[4]
    Plucky lot she cared for idols when I kissed 'er where she stud!
    On the road to Mandalay...

When the mist was on the rice-fields an' the sun was droppin' slow,
She'd git 'er little banjo an' she'd sing "*Kulla-lo-lo!*"[5]
With 'er arm upon my shoulder an' 'er cheek agin' my cheek

---

[1] Moulmein (modern Mawlamyine) is a city on the sea coast of Burma.
[2] The steamboats of the Irrawaddy Flotilla Company used paddle-wheels.
[3] Thibaw Min was the last king of Burma and was deposed in 1885.
[4] Great God Budd – a slang term for Buddha used by Tommy.
[5] *Kalá*: Burmese for stranger or foreigner; the phrase translates to 'Hello stranger.'

We useter watch the steamers an' the *hathis* pilin' teak.[6]
    Elephints a–pilin' teak
    In the sludgy, squdgy creek,
    Where the silence 'ung that 'eavy you was 'arf afraid to speak!
    On the road to Mandalay...

But that's all shove be'ind me – long ago an' fur away,
An' there ain't no 'busses runnin' from the Bank to Mandalay;
An' I'm learnin' 'ere in London what the ten–year soldier tells:
"If you've 'eard the East a–callin', you won't never 'eed naught else."
    No! you won't 'eed nothin' else
    But them spicy garlic smells,
    An' the sunshine an' the palm–trees an' the tinkly temple–bells;
    On the road to Mandalay...

I am sick o' wastin' leather on these gritty pavin'–stones,
An' the blasted Henglish drizzle wakes the fever in my bones;
Tho' I walks with fifty 'ousemaids outer Chelsea to the Strand,
An' they talks a lot o' lovin', but wot do they understand?
    Beefy face an' grubby 'and –
    Law! wot do they understand?
    I've a neater, sweeter maiden in a cleaner, greener land!
    On the road to Mandalay...

Ship me somewheres east of Suez, where the best is like the worst,[7]
Where there aren't no Ten Commandments an' a man can raise a thirst;
For the temple–bells are callin', an' it's there that I would be –
By the old Moulmein Pagoda, looking lazy at the sea;
    On the road to Mandalay,
    Where the old Flotilla lay,
    With our sick beneath the awnings when we went to Mandalay!
    On the road to Mandalay,
    Where the flyin'–fishes play,
    An' the dawn comes up like thunder outer China 'crost the Bay!

Teak, oil, and rubies made Burma (modern day Myanmar) a valuable acquisition for the empire. British rule in Burma began in 1824 as a province of British India and Burma became part of the empire in 1885 until its independence in

---

[6] *Hathi*: Hindi for elephant, also used by Kipling in *The Jungle Book*.

[7] East of Suez – a phrase coined by Kipling to describe an environment for soldiers which was not subject to the strict societal and behavioral conventions of straight-laced Victorian England. Much like the phrase 'What happens in Vegas stays in Vegas'.

1948. There were three Anglo-Burmese Wars (1824, 1852–53, and 1885–87) as well as a number of punitive and expeditionary campaigns, including the Manipur incident.

The capital of British Burma was the city of Rangoon, which lies on the Irrawaddy River. The river runs northward deep into the interior to the city of Mandalay. In order to carry trade up the river into the hinterlands entrepreneurs in Glasgow formed the Irrawaddy Flotilla Company in 1865. The British government hired its steamers to ferry troops up and down the river. The British garrison in Burma comprised mostly infantry and cavalry regiments from the Indian Army and varied in size over the years. The Burma Rifles were raised in 1917 as an Indian Army regiment, but separated in 1937 as an independent regiment.

Kipling exercised considerable poetic license in 'Mandalay' in order to maintain the rhythm and story line. For example, Moulmein does not look eastward at the sea, and China is not across the bay but rather hundreds of miles away over dense and mountainous jungles. Modern readers may be put off by the maudlin tone of the poem, as well as by its pronounced racial overtones and over-the-top use of a constructed vernacular.

Poetry and the Profession of Arms

> For the wind is in the palm-trees, and the temple-bells they say:
> "Come you back, you British soldier; come you back to Mandalay!"

The nostalgia and regret that old soldiers feel for their favourite assignment is palatable in this poem. The immediacy of sounds, breezes, and smells evokes vivid and instant recollections of far-off places, exotic foods, and fascinating people.

> An' I'm learnin' 'ere in London what the ten-year soldier tells:
> "If you've 'eard the East a-callin', you won't never 'eed naught else."

The life an ex-soldier in Victorian England was often difficult and many wound up living in the underbelly of society. Cast adrift and without adequate means, the memories of a better life in a 'cleaner greener land' contrasted with the reality of struggling in the industrialized and polluted warrens of a densely populated northern European city like London.

> Ship me somewheres east of Suez, where the best is like the worst,
> Where there aren't no Ten Commandments an' a man can raise a thirst;
> For the temple-bells are callin', an' it's there that I would be –
> By the old Moulmein Pagoda, looking lazy at the sea;

The call of adventure and exotic lifestyles is an irresistible lure for many ex-soldiers and more than a few become expatriates or, in today's world, contractors working in combat zones.

***

Back to the Army again

Published in the *Pall Mall Gazette* in 1894 and collected in 1896 in *The Seven Seas and Further Barrack-Room Ballads*. The voice is that of ex-soldier Edward Clay, who is trying to reenlist in the army under the name Thomas Parsons.

> I'm 'ere in a ticky ulster an' a broken billycock 'at,
> A-layin' on to the sergeant I don't know a gun from a bat;
> My shirt's doin' duty for jacket, my sock's stickin' out o' my boots,
> An' I'm learnin' the damned old goose-step along o' the new recruits!
> Back to the Army again, sergeant,
> Back to the Army again.
> Don't look so 'ard, for I 'aven't no card,
> I'm back to the Army again!
>
> I done my six years' service. 'Er Majesty sez: "Good-day –
> You'll please to come when you're rung for, an' 'ere's your 'ole back-pay;
> An' fourpence a day for baccy – an' bloomin' gen'rous, too;
> An' now you can make your fortune – the same as your orf'cers do."
>
> Back to the Army again, sergeant,
> Back to the Army again;
> 'Ow did I learn to do right-about turn?
> I'm back to the Army again!
>
> A man o' four-an'-twenty that 'asn't learned of a trade –
> Beside "Reserve" agin' him – 'e'd better be never made.
> I tried my luck for a quarter, an' that was enough for me,
> An' I thought of 'Er Majesty's barracks, an' I thought I'd go an' see.
>
> Back to the Army again, sergeant,
> Back to the Army again;
> 'Tisn't my fault if I dress when I 'alt –
> I'm back to the Army again!
>
> The sergeant arst no questions, but 'e winked the other eye,
> 'E sez to me, "Shun!" an' I shunted, the same as in days gone by;

For 'e saw the set o' my shoulders, an' I couldn't 'elp 'oldin' straight
When me an' the other rookies come under the barrick-gate.

Back to the Army again, sergeant,
Back to the Army again;
'Oo would ha' thought I could carry an' port?
I'm back to the Army again!

I took my bath, an' I wallered – for, Gawd, I needed it so!
I smelt the smell o' the barricks, I 'eard the bugles go.
I 'eard the feet on the gravel – the feet o' the men what drill –
An' I sez to my flutterin' 'eart-strings, I sez to 'em, "Peace, be still!"

Back to the Army again, sergeant,
Back to the Army again;
'Oo said I knew when the *Jumner*[1] was due?
I'm back to the Army again!

I carried my slops to the tailor; I sez to 'im, "None o' your lip!
You tight 'em over the shoulders, an' loose 'em over the 'ip,
For the set o' the tunic's 'orrid." An' 'e sez to me, "Strike me dead,
But I thought you was used to the business!" an' so 'e done what
I said.

Back to the Army again, sergeant,
Back to the Army again.
Rather too free with my fancies? Wot – me?
I'm back to the Army again!

Next week I'll 'ave 'em fitted; I'll buy me a swagger-cane;
They'll let me free o' the barricks to walk on the Hoe again
In the name o' William Parsons, that used to be Edward Clay,
An' – any pore beggar that wants it can draw my four pence a day!

Back to the Army again, sergeant,
Back to the Army again:
Out o' the cold an' the rain, sergeant,
Out o' the cold an' the rain.

'Oo's there?
A man that's too good to be lost you,
A man that is 'andled an' made –

---

[1] Jumner: HMS *Jumna* was a troopship launched in 1866 that made regular scheduled voyages between Britain and India. Soldiers returning to England knew her schedule.

A man that will pay what 'e cost you
In learnin' the others their trade – parade!
You're droppin' the pick o' the Army
Because you don't 'elp 'em remain,
But drives 'em to cheat to get out o' the street
An' back to the Army again!

Modern recruiting stations have two sources of enlistees – those who have never served, and those who have prior service. Both enlistment streams are carefully managed using qualifications such as entrance test scores, physical condition, and age when deciding whether to accept the recruit. Each service determines quotas based how many enlistees are needed annually to be trained for particular military specialities such as infantry, signals, or quartermaster. Each recruiter receives quotas which must be filled, but which sometimes limit the number of qualified recruits who desire the particular opening. The quotas are furthermore broken down into an allocation for every recruiter of the number of initial entry openings and those which may be given to prior service soldiers. It is often difficult for an ex-soldier to return to active service at his or her former grade, and sometimes even to return to the same military occupational specialty.

Recruiters have been known to cheat and rig the system by falsifying the test scores of a recruit or sweeping a criminal record under the rug. In some cases, when a recruiter has an excess of potential recruits, he or she will hold off enlistment until the next month or next quota cycle. Reciprocally, if a recruiter cannot fill the assigned monthly quota he or she might try and slide a prior service applicant into an initial entry slot. There are many way to game the system and turning a blind eye to a recruit's past, as we read in this poem, is one of them.

Poetry and the Profession of Arms

> I'm 'ere in a ticky ulster an' a broken billycock 'at,
> A-layin' on to the sergeant I don't know a gun from a bat;

Dressed in ragged civilian clothing, Edward Clay attempts to convince the recruiting sergeant that he has never served as a soldier.

> A man o' four-an'-twenty that 'asn't learned of a trade –
> Beside "Reserve" agin' him – 'e'd better be never made.

Beyond the idea that being an infantryman does not provide usable civilian job skills, it may seem counter-intuitive that being a reservist is often a liability when trying to find permanent and meaningful civilian employment. The reason for this is because an employer realises that the government might unexpectedly call up the reservist for active service. This causes an immediate problem for the employer, because there is now a hole in the organization and the work still has to get done. Moreover, in today's world, employers are compelled to give the reservist his or her job back, without penalty, when the reservist is released from active service. This makes it even more difficult for the employer to fill the empty position with what amounts to a temporary hire. It is a vicious cycle that continues today as it did in Kipling's time.

> The sergeant arst no questions, but 'e winked the other eye,
> 'E sez to me, "Shun!" an' I shunted, the same as in days gone by;

The recruiting sergeant casually turns a blind eye, but fully understands that Edward Clay is enlisting under false pretences. He pulls a trick to show Clay that he knows full well that he has been a soldier by shouting the command "Shun!", to which Clay unconsciously and automatically snaps to attention.

> In the name o' William Parsons, that used to be Edward Clay,
> An' – any pore beggar that wants it can draw my fourpence a day

Edward Clay is more than willing to give up the meagre retainer that he draws as a reservist in order to get back into uniform. He is also willing to give up his identity and name to become new recruit William Parsons.

> A man that is 'andled an' made –
> A man that will pay what 'e cost you
> In learnin' the others their trade – parade!
> You're droppin' the pick o' the Army
> Because you don't 'elp 'em remain,
> But drives 'em to cheat to get out o' the street
> An' back to the Army again!

Kipling returns to his favourite refrain that soldiers should be paid higher wages and deserve better treatment and conditions. It is inefficient and unconscionable to fully train soldiers over a six-year period and then treat them in such a way as they do not see a future in remaining in the army. Discouraged by low pay and held in low esteem by civilians, too many soldiers become 'time-expired men' and leave the service. Kipling understood the 'value-added' of retaining highly trained men and he understood the return on investment that might be gained by keeping them in the army.

***

The Last of the Light Brigade

Published in the *Saint James Gazette* in April 1890 and later included in definitive editions of Kipling's verse. The voice is that of Kipling reflecting on the survivors of the Charge of the Light Brigade.

> There were thirty million English who talked of England's might,
> There were twenty broken troopers who lacked a bed for the night.
> They had neither food nor money, they had neither service nor trade;
> They were only shiftless soldiers, the last of the Light Brigade.
>
> They felt that life was fleeting; they knew not that art was long,
> That though they were dying of famine, they lived in deathless song.
> They asked for a little money to keep the wolf from the door;
> And the thirty million English sent twenty pounds and four!
>
> They laid their heads together that were scarred and lined and grey;
> Keen were the Russian sabres, but want was keener than they;
> And an old Troop-Sergeant muttered, "Let us go to the man who writes
> The things on Balaclava the kiddies at school recites."
>
> They went without bands or colours, a regiment ten-file strong,
> To look for the Master-singer who had crowned them all in his song;
> And, waiting his servant's order, by the garden gate they stayed,
> A desolate little cluster, the last of the Light Brigade.
>
> They strove to stand to attention, to straighten the toil-bowed back;
> They drilled on an empty stomach, the loose-knit files fell slack;
> With stooping of weary shoulders, in garments tattered and frayed,
> They shambled into his presence, the last of the Light Brigade.
>
> The old Troop-Sergeant was spokesman, and "Beggin' your pardon," he said,
> "You wrote o' the Light Brigade, sir. Here's all that isn't dead.
> An' it's all come true what you wrote, sir, regardin' the mouth of hell;
> For we're all of us nigh to the workhouse, an' we thought we'd call an' tell.
>
> "No, thank you, we don't want food, sir; but couldn't you take an' write
> A sort of 'to be continued' and 'see next page' o'the fight?
> We think that someone has blundered, an' couldn't you tell 'em how?
> You wrote we were heroes once, sir. Please, write we are starving now."

The poor little army departed, limping and lean and forlorn.
And the heart of the Master-singer grew hot with "the scorn of scorn."
And he wrote for them wonderful verses that swept the land like flame,
Till the fatted souls of the English were scourged with the thing called Shame.

O thirty million English that babble of England's might,
Behold there are twenty heroes who lack their food to-night;
Our children's children are lisping to "honour the charge they made –"
And we leave to the streets and the workhouse the charge of the Light Brigade!

Alfred, Lord Tennyson (1809–1902) was Poet Laureate of Great Britain during most of Queen Victoria's reign. Tennyson wrote 'The Charge of the Light Brigade' about the disastrous charge by British cavalry on 25 October 1854 at Balaclava during the Crimean War. Of the 600-odd men who charged, 156 were killed, 122 were wounded and 336 magnificent cavalry horses were killed or had to be destroyed. The poem became an overnight sensation in Britain and the United States, and it was frequently memorized and recited by school children. The poem addressed duty performed under impossible circumstances, bordering on suicide. Tennyson highlighted the criminal negligence of the generals and spoke to the heroism of Britain's magnificent light cavalry regiments. Some of the more well-known couplets include:

"Forward, the Light Brigade!"
Was there a man dismayed?
Not though the soldier knew
Someone had blundered
  Theirs not to make reply,
  Theirs not to reason why,
  Theirs but to do or die.

Stormed at with shot and shell
While horse and hero fell.
They that had fought so well
Came back through the jaws of Death
Back from the mouth of hell,
All that was left of them,
  Left of six hundred.

> When can their glory fade?
> O the wild charge they made!
>   All the world wondered.
> Honour the charge they made!
> Honour the Light Brigade,
>   Noble six hundred!

According to John McGivering and John Radcliffe of the Kipling Society, the twenty-three-year-old Kipling was appalled when he returned to England in 1889 and learned of the plight of the surviving veterans of the Light Brigade. Kipling published 'Tommy' expressing similar sentiments about the treatment of active soldiers in March 1890, and he followed with this poem in April about the treatment of veterans. We might say that Kipling was a one-man engine of conscience, trying to force the British public to respect soldiers and care for veterans. In May 1890, a well-known liberal politician, the Marquess of Hartington, wrote an appeal in *The Times* asking for contributions to the Light Brigade Relief Fund, which was followed by fundraising events. Kipling attended such an event on 24 October, during which thirty Light Brigade survivors appeared on stage at the Empire Theatre.

Poetry and the Profession of Arms

> There were thirty million English who talked of England's might,
> There were twenty broken troopers who lacked a bed for the night.

The plight of homeless veterans, perhaps more prevalent in America today than in Britain, is certainly not a new phenomenon. In Victorian Britain there was sometimes no alternative for veterans than begging or going into the workhouse.

> They asked for a little money to keep the wolf from the door;
> And the thirty million English sent twenty pounds and four!

Kipling detested the niggardly and parsimonious amounts of money that the British public gave to assist veterans. The 1891 population of Britain included 27 million English and six million Scots and Welsh.

> O thirty million English that babble of England's might,
> Behold there are twenty heroes who lack their food to-night;
> Our children's children are lisping to "honour the charge they made —"
> And we leave to the streets and the workhouse the charge of the Light Brigade!

Kipling insults a population who are spared the dangers and consequences of war in an attempt to shame them into shouldering responsibility for veterans. Kipling was exceptionally sensitive to the jingoists who believed that British power and influence lay in its military and naval forces and that these should be used in a heavy-handed interventionist way. A slang term in America today is 'Chickenhawk', which is used to insult politicians and those who would vote for war but would not go themselves nor permit their own children to serve in harm's way.

***

The Veterans

Written for the Gathering of Survivors the Indian Mutiny, Albert Hall, 1907

Published in the London *Morning Post* on 24 December 1907 in honour of the survivors of the Indian Mutiny (and the commemoration of the fiftieth anniversary of its outbreak on 23 December 1857). The voice is that of Kipling himself.

> To-day, across our fathers' graves,
>   The astonished years reveal
> The remnant of that desperate host
>   Which cleansed our East with steel.
>
> Hail and farewell! We greet you here,
>   With tears that none will scorn –
> O Keepers of the House of old,
>   Or ever we were born!
>
> One service more we dare to ask –
>   Pray for us, heroes, pray,
> That when Fate lays on us our task
>   We do not shame the Day!

We share Kipling's theme today when gathering and honouring the survivors of Normandy, Arnhem, or Pearl Harbour as our fathers gathered and honoured the survivors of the Somme, Vimy Ridge, or Passchendaele. We honour these veterans and we honour the difficulty of the task they undertook to accomplish. In retrospect the enormity of their long-ago task seems almost impossibly difficult and dangerous and the battles we fight today seem almost minor in comparison.

The Indian Mutiny (also called the Sepoy Rebellion) was a seminal event for the British empire and an earth-shattering experience for British soldiers, their families, and civilians who were caught up in it in 1857. It seemed to happen spontaneously, although the root causes were long in the making. The excesses and inhuman violence visited on Westerners caught by the rebels was monstrous and widely publicised by the British press. And it was narrowly put down by the British and East India Company armies. Using Wellington's words about Waterloo to describe the Indian Mutiny – 'It was a near run thing.'

Kipling ends with a prayer of sorts, which speaks to his generation's uncertainty that they might not be capable of such heroism and sacrifice as the country demonstrated during the Indian Mutiny. The irony, of course, is that Fate did lay an even more difficult task on Kipling's generation (and their children) with the First World War. The incredible will and sacrifice necessary to sustain the slaughter in the trenches of France from 1914 to 1918 is almost unimaginable today.

Chapter 8

Lessons Learned
the Hard Way

Introduction

Kipling was a keen observer of the human condition and reflected on how people absorbed and processed the lessons of their experiences. The early defeats and ultimate effort and costs of the Second Anglo-Boer War especially troubled Kipling, the British people, and the British government. It can be accurately stated that the lessons learned in that war led directly to the Haldane Reforms of 1906–08, which, in turn, led to the successful deployment of a modern British Expeditionary Force to France in 1914. Kipling was also particularly interested in how the experience of combat and war was processed by individuals as well as by militaries.

Kipling considered, in metaphorical terms, the danger of Russia and warned against her. He attempted to inform the United States about the hard-won lessons and consequences of conquering an empire. Kipling also commented on the dilemma of kinship and friendship when these conflict with one's duty in combat. The final poem in this chapter deals with defeat and cowardice under fire, and the life-long legacy of living with that knowledge. The poems I have selected for this chapter are 'The Lesson', 'The Truce of the Bear', 'The White Man's Burden', '"Snarleyow"', and 'That Day'.

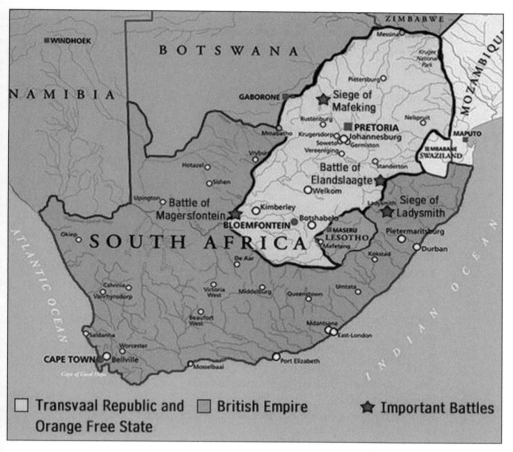

Engagements, Second Anglo–Boer War. Surrounded by British territory and cut off from the sea by Portuguese colonies, the British victory over the Boers seemed like a foregone conclusion. However, the use of guerrilla tactics by the Boers made victory an expensive endeavour for Britain and its empire. Map courtesy of History Plex.

The Lesson

1899–1902

(Boer War)

Kipling was already at work on this poem in February 1901 and it was published in *The Times* in July. It was collected and published in *The Five Nations* in 1903. The voice is that of Kipling himself commenting on the results of the Second Anglo–Boer War.

> *Let us admit it fairly, as a business people should,*
> *We have had no end of a lesson: it will do us no end of good.*

Not on a single issue, or in one direction or twain,
But conclusively, comprehensively, and several times and again,
Were all our most holy illusions knocked higher than Gilderoy's kite.
We have had a jolly good lesson, and it serves us jolly well right!

This was not bestowed us under the trees, nor yet in the shade of
a tent,
But swingingly, over eleven degrees of a bare brown continent.
From Lamberts to Delagoa Bay, and from Pietersburg to Sutherland,
Fell the phenomenal lesson we learned – with a fullness accorded
no other land.

It was our fault, and our very great fault, and not the judgment
of Heaven.
We made an Army in our own image, on an island nine by seven,
Which faithfully mirrored its makers' ideals, equipment, and
mental attitude –
And so we got our lesson: and we ought to accept it with gratitude.

We have spent two hundred million pounds to prove the fact once
more,
That horses are quicker than men afoot, since two and two make
four;
And horses have four legs, and men have two legs, and two into
four goes twice,
And nothing over except our lesson – and very cheap at the price.

For remember (this our children shall know: we are too near for
that knowledge)
Not our mere astonished camps, but Council and Creed and
College –
All the obese, unchallenged old things that stifle and overlie us –
Have felt the effects of the lesson we got – an advantage no money
could buy us!

Then let us develop this marvellous asset which we alone command,
And which, it may subsequently transpire, will be worth as much
as the Rand.
Let us approach this pivotal fact in a humble yet hopeful mood –
We have had no end of a lesson, it will do us no end of good!

It was our fault, and our very great fault – and now we must turn
it to use.
We have forty million reasons for failure, but not a single excuse.

So the more we work and the less we talk the better results we
shall get –
We have had an Imperial lesson; it may make us an Empire yet!

Britain entered the twentieth century with a military staff and training
establishment that dated back to the Napoleonic Wars. While the Cardwell and
Childers reforms of the 1880s had changed the regimental and militia systems,
nothing had been done to create higher-level army staffs and national-level
staffs. Moreover, the curriculum at the army's staff college at Camberley was
out-of-date and focused on the campaigns of the American Civil War rather
than on the then current German and French command and staff processes.
The early defeats and ultimate costs of the Second Anglo-Boer War provided
much incentive for another round of army reforms.

In December 1905, Viscount Sir Richard Haldane became Secretary of
State for War and he brought the British Army into the twentieth century. In
1906, Haldane created a standing expeditionary force of six infantry divisions
and one cavalry division for service on the Continent. He followed this with
the Territorial and Reserve Forces Act of 1907, which consolidated the militia
into fourteen territorial infantry divisions and fourteen cavalry brigades.
Reforms standardizing training and doctrine soon followed, and the Imperial
General Staff was reorganized along modern lines as well. By 1914 Britain
had a small, but well-trained, expeditionary army backed up by substantial
and well-organized reserves.

Poetry and the Profession of Arms

Let us admit it fairly, as a business people should,
We have had no end of a lesson: it will do us no end of good.

The first step in moving on past disasters is to assess them fairly. The modern
military conducts After Action Reviews (AAR) in which one asks 'What was
supposed to happen?', 'What did happen.' and 'What do we do about it?'

This was not bestowed us under the trees, nor yet in the shade of a tent,
But swingingly, over eleven degrees of a bare brown continent.

The British and the Boers fought their war over a vast area encompassing
some eleven degrees of latitude (22°S to 33°S) in an area roughly 900 by
400 miles. The lessons of the war were not academic, but were learned 'the
hard way' in campaigns of manoeuvre in large-scale operational and tactical
environments.

> We have spent two hundred million pounds to prove the fact once more,
> That horses are quicker than men afoot, since two and two make four;
> And horses have four legs, and men have two legs, and two into four
> goes twice,
> And nothing over except our lesson – and very cheap at the price.

Kipling's tongue-in-cheek remarks about horses being quicker than men speaks to the deployment of large numbers of infantrymen who proved redundant at the conclusion of the conventional phase of the war. As we have seen previously, the creation of mounted infantry solved that problem. Modern soldiers might consider whether the force that is deployed is appropriate to the task in terms of mobility and equipment.

> For remember (this our children shall know: we are too near for that
> knowledge)
> Not our mere astonished camps, but Council and Creed and College –
> All the obese, unchallenged old things that stifle and overlie us –
> Have felt the effects of the lesson we got – an advantage no money
> could buy us!

It is difficult for practitioners in the current generation to find fault with their own tactics and often it is the following generations that recognize problems. Kipling challenges his contemporaries to move past this and examine the 'obese and unchallenged old things'. The lessons learned therein are priceless.

***

The Truce of the Bear
1898

Published in *Literature* on 1 October 1898 and collected in *The Five Nations* in 1903. The voice is that of a hunting guide who underestimates the intentions of an adversary. Many readers interpret the poem as an allegorical lesson and warning not to trust Russia.

> Yearly, with tent and rifle, our careless white men go
> By the Pass called Muttianee, to shoot in the vale below.
> Yearly by Muttianee he follows our white men in –
> Matun, the old blind beggar, bandaged from brow to chin.
>
> Eyeless, noseless, and lipless – toothless, broken of speech,
> Seeking a dole at the doorway he mumbles his tale to each;
> Over and over the story, ending as he began:
> "Make ye no truce with Adam-zad – the Bear that walks like a Man!

"There was a flint in my musket – pricked and primed was the pan,
When I went hunting Adam-zad – the Bear that stands like a Man.
I looked my last on the timber, I looked my last on the snow,
When I went hunting Adam-zad fifty summers ago!

"I knew his times and his seasons, as he knew mine, that fed
By night in the ripened maize field and robbed my house of bread.
I knew his strength and cunning, as he knew mine, that crept
At dawn to the crowded goat-pens and plundered while I slept.

"Up from his stony playground – down from his well-digged lair –
Out on the naked ridges ran Adam-zad the Bear –
Groaning, grunting, and roaring, heavy with stolen meals,
Two long marches to northward, and I was at his heels!

"Two long marches to northward, at the fall of the second night,
I came on mine enemy Adam-zad all panting from his flight.
There was a charge in the musket – pricked and primed was the pan –
My finger crooked on the trigger – when he reared up like a man.

"Horrible, hairy, human, with paws like hands in prayer,
Making his supplication rose Adam-zad the Bear!
I looked at the swaying shoulders, at the paunch's swag and swing,
And my heart was touched with pity for the monstrous, pleading
thing.

"Touched with pity and wonder, I did not fire then...
I have looked no more on women – I have walked no more with men.
Nearer he tottered and nearer, with paws like hands that pray –
From brow to jaw that steel-shod paw, it ripped my face away!

"Sudden, silent, and savage, searing as flame the blow –
Faceless I fell before his feet, fifty summers ago.
I heard him grunt and chuckle – I heard him pass to his den.
He left me blind to the darkened years and the little mercy of men.

"Now ye go down in the morning with guns of the newer style,
That load (I have felt) in the middle and range (I have heard) a
mile?
Luck to the white man's rifle, that shoots so fast and true,
But – pay, and I lift my bandage and show what the Bear can do!"

(Flesh like slag in the furnace, knobbed and withered and grey –
Matun, the old blind beggar, he gives good worth for his pay.)
"Rouse him at noon in the bushes, follow and press him hard –
Not for his ragings and roarings flinch ye from Adam-zad.

"But (pay, and I put back the bandage) *this* is the time to fear,
When he stands up like a tired man, tottering near and near;
When he stands up as pleading, in wavering, man-brute guise,
When he veils the hate and cunning of his little, swinish eyes;

"When he shows as seeking quarter, with paws like hands in prayer
That is the time of peril – the time of the Truce of the Bear!"

Eyeless, noseless, and lipless, asking a dole at the door,
Matun, the old blind beggar, he tells it o'er and o'er;
Fumbling and feeling the rifles, warming his hands at the flame,
Hearing our careless white men talk of the morrow's game;

Over and over the story, ending as he began: –
"There is no truce with Adam-zad, the Bear that looks like a Man!"

This is a tongue-in-cheek rousing ballad that many readers find compelling when juxtaposed into the modern world with regard to Russia. When this poem was written Britain and Russia were vying for regional dominance in what was called the 'Great Game' in central Asia. The Entente Cordiale was yet to be signed (1904) and it was this document that transformed the Anglo-Russian relationship into a quasi-alliance. Traditionally in the Western vernacular Russia was, and is, portrayed symbolically as a great bear, and many readers take Kipling's poem as a metaphorical warning never to trust the Russians under any circumstances.

***

The White Man's Burden
1899
The United States and the Philippine Islands

Published in *The Times* in February 1899 after the American conquest of the Philippines during the Spanish-American War (April–August 1898). The voice is that of a wiser older brother giving advice to an inexperienced younger brother.

Take up the White Man's burden –
    Send forth the best ye breed –
Go bind your sons to exile
    To serve your captives' need;

To wait in heavy harness
   On fluttered folk and wild –
Your new–caught, sullen peoples,
   Half devil and half child.

Take up the White Man's burden –
   In patience to abide,
To veil the threat of terror
   And check the show of pride;
By open speech and simple,
   An hundred times mad plain.
To seek another's profit,
   And work another's gain.

Take up the White Man's burden –
   The savage wars of peace –
Fill full the mouth of Famine
   And bid the sickness cease;
And when your goal is nearest
   The end for others sought,
Watch Sloth and heathen Folly
   Bring all your hope to nought.

Take up the White Man's burden –
   No tawdry rule of kings,
But toil of serf and sweeper –
   The tale of common things.
The ports ye shall not enter,
   The roads ye shall not tread,
Go make them with your living,
   And mark them with your dead!

Take up the White Man's burden –
   And reap his old reward:
The blame of those ye better,
   The hate of those ye guard –
The cry of hosts ye humour
   (Ah, slowly!) toward the light: –
"Why brought ye us from bondage,
   "Our loved Egyptian night?"[1]

---

[1] Another biblical reference from the book of Exodus. After being led into the wilderness the Israelites complained to Moses that they were starving and homeless and at least had homes and food living as slaves under Pharaoh.

Take up the White Man's burden –
  Ye dare not stoop to less –
Nor call too loud on freedom
  To cloak your weariness;
By all ye cry or whisper,
  By all ye leave or do,
The silent, sullen peoples
  Shall weigh your Gods and you.

Take up the White Man's burden –
  Have done with childish days –
The lightly proffered laurel,
  The easy, ungrudged praise.
Comes now, to search your manhood
  Through all the thankless years,
Cold-edged with dear-bought wisdom,
  The judgment of your peers!

At the Columbian Exposition in Chicago in 1893 American historian Frederick Jackson Turner delivered a speech advancing his 'frontier thesis.' Turner argued that the frontier had closed and with it a chapter in American history defined by rugged individuals who fought Indians and tamed the frontier. Furthermore, Turner asserted that Americans had been an inwardly focused people who must now turn their energies and aspirations outward. Events validated Turner's thesis when the United States seized Cuba, Puerto Rico, and the Philippines from Spain in 1898, thus launching America on a path leading to internationalism.

Kipling saw this as the birth of an American empire, in which the newly-seized Spanish islands would become colonies or possessions like the colonies of the British Empire. Since Americans had no experience administering colonies Kipling warns the United States about its moral obligations and humanitarian responsibilities when dealing with its 'new caught' colonial peoples.

Unfortunately, 'The White Man's Burden' itself became an unintended smirch on Western civilization, because it is packed full of demeaning phrases about native peoples and their cultures. Readers today tend to focus on the imposition of Anglo-centric themes, which Kipling presents as a better way of life for native inhabitants. In fact, Kipling deeply believed that the British Empire was bringing the benefits of English civilization to non-Western peoples (whether they wanted it or not!). I think that Kipling believed that such English ideas as individual rights, representative government, the rule of law and a system of courts, schools, and modern infrastructure counter-balanced the oppressions and contradictions of the colonial system. Niall

Ferguson's 2003 book *Empire, How Britain Made the Modern World* advances this thesis about the valuable legacies of benevolent British rule.

Poetry and the Profession of Arms

> Take up the White Man's burden –
> Send forth the best ye breed –
> Go bind your sons to exile
> To serve your captives' need;
> To wait in heavy harness
> On fluttered folk and wild –
> Your new-caught, sullen peoples,
> Half devil and half child.

Britain's Indian Civil Service was a life-long career that took well-qualified and sincere Britons to the sub-continent for twenty years or more. While there were 'perks' involved (such as servants and inexpensive living), it is important to remember that the Indian Civil Service incurred not a small amount of sacrifice and hard work. Similarly, serving soldiers and their government agency counterparts today can expect to spend a substantial number of years in what amounts to quasi-permanent exile in distant lands.

> Take up the White Man's burden –
> Have done with childish days –
> The lightly proffered laurel,
> The easy, ungrudged praise.
> Comes now, to search your manhood
> Through all the thankless years,
> Cold-edged with dear-bought wisdom,
> The judgment of your peers!

The Spanish-American War was short and easy. In truth, the United States acquired its 'empire' on the cheap from Spain, which was, by 1898, a semi-bankrupt and unindustrialized country. Kipling noted this, but cautioned the Americans that the world would watch and judge how they handled the responsibilities of empire.

***

"Snarleyow"

First published in the *National Observer* in November 1890 and collected in *Barrack Room Ballads and Other Verses* in 1892. The voice is that of a regular army gunner reflecting on what he has learned about the nature of combat.

This 'appened in a battle to a batt'ry of the corps
Which is first among the women an' amazin' first in war;
An' what the bloomin' battle was I don't remember now,
But Two's off-lead 'e answered to the name o' *Snarleyow*.[1]
   Down in the Infantry, nobody cares;
   Down in the Cavalry, Colonel 'e swears;
   But down in the lead with the wheel at the flog
   Turns the bold Bombardier to a little whipped dog!

They was movin' into action, they was needed very sore,
To learn a little schoolin' to a native army corps,
They 'ad nipped against an uphill, they was tuckin' down the brow,
When a tricky, trundlin' roundshot give the knock to *Snarleyow*.[2]

They cut 'im loose an' left 'im – 'e was almost tore in two –
But he tried to follow after as a well-trained 'orse should do;
'E went an' fouled the limber, an' the Driver's Brother squeals:
"Pull up, pull up for *Snarleyow* – 'is head's between 'is 'eels!"

The Driver 'umped 'is shoulder, for the wheels was goin' round,
An' there ain't no "Stop, conductor!" when a batt'ry's changin' ground;
Sez 'e: "I broke the beggar in, an' very sad I feels,
But I couldn't pull up, not for *you* – your 'ead between your 'eels!"

'E 'adn't 'ardly spoke the word, before a droppin' shell
A little right the batt'ry an' between the sections fell;
An' when the smoke 'ad cleared away, before the limber wheels,
There lay the Driver's Brother with 'is 'ead between 'is 'eels.

Then sez the Driver's Brother, an' 'is words was very plain,
"For Gawd's own sake get over me, an' put me out o' pain."
They saw 'is wounds was mortal, an' they judged that it was best,
So they took an' drove the limber straight across 'is back an' chest.

The Driver 'e give nothin' 'cept a little coughin' grunt,
But 'e swung 'is 'orses 'andsome when it came to "Action Front!"[3]
An' if one wheel was juicy, you may lay your Monday head[4]
'Twas juicier for the niggers when the case begun to spread.[5]

---

[1] Two's off-lead: horse artillery was drawn by six horse teams harnessed in pairs. The subject of the poem is the Number 2 gun off-side lead horse who is named Snarleyow.

[2] Roundshot: a cannon ball.

[3] Action Front: an artillery command used to orient the guns to engage the enemy immediately to their front.

[4] Monday head. A Monday morning hangover.

[5] Modern sensibilities may take offense at the use of the word nigger, but, in this context, it means natives who were engaged with case shot (an anti-personnel shell composed of a canister filled with musket balls).

The moril of this story, it is plainly to be seen:
You 'avn't got no families when servin' of the Queen –
You 'avn't got no brothers, fathers, sisters, wives, or sons –
If you want to win your battles take an' work your bloomin' guns!
    Down in the Infantry, nobody cares;
    Down in the Cavalry, Colonel 'e swears;
    But down in the lead with the wheel at the flog
    Turns the bold Bombardier to a little whipped dog!

"Snarleyow" is a humorous and tongue-in-cheek ballad about the nature of close relationships in combat. In the poem the driver has an affection for a horse he has trained and cared for, and when the horse is badly wounded the driver's brother asks him to stop and help the horse. The driver, evidently older and more experienced, replies that in the heat of battle the gun team cannot stop for any reason. Immediately thereafter the driver's brother is mortally wounded and, recognizing the truth of his brother's words, asks the driver to put him out of his misery.

Poetry and the Profession of Arms

The moril of this story, it is plainly to be seen:
You 'avn't got no families when servin' of the Queen –
You 'avn't got no brothers, fathers, sisters, wives, or sons –
If you want to win your battles take an' work your bloomin' guns!

Soldiers recognize the inherent dangers of close relationships in battle. For this reason it is unwise to serve in a unit with a sibling or a spouse. While soldiers care for their comrades and treat the wounded, they realize that the mission comes first. The defeat of the enemy is more important than the welfare of individuals.

***

That Day

Kipling met a sergeant of the Royal Berkshire Regiment while on holiday in Bermuda in 1894, who told him the story of what happened when a wing of his brigade was wiped out at the Battle of Maiwand. The poem was first published in the *Pall Mall Gazette* on 25 April 1895. The voice is that of a survivor who is ashamed of his conduct on the field of battle.

It got beyond all orders an' it got beyond all 'ope;
    It got to shammin' wounded an' retirin' from the 'alt.

'Ole companies was lookin' for the nearest road to slope;
　　It were just a bloomin' knock-out – an' our fault!

Now there ain't no chorus 'ere to give,
　　Nor there ain't no band to play;
An' I wish I was dead 'fore I done what I did,
　　Or seen what I seed that day!

We was sick o' bein' punished, an' we let 'em know it, too;
　　An' a company-commander up an' 'it us with a sword,
An' some one shouted "'Ook it!" an' it come to *sove-ki-poo*,[1]
　　An' we chucked our rifles from us – O my Gawd!

There was thirty dead an' wounded on the ground we wouldn't
keep –
　　No, there wasn't more than twenty when the front begun to go –
But, Christ! along the line o' flight they cut us up like sheep,
　　An' that was all we gained by doin' so!

I 'eard the knives be'ind me, but I dursn't face my man,
　　Nor I don't know where I went to, 'cause I didn't 'alt to see,
Till I 'eard a beggar squealin' out for quarter as 'e ran,
　　An' I thought I knew the voice an' – it was me!

We was 'idin' under bedsteads more than 'arf a march away:
　　We was lyin' up like rabbits all about the country-side;
An' the Major cursed 'is Maker 'cause 'e'd lived to see that day,
　　An' the Colonel broke 'is sword acrost, an' cried.

We was rotten 'fore we started – we was never disciplined;
　　We made it out a favour if an order was obeyed.
Yes, every little drummer 'ad 'is rights an' wrongs to mind,
　　So we had to pay for teachin'—an' we paid!

The papers 'id it 'andsome, but you know the Army knows;
　　We was put to groomin' camels till the regiments withdrew,
An' they gave us each a medal for subduin' England's foes,
　　An' I 'ope you like my song – because it's true!

Now there ain't no chorus 'ere to give,
　　Nor there ain't no band to play;
An' I wish I was dead 'fore I done what I did,
　　Or seen what I seed that day!

---

[1] *sove-ki-poo*: Tommy's pronunciation of the French phrase *sauve qui peut* – meaning 'every man for himself.'

The Afghans defeated the British at Maiwand on 27 July 1880 during the Second Afghan War. During the battle the British left wing (composed of Indian regiments) collapsed, leaving the 66th Foot's (Berkshires) flank exposed to disaster. Defeat turned into a rout, during which 140 soldiers of the Berkshires made a stand on the south side of the battlefield at the Mundabad Ravine. They were forced back again, but fifty-six men made it into a walled garden at Khig where they made a bitter last stand against overwhelming odds. The famous 'Last Eleven' (two officers and nine soldiers) went down fighting while making a heroic charge out of the garden. The regimental dog, Bobbie, survived the battle and the fictional character Dr John Watson (Sherlock Holmes' steadfast companion), on attachment from his own 5th Regiment of Foot (the Northumberland Fusiliers) was wounded while serving with the Berkshires at Maiwand. The Queen's Colours and the Regimental Colours of 66th Foot, later the Royal Berkshire Regiment, were captured 'that day'.

However, Kipling did not choose to write a poem about the incredible courage and heroism of the Berkshires or the 'Last Eleven.' Rather he chose to write about a survivor representative of the soldiers who panicked and fled the field. During the battle the Berkshires were brigaded with the 1st and 30th Bombay Native Infantry Regiments and the Number 2 Company of the Bombay Miners and Sappers. Whether Kipling was writing about a cowardly Berkshire or Indian soldier is unknown today.

Poetry and the Profession of Arms

> We was rotten 'fore we started—we was never disciplined;
>> We made it out a favour if an order was obeyed.
> Yes, every little drummer 'ad 'is rights an' wrongs to mind,
>> So we had to pay for teachin' – an' we paid!

The first phrase of this stanza was quoted directly by American official historian Russell A. Gugeler in his opening chapter 'Withdrawal Action' in *Combat Actions in Korea* to describe the condition of US Army units fighting in Korea in July 1950. These units came from the American occupation forces in Japan, which were minimally trained, poorly disciplined, and soft from years of easy living in post-war Japan. The army's 24th Infantry and 1st Cavalry Divisions were committed piecemeal with outdated equipment, which made things worse, but all historians agree that it was the condition of the officers and men that doomed them to defeat at the hands of the well-trained North Korean Army. Both divisions fragmented and disintegrated under fire and are today, in the American command and staff colleges, used as case studies in failure by commanders to prepare soldiers for war.

This verse speaks to the opposite of the themes in 'The 'eathen', which detailed the importance of training and discipline. In combat the lack of discipline most often leads to defeat and, according to Kipling's source, in this regiment the men were coddled and appeased in order to get them to work. The bitter lesson learned in catastrophic defeat and rout is that discipline is the soul of an army.

> The papers 'id it 'andsome, but you know the Army knows;
>> We was put to groomin' camels till the regiments withdrew,
> An' they gave us each a medal for subduin' England's foes,
>> An' I 'ope you like my song – because it's true!

> *Now there ain't no chorus 'ere to give,*
>> *Nor there ain't no band to play;*
> *An' I wish I was dead 'fore I done what I did,*
>> *Or seen what I seed that day!*

Kipling is savage in his retelling of the shame and anguish felt by defeated soldiers who have let their comrades down. Much like the defeated commanders in 'Stellenbosch', the survivors of the rout were given meaningless tasks in the rear after the battle. In spite of being awarded a campaign medal, this particular survivor regrets his conduct and this is a life-long legacy which will never heal.

Chapter 9

Patriotism Imagined – Kipling's England

Introduction

This chapter highlights Kipling's rose-tinted views on his British homeland and his sentimental affection for England. These poems present a pastoral and quiet England that existed in memory and in Kipling's imagination. This particular England... Kipling's England... was an idealized island kingdom that was worth fighting and dying for. His sense that the British people did not appreciate their heritage shines through in these poems. Kipling also had strong notions of what the Union Jack represented and what it meant for the larger world. The reader must keep in mind that, in Kipling's time – especially in the pre-1914 timeframe – the British Empire appeared impregnable and enduring.

Kipling's historical poems about his England and its history are reminiscent of Sir Winston Churchill's later multi-volume *A History of The English-Speaking Peoples*, which Churchill published in the mid-1950s. Churchill's work is richly and romantically written, and in his own words, 'aims rather to present a personal view on the processes whereby English-speaking peoples throughout the world have achieved their distinctive position and character.' Intellectually Kipling and Churchill shared common understandings of their heritage and a Victorian lens through which they viewed British history. In this manner both Kipling and Churchill demonstrated that they were imperialists to their marrow and justifiably proud of the achievements of Britons building a world-wide empire.

Historical counties of England. Readers unfamiliar with the counties of England will easily find Sussex on the southern coast along the English Channel. Map courtesy of the BBC.

The poems I have selected for this chapter are 'Puck's Song', 'Sussex', 'The Way through the Woods', and 'The English Flag'. Other similar poems which may be found on the Kipling Society's superb website and which I recommend to the reader are 'The Roman Centurion's Song', 'The Dane-Geld', 'The Reeds at Runnymede', 'Edgehill Fight', and 'The Dutch in the Medway'.

Puck's Song

This poem was first published in 1906 in *Puck of Pook's Hill*, in association with the story 'Weyland's Sword'. The voice is that of a whimsical storyteller pointing out landmarks to his listener, which identify the rich history of the island.

See you the ferny ride that steals
Into the oak-woods far?
O that was whence they hewed the keels
That rolled to Trafalgar.

And mark you where the ivy clings
To Bayham's mouldering walls?
O there we cast the stout railings
That stand around St Paul's.

See you the dimpled track that runs
All hollow through the wheat?
O that was where they hauled the guns
That smote King Philip's fleet.

(Out of the Weald, the secret Weald,[1]
Men sent in ancient years,
The horse-shoes red at Flodden Field,
The arrows at Poitiers!)

See you our little mill that clacks,
So busy by the brook?
She has ground her corn and paid her
Ever since Domesday Book.

See you our stilly woods of oak,
And the dread ditch beside?
O that was where the Saxons broke
On the day that Harold died.

See you the windy levels spread
About the gates of Rye?
O that was where the Northmen fled,
When Alfred's ships came by.

---

[1] Weald: an area in southeast England covered in forest in ancient times but today 'jumbled, tumbled country, small mixed farms, and small fields interspersed with woodland.'

See you our pastures wide and lone,
Where the red oxen browse?
O there was a City thronged and known,
'Ere London boasted a house.

And see you after rain, the trace
Of mound and ditch and wall?
O that was a Legion's camping-place,
When Caesar sailed from Gaul.

And see you marks that show and fade,
Like shadows on the Downs?
O they are the lines the Flint Men made,
To guard their wondrous towns.

Trackway and Camp and City lost,
Salt Marsh where now is corn –
Old Wars, old Peace, old Arts that cease,
And so was England born!

She is not any common Earth,
Water or wood or air,
But Merlin's Isle of Gramarye,
Where you and I will fare!

Kipling's deep sense of history as a continuum and platform for understanding time and space for modern readers is evident in this poem. It is constructed in reverse chronology of British history: as the reader proceeds backwards through the verses from 1906 to 5,000 BC, they proceed from Kipling's present into the distant and long-forgotten past. A British reader (and many Americans in the nineteenth century as well) would have easily understood the historical references contained in these verses.

The poem begins with the reader looking back 100 years from 1906 to the Battle of Trafalgar (a great naval victory against the French and Spanish in 1805) when the wooden walls and iron men of the Royal Navy's ships defeated the enemies of Great Britain. The verse following reveals that the railings in the dome of St Paul's Cathedral in London (designed by Christopher Wren in the late 1660s), were made nearby.

King Phillip II launched the Spanish Armada against England in 1588 and the small, but well-manned and gunned ships of Elizabeth's Royal Navy defeated it and sent its remnants back to Spain. At Flodden Field in 1513, an English army, under the Earl of Surrey, defeated the invading Scots under King James IV. The Battle of Poitiers in 1356 was an English victory over the

French. Similarly to the earlier Battle of Crécy in 1346 and the later Battle of Agincourt in 1415, the victory at Poitiers was possible through the prowess of English longbow men, who defeated the heavily armoured and far more numerous French knights.

William the Conqueror defeated the Anglo–Saxon King Harold at the Battle of Hastings in 1066 and went on to impose Norman rule in England. After the conquest William ordered a census and inventory taken of his newly acquired lands (for the purpose of imposing taxes), the outcome of which was the Domesday Book in 1086. The Domesday Book was a complete survey of the land, possessions (including animals), and buildings in England and the king assessed taxes based on this comprehensive survey.

In 876 King Alfred threw back the Danes (the Northmen) who attempted to invade England. Much earlier Julius Caesar invaded England twice, in 55 and 54 BC, and his legions built classic Roman military camps on the island. These camps were characterized by a signature *fossa vallumque*, or wall and ditch. When constructing their camps Roman legionnaires dug a protective ditch and piled the dirt into earthen ramparts. On top of the rampart they placed sharp wooden stakes pointed outwards. Even earlier, several thousand years before the Romans invaded Britain, Neolithic men using flint axes and knives inhabited the island, and the Downs still show traces of their towns and encampments. Kipling ends this poem by invoking memories of Merlin and King Arthur. In doing so he endows the island with mystical qualities and reminds the reader of the uniqueness of England.

***

Sussex

1902

Kipling's first permanent home in England was Bateman's in Sussex, which became the background locale for many of his subsequent poems and stories. He appears to have written this poem in 1902 and it was reprinted widely thereafter. The voice is that of a nostalgic resident of the county of Sussex reflecting on the history and natural beauty of his home.

> God gave all men all earth to love,
>   But, since our hearts are small
> Ordained for each one spot should prove
>   Belovèd over all;
> That, as He watched Creation's birth,
>   So we, in godlike mood,

May of our love create our earth
    And see that it is good.

So one shall Baltic pines content,
    As one some Surrey glade,
Or one the palm-grove's droned lament
    Before Levuka's Trade.[1]
Each to his choice, and I rejoice
    The lot has fallen to me
In a fair ground – in a fair ground –
    Yea, Sussex by the sea!

No tender-hearted garden crowns,
    No bosomed woods adorn
Our blunt, bow-headed, whale-backed Downs,
    But gnarled and writhen thorn –
Bare slopes where chasing shadows skim,
    And, through the gaps revealed,
Belt upon belt, the wooded, dim,
    Blue goodness of the Weald.

Clean of officious fence or hedge,
    Half-wild and wholly tame,
The wise turf cloaks the white cliff-edge
    As when the Romans came.
What sign of those that fought and died
    At shift of sword and sword?
The barrow[2] and the camp abide,
    The sunlight and the sward.

Here leaps ashore the full Sou'west
    All heavy-winged with brine,
Here lies above the folded crest
    The Channel's leaden line,
And here the sea-fogs lap and cling,
    And here, each warning each,
The sheep-bells and the ship-bells ring
    Along the hidden beach.

We have no waters to delight
    Our broad and brookless vales –

---

[1] Levuka's Trade: a steady trade wind that sweeps the Fiji Islands.
[2] Barrow: prehistoric burial mound.

Only the dewpond on the height[3]
    Unfed, that never fails –
Whereby no tattered herbage tells
    Which way the season flies –
Only our close-bit thyme that smells
    Like dawn in Paradise.

Here through the strong and shadeless days
    The tinkling silence thrills;
Or little, lost, Down churches praise
    The Lord who made the hills:
But here the Old Gods guard their round,
    And, in her secret heart,
The heathen kingdom Wilfrid found[4]
    Dreams, as she dwells, apart.

Though all the rest were all my share,
    With equal soul I'd see
Her nine-and-thirty sisters fair,[5]
    Yet none more fair than she.
Choose ye your need from Thames to Tweed,
    And I will choose instead
Such lands as lie 'twixt Rake and Rye,
    Black Down and Beachy Head.

I will go out against the sun
    Where the rolled scarp retires,
And the Long Man of Wilmington[6]
    Looks naked toward the shires;
And east till doubling Rother crawls
    To find the fickle tide,
By dry and sea-forgotten walls,
    Our ports of stranded pride.

I will go north about the shaws[7]
    And the deep ghylls[8] that breed
Huge oaks and old, the which we hold

---

[3] Dewpond: small man-made reservoirs on hilltops constructed to catch and hold water.
[4] Wilfrid: a Christian priest shipwrecked on the Sussex coast in 669.
[5] Historically there are 39 counties in England. Why Kipling did not use eight and thirty sisters is unknown.
[6] The Long Man of Wilmington. A giant 240 foot figure cut into the turf to expose the white chalk on Windover Hill.
[7] Shaws: groves or thickets on a steep hillside.
[8] Ghylls: steep-sided clefts in hillsides.

No more than Sussex weed;
Or south where windy Piddinghoe's
    Begilded dolphin veers,[9]
And red beside wide-bankèd Ouse
    Lie down our Sussex steers.

So to the land our hearts we give
    Til the sure magic strike,
And Memory, Use, and Love make live
    Us and our fields alike –
That deeper than our speech and thought,
    Beyond our reason's sway,
Clay of the pit whence we were wrought
    Yearns to its fellow-clay.

God gives all men all earth to love,
    But, since man's heart is small,
Ordains for each one spot shall prove
    Belovèd over all.
Each to his choice, and I rejoice
    The lot has fallen to me
In a fair ground – in a fair ground –
    Yea, Sussex by the sea!

This romantic view of Kipling's adopted home is self-explanatory and speaks to the affection and comfort that he felt about Sussex. The poem reminds the author in its rhyming words of American author Edgar Allen Poe's last poem, written in 1849, called 'Annabel Lee'.

***

The Way Through the Woods

Published in *Rewards and Fairies* in 1910. The voice is that of an observer caught in a moment of sublime mystery.

They shut the road through the woods
Seventy years ago.
Weather and rain have undone it again,
And now you would never know
There was once a road through the woods

---

[9] The Piddinghoe village church has a weathervane in the shape of a sea trout. Whether Kipling deliberately misidentified this landmark is unknown.

Before they planted the trees.
It is underneath the coppice and heath,
And the thin anemones.
Only the keeper sees
That, where the ring-dove broods,
And the badgers roll at ease,
There was once a road through the woods.

Yet, if you enter the woods
Of a summer evening late,
When the night-air cools on the trout-ringed pools
Where the otter whistles his mate.
(They fear not men in the woods,
Because they see so few)
You will hear the beat of a horse's feet,
And the swish of a skirt in the dew,
Steadily cantering through
The misty solitudes,
As though they perfectly knew
The old lost road through the woods...
But there is no road through the woods!

This is a purely romantic and mystical poem, which hints at haunting spirits enduring in a place long after death. This was a common theme in the Victorian age, which saw the emergence of the Spiritualism movement. While not entirely caught up in these public phenomena, Kipling became interested in spiritualism and the afterlife when his son was killed in 1915 during the First World War. His tale 'A Madonna of the Trenches' demonstrates his interest.

Reflecting the *zeitgeist* of the age is the story of the Cottingley Fairies, a clever hoax perpetrated by two cousins and presented as authentic evidence of wayward spirits. The cousins took five photographs in 1917 of what were purported to be fairies, but which were later proven to be frauds. Kipling's sister Trix, who suffered from mental illness, was interested in psychic phenomena and dabbled in spiritualism.

***

The English Flag

1891

First published in the *Saint James Gazette* in 1891, the poem was republished in several magazines in the 1890s and collected in a number of poetry editions.

Kipling asks the question, 'What is the Flag of England?' The voices in reply are those of the four winds, which carry the flag aloft across the globe.

> *Above the portico a flag-staff, bearing the*
> *Union Jack, remained fluttering in the flames*
> *for some time, but ultimately when it fell the*
> *crowds rent the air with shouts, and seemed to*
> *see significance in the incident. – DAILY PAPERS.*

Winds of the World, give answer! They are whimpering to and fro –
And what should they know of England who only England know? –
The poor little street-bred people that vapour and fume and brag,
They are lifting their heads in the stillness to yelp at the English
Flag!

Must we borrow a clout from the Boer – to plaster anew with dirt?
An Irish liar's bandage, or an English coward's shirt?
We may not speak of England; her Flag's to sell or share.
What is the Flag of England? Winds of the World, declare!

The North Wind blew: – "From Bergen my steel-shod vanguards go;
"I chase your lazy whalers home from the Disko floe;
"By the great North Lights above me I work the will of God,
"And the liner splits on the ice-field or the Dogger fills with cod.

"I barred my gates with iron, I shuttered my doors with flame,
"Because to force my ramparts your nutshell navies came;
"I took the sun from their presence, I cut them down with my blast,
"And they died, but the Flag of England blew free ere the spirit
passed.

"The lean white bear hath seen it in the long, long Arctic night,
"The musk-ox knows the standard that flouts the Northern Light:
"What is the Flag of England? Ye have but my bergs to dare,
"Ye have but my drifts to conquer. Go forth, for it is there!"

The South Wind sighed: – "From the Virgins my mid-sea course
was ta'en
"Over a thousand islands lost in an idle main,
"Where the sea-egg flames on the coral and the long-backed
breakers croon
"Their endless ocean legends to the lazy, locked lagoon.

"Strayed amid lonely islets, mazed amid outer keys,
"I waked the palms to laughter – I tossed the scud in the breeze –
"Never was isle so little, never was sea so lone,
"But over the scud and the palm-trees an English flag was flown.

"I have wrenched it free from the halliard to hang for a wisp on
the Horn;
"I have chased it north to the Lizard – ribboned and rolled and
torn;
"I have spread its fold o'er the dying, adrift in a hopeless sea;
"I have hurled it swift on the slaver, and seen the slave set free.

"My basking sunfish know it, and wheeling albatross,
"Where the lone wave fills with fire beneath the Southern Cross.
"What is the Flag of England? Ye have but my reefs to dare,
"Ye have but my seas to furrow. Go forth, for it is there!"

The East Wind roared: – "From the Kuriles, the Bitter Seas, I come,
"And me men call the Home-Wind, for I bring the English home.
"Look – look well to your shipping! By the breath of my mad typhoon
"I swept your close-packed Praya and beached your best at Kowloon!

"The reeling junks behind me and the racing seas before,
"I raped your richest roadstead – I plundered Singapore!
"I set my hand on the Hoogli; as a hooded snake she rose,
"And I flung your stoutest steamers to roost with the startled crows.

"Never the lotus closes, never the wild-fowl wake,
"But a soul goes out on the East Wind that died for England's
sake –
"Man or woman or suckling, mother or bride or maid –
"Because on the bones of the English the English Flag is stayed.

"The desert-dust hath dimmed it, the flying wild-ass knows,
"The scared white leopard winds it across the taintless snows.
"What is the Flag of England? Ye have but my sun to dare,
"Ye have but my sands to travel. Go forth, for it is there!"

The West Wind called: – "In squadrons the thoughtless galleons fly
"That bear the wheat and cattle lest street-bred people die.
"They make my might their porter, they make my house their path,
"Till I loose my neck from their rudder and whelm them all in
my wrath.

"I draw the gliding fog-bank as a snake is drawn from the hole,
"They bellow one to the other, the frighted ship-bells toll,
"For day is a drifting terror till I raise the shroud with my breath,
"And they see strange bows above them and the two go locked to
death.

"But whether in calm or wrack-wreath, whether by dark or day,
"I heave them whole to the conger or rip their plates away,
"First of the scattered legions, under a shrieking sky,
"Dipping between the rollers, the English Flag goes by.

"The dead dumb fog hath wrapped it – the frozen dews have kissed –
"The naked stars have seen it, a fellow-star in the mist.
"What is the Flag of England? Ye have but my breath to dare,
"Ye have but my waves to conquer. Go forth, for it is there!"

According to John McGivering of the Kipling Society 'The English Flag'
was written only months after young Kipling's return from India and shortly
before he wrote 'The Last of the Light Brigade'. Both poems criticise the self-
centredness of the British people, and both poems highlight the sacrifice of
those who defended the empire and flag. The English flag itself is composed
only of the red cross of Saint George on a field of white; however, Kipling's
odd introductory headnote (allegedly taken from daily papers) affirms that
the subject of the poem is the Union Flag (which represents all of the United
Kingdom).

'The English Flag' is one of Kipling's most patriotic and jingoistic poems
and, in addition to these themes, the poem highlights the adventurous spirit
and wanderlust of the English people. Geography is a consistent theme in
many of Kipling's poems and this is no exception. The four winds carry the
English flag across the continents and the seas of the globe, and neither arctic
cold, desert heat, storms, fog-banks, dust clouds, or ice floes can stop the
Union Jack from flying proudly in the wind. The verses affirm again and
again the incredibly difficult and dangerous task of planting the English
flag around the globe. I believe that Kipling's intent was to use the flag as a
metaphor to honour the Britons who had left the safety of the home islands to
build an empire upon which the sun never set.

Poetry and the Profession of Arms

Winds of the World, give answer! They are whimpering to and fro –
And what should they know of England who only England know? –
The poor little street-bred people that vapour and fume and brag,
They are lifting their heads in the stillness to yelp at the English Flag!

This verse contains one of my personal favourite lines from Kipling 'And what should they know of England who only England know?' It is a profound sentiment, echoed by many who have served their country overseas and gone into harm's way. Kipling follows this with insulting comments about the people of his country who are full of ignorance and hot air. We are immediately reminded of 'thirty million English that babble of England's might' from 'The Last of The Light Brigade'. Kipling felt that the majority of his countrymen did not understand what Britain's flag stood for, and, moreover, had simply not earned the right to express unbridled adulation for it either.

It is not uncommon for American soldiers to note that many civilians and politicians wear American flag lapel pins, and they wonder what sacrifices those individuals have made. It is also very common for veterans to believe, because of their experiences abroad and in combat, that they have a more profound appreciation of patriotism and duty than their civilian counterparts.

Chapter 10

Patriotism Experienced – The Reality of Modern War

Introduction

There is no question that Rudyard Kipling suffered a life-changing loss when his only son, John Kipling, was declared missing in action at the Battle of Loos on 27 September 1915. While this was a shock to Kipling personally, he continued to support the war effort, but his later work reflected a more critical view of unquestioning patriotism and of war.

On 2 September 1914 the British government convened a meeting of twenty-five prominent British writers, including Kipling, Sir Arthur Conan Doyle, H.G. Wells, John Buchan, and Thomas Hardy, among others. These men agreed to support the war by writing publications shaming Germany and they joined what became the War Propaganda Bureau at Wellington House. Their first effort appeared in early 1915, entitled *Report on Alleged German Outrages* (in Belgium). That Kipling was predisposed to do this is reflected in the first poem in this chapter, "'For All We Have and Are'", which was published, coincidentally, on the same day that he met with his fellow authors. The poem presents the Germans as 'Huns at the gate'. Kipling became an ardent advocate of the war, which he had predicted would come and which he came to believe was a battle for civilization.

When the army declared his son missing in action Kipling became even more vociferous in his hostility toward Germany. However, by 1917, the

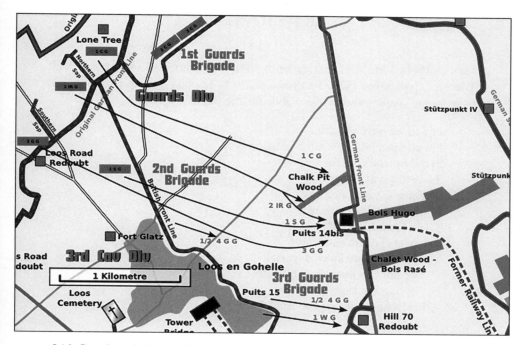

Irish Guards at the Battle of Loos. The attacks of the Guards Division on 27 September 1915 are shown on this map. John Kipling's battalion is shown in the centre as II IR G. John died on this day somewhere in the vicinity of Chalk Pit Woods. Map courtesy of the University of Texas at Austin.

reality of the country's massive casualties from trench warfare in France likely caused Kipling to reframe his thoughts on the glory of war and to question the decisions of the British government.

The theme of this chapter is to examine how citizens process the true meaning of patriotism when they are themselves caught up in war. Flag-waving is easy when a citizen is not personally invested, and does not have family members or close friends fighting in the war. Sacrifice hits closer to home when large casualty returns are published in the newspapers. In turn, personal reactions to loss run the gamut from becoming an anti-war protester to increasing one's personal resolve and dedication to winning the war regardless of the costs.

The poems I have selected for this chapter are "'For All We Have and Are'", 'Lord Roberts', 'My Boy Jack', 'The Children', 'Gethsemane', and 'Epitaphs of the War'. Other similar poems, which may be found on the Kipling Society's website and which I recommend to the reader, are 'A Death Bed' and 'Justice'.

"For All We Have and Are"

1914

First published in *The Times* a month after the outbreak of the First World War on 2 September 1914. The voice is that of Kipling himself issuing a call to arms and steeling the British public for the sacrifices yet to come.

For all we have and are,
For all our children's fate,
Stand up and take the war.
The Hun is at the gate!
Our world has passed away,
In wantonness o'erthrown.
There is nothing left to-day
But steel and fire and stone!
    Though all we knew depart,
    The old Commandments stand: –
    "In courage kept your heart,
    In strength lift up your hand."

Once more we hear the word
That sickened earth of old: –
"No law except the Sword
Unsheathed and uncontrolled."
Once more it knits mankind,
Once more the nations go
To meet and break and bind
A crazed and driven foe.

Comfort, content, delight,
The ages' slow-bought gain,
They shrivelled in a night.
Only ourselves remain
To face the naked days
In silent fortitude,
Through perils and dismays
Renewed and re-renewed.
    Though all we made depart,
    The old Commandments stand: –
    "In patience keep your heart,
    In strength lift up your hand."

No easy hope or lies
Shall bring us to our goal,
But iron sacrifice
Of body, will, and soul.
There is but one task for all –
One life for each to give.
What stands if Freedom fall?
Who dies if England live?

Poetry and the Profession of Arms

No easy hope or lies
Shall bring us to our goal,
But iron sacrifice
Of body, will, and soul.

Kipling reminds us that large-scale war incurs incredible sacrifices in order to secure victory. However, the major powers of the world have not seen what is called a 'total war' since 1945, and we have forgotten what sacrifice on such a scale means. In truth, the wars of today are more properly called 'limited war', which costs relatively little in terms of human and financial capital. It is possible these days for the public to keep the war at bay and to continue with day-to-day life without sacrificing anything. Soldiers today recognize this and they are acutely aware that their personal sacrifices are not shared by their civilian counterparts.

***

Lord Roberts
Died in France 1914

Kipling returned to one of his favourite subjects by publishing 'Lord Roberts' in October 1915. Roberts died on 14 October 1914 of pneumonia while visiting the Indian Corps on the Western Front in France. The voice is that of Kipling, praising the life and passing of Lord Roberts.

He passed in the very battle-smoke
Of the war that he had descried.
Three hundred mile of cannon spoke
When the Master-Gunner died.

He passed to the very sound of the guns;
But, before his eye grew dim,

He had seen the faces of the sons
Whose sires had served with him,

He had touched their sword-hilts and greeted
With the old sure word of praise;
And there was virtue in touch and speech
As it had been in old days.

So he dismissed them and took his rest,
And the steadfast spirit went forth
Between the adoring East and West
And the tireless guns of the North.

Clean, simple, valiant, well-beloved,
Flawless in faith and fame,
Whom neither ease nor honours moved
An hair's-breadth from his aim.

Never again the war-wise face,
The weighed and urgent word
That pleaded in the market-place –
Pleaded and was not heard!

Yet from his life a new life springs
Through all the hosts to come,
And Glory is the least of things
That follow this man home.

After 1902 Lord Roberts was an ardent advocate of compulsory service for home defence. He was also an enthusiastic supporter of Baden-Powell's Boy Scout movement. By 1912, Roberts began warning that Germany had become an active enemy of Britain, which now faced a surprise invasion by the German army and navy. He was aided in this effort through the publication of such books as Erskin Childer's *The Riddle of the Sands* and William Le Queux's *The Invasion of 1910*. When war arrived in August 1914, Roberts appeared as something of a Cassandra-like prophet, whose dire warnings were not heeded by the British government.

Having served so long in India, and with so much experience leading soldiers, Roberts was a natural to send to France to inspire the Sepoys of the Indian Corps, which was composed of the 3rd (Lahore) and 7th (Meerut) Infantry Divisions. The eighty-two-year-old Roberts put on his uniform to visit and inspect the men of the Indian Army. It was his last hurrah and he contracted pneumonia in chilly, rainy north-eastern France. Lord Roberts died in St Omer on 14 October 1914.

***

My Boy Jack
1914–18

Published simultaneously on 19 October 1916 in *The Times*, *Daily Telegraph*, and the *New York Times*. The voice is that of a father mourning his son who is missing in action.

"Have you news of my boy Jack?"
   Not this tide.
"When d'you think that he'll come back?"
   Not with this wind blowing, and this tide.

"Has anyone else had word of him?"
   Not this tide.
For what is sunk will hardly swim,
   Not with this wind blowing, and this tide.

"Oh, dear, what comfort can I find?"
   None this tide,
   Nor any tide,
Except he did not shame his kind –
   Not even with that wind blowing, and that tide.

Then hold your head up all the more,
   This tide,
   And every tide;
Because he was the son you bore,
   And gave to that wind blowing and that tide!

Many readers will surmise that Kipling is writing about his personal loss. However, scholarship by the Kipling Society suggests that this is an incorrect view, because Kipling and the family always called John Kipling 'John' and *never* 'Jack'. Moreover, Kipling published this poem alongside an article from *Destroyers at Jutland*. Combined with the maritime references in the verses, it seems likely that Kipling wrote this poem as a tribute to those sailors lost at the Battle of Jutland (31 May–1 June 1916).

Poetry and the Profession of Arms

> "Oh, dear, what comfort can I find?"
> *None this tide,*
> *Nor any tide,*
> *Except he did not shame his kind –*

Like many English families, Kipling struggled with the uncertainty of what had happened to his son, who was declared missing in action at the front. John Kipling was almost certainly dead and never coming home – and Kipling knew it. The only comfort that Kipling could find was that his son did his duty when his generation was called to the colours.

***

The Children
1914–18

First published in 1917 in *A Diversity of Creatures*. This is the plural and collective voice of patriotic British citizens who lost a generation of children in the First World War.

> These were our children who died for our lands: they were dear in our sight.
> We have only the memory left of their home-treasured sayings and laughter.
> The price of our loss shall be paid to our hands, not another's hereafter.
> Neither the Alien nor Priest shall decide on it. That is our right.
> *But who shall return us the children?*

> At the hour the Barbarian chose to disclose his pretences,
> And raged against Man, they engaged, on the breasts that they bared for us,
> The first felon-stroke of the sword he had long-time prepared for us –
> Their bodies were all our defence while we wrought our defences.

> They bought us anew with their blood, forbearing to blame us,
> Those hours which we had not made good when the Judgment o'ercame us.
> They believed us and perished for it. Our statecraft, our learning
> Delivered them bound to the Pit and alive to the burning

Whither they mirthfully hastened as jostling for honour –
Nor since her birth has our Earth seen such worth loosed upon
her.

Nor was their agony brief, or once only imposed on them.
    The wounded, the war-spent, the sick received no exemption:
    Being cured they returned and endured and achieved our
redemption,
Hopeless themselves of relief, till Death, marvelling, closed on
them.

That flesh we had nursed from the first in all cleanness was given
To corruption unveiled and assailed by the malice of Heaven –
By the heart-shaking jests of Decay where it lolled in the wires –
To be blanched or gay-painted by fumes – to be cindered by fires –
To be senselessly tossed and retossed in stale mutilation
From crater to crater. For that we shall take expiation.
    But who shall return us our children?

Poetry and the Profession of Arms

They believed us and perished for it. Our statecraft, our learning
Delivered them bound to the Pit and alive to the burning

Few people in society today have lost children to the wars of the twenty-first century. Thus the sentiments expressed by Kipling in this verse will likely resonate more with professional soldiers. This is because the professional Western armies of today are something of a family business, in that the children of serving military members often themselves become soldiers. No citizen is more aware of the penalties of bad civilian leadership and flawed decision-making leading to war than a soldier who has lost a child to the chaos of war.

***

Gethsemane
1914–18

First collected in *The Years Between*, published in 1919. The voice is that of a soldier reflecting on his approaching death.

The Garden called Gethsemane
    In Picardy it was,

And there the people came to see
   The English soldiers pass.
We used to pass – we used to pass
   Or halt, as it might be,
And ship our masks in case of gas
   Beyond Gethsemane.

The Garden called Gethsemane,
   It held a pretty lass,
But all the time she talked to me
   I prayed my cup might pass.
The officer sat on the chair,
   The men lay on the grass,
And all the time we halted there
   I prayed my cup might pass.

It didn't pass – it didn't pass –
   It didn't pass from me.
I drank it when we met the gas
   Beyond Gethsemane.

It was in the Garden of Gethsemane, at the foot of the Mount of Olives, that Jesus Christ spent his last night before his crucifixion. Praying there with Peter, John, and James, Jesus knew that his death was imminent and he asked God to let the cup of death pass him by. However, in the end, Jesus acknowledged his fate by remarking 'If this cup cannot pass by, but I must drink it, your will be done!'

Poetry and the Profession of Arms

But all the time she talked to me
   I prayed my cup might pass.
The officer sat on the chair,
   The men lay on the grass,
And all the time we halted there
   I prayed my cup might pass.

There is an expression that 'there are no atheists in foxholes'. While not entirely true, most soldiers in combat do pray that they will not die or be wounded. It is an unavoidable consequence of the experience of combat. An affirmed church-goer will pray to God and an agnostic or atheist will simply consider the odds and hope for the best. It is a universal truth that, in combat, every combatant thinks about his or her own death at some point.

***

Epitaphs of the War
1914–18

First published in *The Years Between* in 1919 and modelled after ancient tomb inscriptions. The voice changes from verse to verse between the first person and the third person.

"EQUALITY OF SACRIFICE"

A. "I was a Have." B. "I was a 'have-not.'"
(Together). "What hast thou given which I gave not?"

A SERVANT

We were together since the War began.
He was my servant – and the better man.

A SON

My son was killed while laughing at some jest. I would I knew
What it was, and it might serve me in a time when jests are few.

AN ONLY SON

I have slain none except my Mother. She
(Blessing her slayer) died of grief for me.

EX-CLERK

Pity not! The Army gave
Freedom to a timid slave:
In which Freedom did he find
Strength of body, will, and mind:
By which strength he came to prove
Mirth, Companionship, and Love:
For which Love to Death he went:
In which Death he lies content.

THE WONDER

Body and Spirit I surrendered whole
To harsh Instructors—and received a soul...
If mortal man could change me through and through
From all I was – what may The God not do?

HINDU SEPOY IN FRANCE

This man in his own country prayed we know not to what Powers.
We pray Them to reward him for his bravery in ours.

THE COWARD

I could not look on Death, which being known,
Men led me to him, blindfold and alone.

SHOCK

My name, my speech, myself I had forgot.
My wife and children came – I knew them not.
I died. My Mother followed. At her call
And on her bosom I remembered all.

A GRAVE NEAR CAIRO

Gods of the Nile, should this stout fellow here
Get out – get out! He knows not shame nor fear.

PELICANS IN THE WILDERNESS
(A Grave near Haifa)

The blown sand heaps on me, that none may learn
    Where I am laid for whom my children grieve...
O wings that beat at dawning, ye return
    Out of the desert to your young at eve!

TWO CANADIAN MEMORIALS
    I

We giving all gained all.
    Neither lament us nor praise.
Only in all things recall,
    It is Fear, not Death that slays.

    II

From little towns in a far land we came,
    To save our honour and a world aflame.
By little towns in a far land we sleep;
    And trust that world we won for you to keep!

THE FAVOUR

Death favoured me from the first, well knowing I could not endure
    To wait on him day by day. He quitted my betters and came

Whistling over the fields, and, when he had made all sure,
  "Thy line is at end," he said, "but at least I have saved its name."

THE BEGINNER

On the first hour of my first day
  In the front trench I fell.
(Children in boxes at a play
  Stand up to watch it well.)

R.A.F. (AGED EIGHTEEN)

Laughing through clouds, his milk-teeth still unshed,
Cities and men he smote from overhead.
His deaths delivered, he returned to play
Childlike, with childish things now put away.

THE REFINED MAN

I was of delicate mind. I stepped aside for my needs,
  Disdaining the common office. I was seen from afar and killed...
How is this matter for mirth? Let each man be judged by his deeds.
  I have paid my price to live with myself on the terms that I willed.

NATIVE WATER-CARRIER (M.E.F.)

Prometheus brought down fire to men,
  This brought up water.
The Gods are jealous – now, as then,
  Giving no quarter.

BOMBED IN LONDON

On land and sea I strove with anxious care
To escape conscription. It was in the air!

THE SLEEPY SENTINEL

Faithless the watch that I kept: now I have none to keep.
I was slain because I slept: now I am slain I sleep.
Let no man reproach me again, whatever watch is unkept –
I sleep because I am slain. They slew me because I slept.

BATTERIES OUT OF AMMUNITION

If any mourn us in the workshop, say
We died because the shift kept holiday.

COMMON FORM

If any question why we died,
Tell them, because our fathers lied.

A DEAD STATESMAN

I could not dig: I dared not rob:
Therefore I lied to please the mob.
Now all my lies are proved untrue
And I must face the men I slew.
What tale shall serve me here among
Mine angry and defrauded young?

THE REBEL

If I had clamoured at Thy Gate
    For gift of Life on Earth,
And, thrusting through the souls that wait,
    Flung headlong into birth –
Even then, even then, for gin and snare
    About my pathway spread,
Lord, I had mocked Thy thoughtful care
    Before I joined the Dead!
But now? ...I was beneath Thy Hand
    Ere yet the Planets came.
And now – though Planets pass, I stand
    The witness to Thy shame!

THE OBEDIENT

Daily, though no ears attended,
    Did my prayers arise.
Daily, though no fire descended,
    Did I sacrifice.
Though my darkness did not lift,
    Though I faced no lighter odds,
Though the Gods bestowed no gift,
    None the less,
None the less, I served the Gods!

A DRIFTER OFF TARENTUM

He from the wind-bitten North with ship and companions descended,
    Searching for eggs of death spawned by invisible hulls.

Many he found and drew forth. Of a sudden the fishery ended
   In flame and a clamours breath known to the eye-pecking gulls.

DESTROYERS IN COLLISION
For Fog and Fate no charm is found
   To lighten or amend.
I, hurrying to my bride, was drowned –
   Cut down by my best friend.

CONVOY ESCORT
I was a shepherd to fools
   Causelessly bold or afraid.
They would not abide by my rules.
   Yet they escaped. For I stayed.

UNKNOWN FEMALE CORPSE
Headless, lacking foot and hand,
Horrible I come to land.
I beseech all women's sons
Know I was a mother once.

RAPED AND REVENGED
One used and butchered me: another spied
Me broken – for which thing an hundred died.
So it was learned among the heathen hosts
How much a freeborn woman's favour costs.

SALONIKAN GRAVE
I have watched a thousand days
Push out and crawl into night
Slowly as tortoises.
Now I, too, follow these.
It is fever, and not the fight –
Time, not battle, that slays.

THE BRIDEGROOM
Call me not false, beloved,
   If, from thy scarce-known breast
So little time removed,
   In other arms I rest.

For this more ancient bride,
   Whom coldly I embrace,
Was constant at my side
   Before I saw thy face.

Our marriage, often set –
   By miracle delayed –
At last is consummate,
   And cannot be unmade.

Live, then, whom Life shall cure,
   Almost, of Memory,
And leave us to endure
   Its immortality.

V.A.D. (MEDITERRANEAN)[1]

Ah, would swift ships had never been, for then we ne'er had found,
These harsh Aegean rocks between, this little virgin drowned,
Whom neither spouse nor child shall mourn, but men she nursed through pain
And – certain keels for whose return the heathen look in vain.

ACTORS
On a Memorial Tablet in Holy Trinity Church,
Stratford-on-Avon

We counterfeited once for your disport
   Men's joy and sorrow: but our day has passed.
We pray you pardon all where we fell short –
   Seeing we were your servants to this last.

JOURNALISTS
On a Panel in the Hall of the Institute of Journalists

We have served our day.

Poetry and the Profession of Arms

There are an abundant themes in 'Epitaphs of the War' that will resonate with soldiers. These include carelessness, unsung courage, cowardice, sacrifice, duty, and irony.

---

[1] V.A.D. Voluntary Aid Detachment. Auxiliary Nurses who served for the duration of the war.

> On the first hour of my first day
>> In the front trench I fell.
> (Children in boxes at a play
>> Stand up to watch it well.)

In combat it is sometimes the case that carelessness gets a soldier killed quicker than enemy action. In 'The Beginner', standing up in the trench to watch is a death sentence.

> Faithless the watch that I kept: now I have none to keep.
> I was slain because I slept: now I am slain I sleep.

A similar theme emerges in 'The Sleepy Sentinel', in which a soldier carelessly falls asleep on guard watch and is killed as a result.

> I was of delicate mind. I stepped aside for my needs,
>> Disdaining the common office. I was seen from afar and killed.

Soldiers exercising personal hygiene in the field are rarely afforded privacy and those requiring privacy sometimes put themselves at risk. In 'The Refined Man' a soldier's attempt to find a private location for defecation results in his death.

> If any question why we died,
> Tell them, because our fathers lied.

In 'Common Form' Kipling repeats the questions he previously raised in 'The Children'.

> I was a shepherd to fools
>> Causelessly bold or afraid.
> They would not abide by my rules.
>> Yet they escaped. For I stayed.

Combat soldiers running convoy escort duty on dangerous roads will recognize the problem of errant drivers being convoyed (on land) who disregard stringent rules designed to keep them safe. In 'Convoy Escort' an escorting destroyer doing its duty pays the price for the indiscipline of merchantmen.

> This man in his own country prayed we know not to what Powers.
> We pray Them to reward him for his bravery in ours.

In 'Hindu Sepoy in France' Kipling pays tribute to the bravery of Indian Army soldiers who came thousands of miles from the subcontinent to fight the Germans in France.

> On land and sea I strove with anxious care
> To escape conscription. It was in the air!

The irony of draft dodgers being killed by enemy bombs on the supposedly safe streets of London cannot but raise a smile with combat soldiers.

> I could not look on Death, which being known,
> Men led me to him, blindfold and alone.

Irony is also the theme of Kipling's 'The Coward', in which a soldier fearing death deserts, only to be caught and shot before a firing squad.

Chapter 11

Kipling for Fun

Introduction

A number of my favourite Kipling poems have no bearing on the Profession of Arms. However, many of them are well-known and beloved by the English-speaking world and, I think, deserve a place in this book. These poems reflect Kipling's sense of humour, his finely tuned sense of irony, and his sense of order and place. In a sense these are advisory verses about the reality of the human condition and about how to get along inside that dynamic. And, as the Profession of Arms is functionally dependent on the human condition, soldiers might consider and reflect on the ideas which Kipling presents in these poems.

The poems I have selected for this chapter are 'A Study of an Elevation In Indian Ink', 'In the Neolithic Age', 'The Law of the Jungle', 'Prelude', 'If', and 'When Earth's Last Picture is Painted'. Other similar poems, which may be found on the Kipling Society's superb website and which I recommend to the reader, are 'The Thousandth Man', 'Tomlinson', and 'The Vampire'.

Study of an Elevation, In Indian Ink

This poem first appeared in the *Civil and Military Gazette,* 16 February 1886, and in the *Pioneer* two days later. It was subsequently collected in *Departmental Ditties.* The voice is that of a man lamenting the baffling rise of a younger, incompetent man.

This ditty is a string of lies.
    But – how the deuce did Gubbins[1] rise?

Potiphar Gubbins, C.E.[2]
    Stands at the top of the tree;
And I muse in my bed on the reasons that led
    To the hoisting of Potiphar G.

Potiphar Gubbins, C.E.,
    Is seven years junior to Me;
Each bridge that he makes either buckles or breaks,
    And his work is as rough as he.

Potiphar Gubbins, C.E.,
    Is coarse as a chimpanzee;
And I can't understand why you gave him your hand,
    Lovely Mehitabel Lee.

Potiphar Gubbins, C.E.,
    Is dear to the Powers that Be;
For They bow and They smile in an affable style,
    Which is seldom accorded to Me.

Potiphar Gubbins, C.E.,
    Is certain as certain can be
Of a highly paid post which is claimed by a host
    Of seniors – including Me.

Careless and lazy is he,
    Greatly inferior to Me.
What is the spell that you manage so well,
    Commonplace Potiphar G.?

Lovely Mehitabel Lee,
    Let me inquire of thee,
Should I have riz to where Potiphar is,
    Hadst thou been mated to Me?

Poetry and the Profession of Arms

Every serving soldier knows a comrade-in-arms like Gubbins, whose
promotions defy understanding. When a Gubbins moves ahead of you it often

---

[1] Gubbins: British slang for a foolish or silly person. Also used as slang term for something which is untidy.
[2] C.E.: Civil Engineer.

causes severe anxiety and anger. The poem points out the importance of a spouse in the military and in the civil service. Armies often expect a 'two-for-one' commander, whose spouse is committed to the advancement of the officer's career. Participation by spouses in voluntary activities such as the officers' wives club, regimental charities, wounded warrior centres, and family support groups for deployed soldiers are incredibly valuable to unit effectiveness and are thus are an important advantage in moving up the promotion ladder.

***

In the Neolithic Age
1895

This light-hearted poem was first published without a title as a heading for *My First Book* in the *San Francisco Examiner* on 31 December 1896 and in the *Civil and Military Gazette* on the same day. It was first collected in 1896 in *The Seven Seas*. The voice is that of a savage Neolithic singer who is reincarnated in today's world.

In the Neolithic Age savage warfare did I wage
    For food and fame and woolly horses' pelt.
I was singer to my clan in that dim, red Dawn of Man,
    And I sang of all we fought and feared and felt.

Yea, I sang as now I sing, when the Prehistoric spring
    Made the piled Biscayan ice-pack split and shove;
And the troll and gnome and dwerg, and the Gods of Cliff and Berg
    Were about me and beneath me and above.

But a rival, of Solutré,[1] told the tribe my style was *outré* —[2]
    'Neath a tomahawk, of diorite, he fell
And I left my views on Art, barbed and tanged, below the heart
    Of a mammothistic etcher at Grenelle.[3]

Then I stripped them, scalp from skull, and my hunting-dogs fed full,
    And their teeth I threaded neatly on a thong;
And I wiped my mouth and said, "It is well that they are dead,
    For I know my work is right and theirs was wrong."

---

[1] Solutré: A limestone rock escarpment in France known for its prehistoric remains.
[2] *Outré*: Unusual or startling.
[3] Grenelle: in southwestern France and continuously inhabited since prehistoric times.

But my Totem saw the shame; from his ridgepole-shrine he came,
　　And he told me in a vision of the night: –
"There are nine and sixty ways of constructing tribal lays,
　　And every single one of them is right!".......

***

Then the silence closed upon me till They put new clothing on me
　　Of whiter, weaker flesh and bone more frail;
And I stepped beneath Time's finger, once again a tribal singer,
　　And a minor poet certified by Traill![4]

Still they skirmish to and fro, men my messmates on the snow
　　When we headed off the aurochs turn for turn;
When the rich Allobrogenses[5] never kept amanuenses,
　　And our only plots were piled in lakes at Berne.[6]

Still a cultured Christian age sees us scuffle, squeak, and rage,
　　Still we pinch and slap and jabber, scratch and dirk;
Still we let our business slide – as we dropped the half-dressed
hide –
　　To show a fellow-savage how to work.

Still the world is wondrous large, – seven seas from marge to
marge –
　　And it holds a vast of various kinds of man;
And the wildest dreams of Kew[7] are the facts of Khatmandhu,[8]
　　And the crimes of Clapham[9] chaste in Martaban.[10]

Here's my wisdom for your use, as I learned it when the moose
　　And the reindeer roamed where Paris roars to-night: –
"There are nine and sixty ways of constructing tribal lays,
　　"And – every – single – one – of – them – is – right!"

This poem is one of my favourite verses from Kipling. Every time I read it I chuckle and think of somebody I've known in my life who does this. The poem is in two voices. The first voice is that of a prehistoric singer in a clan who is

---

[4] Traill: Henry Duff Traill (1842–1900). A British editor and author who wrote reviews of literature and poetry.

[5] Allobrogenses (Allobroges): an ancient Gallic tribe living in the Rhône Valley and Switzerland.

[6] Ancient Swiss lake-dwellers at Berne lived on artificial islands in the lakes.

[7] Kew. A district of London.

[8] Kathmandu. The capital city of Nepal.

[9] Clapham. A district of London, which in Kipling's time was a very rough neighbourhood.

[10] Martaban. Today known as Mottama, Myanmar, a town in Burma.

intolerant of taking advice or listening to criticism. Moreover, he responds to commentary on his work by killing his critics! To his shame his totem visits him in the night and tells him that there are many ways to write and sing songs and that they *all* have value. The second voice is that of the prehistoric singer who is now reincarnated as a poet. He notes that even today humans are disinclined to listen to criticism. In the end, Kipling notes that we all will often seek to impose our own unasked-for judgements and values on others.

Poetry and the Profession of Arms

> Still a cultured Christian age sees us scuffle, squeak, and rage,
>> Still we pinch and slap and jabber, scratch and dirk;
> Still we let our business slide – as we dropped the half-dressed hide –
>> To show a fellow-savage how to work.

> Here's my wisdom for your use, as I learned it when the moose
>> And the reindeer roamed where Paris roars to-night: –
>> *"There are nine and sixty ways of constructing tribal lays,*
>> *"And – every – single – one – of – them – is – right!"*

Kipling reminds us that we often 'have a better idea' for our fellows. In the military soldiers might well remember that for any particular tactical problem there are a number of courses of action available. In particular, for commanders and leaders, it is hard to let subordinates make mistakes, but this is critical to the professional development of younger leaders. The 80 per cent solution arrived at by a subordinate is often a better outcome for the long-term interests of the service than your own 95 per cent solution imposed on your subordinate.

***

The Law of the Jungle
"How Fear Came" – The Second Jungle Book

Published in *The Jungle Book* in 1894. The voice is that of Baloo giving Mowgli a code of behaviour for survival in the jungle.

> *Now this is the Law of the Jungle – as old and as true as the sky;*
> *And the Wolf that shall keep it may prosper, but the Wolf that shall break it must die.*

> *As the creeper that girdles the tree-trunk the Law runneth forward and back –*

For the strength of the Pack is the Wolf, and the strength of the Wolf is the Pack.

Wash daily from nose-tip to tail-tip; drink deeply, but never too deep;
And remember the night is for hunting, and forget not the day is for sleep.

The Jackal may follow the Tiger, but, Cub, when thy whiskers are grown,
Remember the Wolf is a Hunter – go forth and get food of thine own.

Keep peace with Lords of the Jungle – the Tiger, the Panther, and Bear.
And trouble not Hathi the Silent, and mock not the Boar in his lair.

When Pack meets with Pack in the Jungle, and neither will go from the trail,
Lie down till the leaders have spoken – it may be fair words shall prevail.

When ye fight with a Wolf of the Pack, ye must fight him alone and afar,
Lest others take part in the quarrel, and the Pack be diminished by war.

The Lair of the Wolf is his refuge, and where he has made him his home,
Not even the Head Wolf may enter, not even the Council may come.

The Lair of the Wolf is his refuge, but where he has digged it too plain,
The Council shall send him a message, and so he shall change it again.

If ye kill before midnight, be silent, and wake not the woods with your bay,
Lest ye frighten the deer from the crop, and your brothers go empty away.

Ye may kill for yourselves, and your mates, and your cubs as they need, and ye can;
But kill not for pleasure of killing, and *seven* times *never kill Man!*

If ye plunder his Kill from a weaker, devour not all in thy pride;
Pack-Right is the right of the meanest; so leave him the head and
the hide.

The Kill of the Pack is the meat of the Pack. Ye must eat where
it lies;
And no one may carry away of that meat to his lair, or he dies.

The Kill of the Wolf is the meat of the Wolf. He may do what he will;
But, till he has given permission, the Pack may not eat of that Kill.

Cub-Right is the right of the Yearling. From all of his Pack he
may claim
Full-gorge when the killer has eaten; and none may refuse him
the same.

Lair-Right is the right of the Mother. From all of her year she
may claim
One haunch of each kill for her litter, and none may deny her the
same.

Cave-Right is the right of the Father – to hunt by himself for his
own:
He is freed of all calls to the Pack; he is judged by the Council
alone.

Because of his age and his cunning, because of his gripe and his
paw,
In all that the Law leaveth open, the word of your Head Wolf is
Law.

Now these are the Laws of the Jungle, and many and mighty are they;
But the head and the hoof of the Law and the haunch and the hump
is – Obey!

This Kipling classic is instantly recognizable to almost everyone in the
English-speaking world, and its quoted couplets are found in such diverse
motifs as Disney movies and the Boy Scouts.

Poetry and the Profession of Arms

There are fictional loner heroes such as John Rambo who embody the
individual warrior ethos and exemplify the idea that singularly competent
individuals can win engagements and battles all by themselves. It is true that

sometimes individuals provide the courage and heroic acts which tip the fight toward victory. However, professional soldiers must always remember that victory in battle is a collective endeavour. Individuals do not survive long in combat, because survival in combat depends on the group. For example, a soldier cannot remain awake continuously, nor can he or she 'mutually support' him or herself. Kipling's message in this poem is not 'kill or be killed'; rather it is about survival by being a member of a group.

Baloo's advice to Mowgli is to obey the commands of the elders, obey the rules, do your part well, take care of the weaker members, put the welfare of the group before yourself, and stay in your own lane. Modern military codes of conduct and ethical guidelines say much the same thing and are designed to strengthen the group.

***

Prelude
(to Departmental Ditties)

First published in the fourth edition of *Departmental Ditties and Other Verses* in February 1890. The voice is that of Kipling himself reflecting on how he has collected his stories for the enjoyment of Britons in the home islands.

> I have eaten your bread and salt.
>   I have drunk your water and wine.
> In deaths ye died I have watched beside,
>   And the lives ye led were mine.
>
> Was there aught that I did not share
>   In vigil or toil or ease, –
> One joy or woe that I did not know,
>   Dear hearts across the seas?
>
> I have written the tale of our life
>   For a sheltered people's mirth,
> In jesting guise – but ye are wise,
>   And ye know what the jest is worth.

This poem is included simply to reaffirm Kipling's deep-rooted belief that the British were a 'sheltered people' who were weaker, softer, and not as quite tough as their fellows living in the overseas empire. Kipling died in 1936 before such famous encounters as Dunkirk and the Battle of Britain, and one cannot help but wonder if he might have changed his opinion of British home-islanders if confronted with the direct evidence of their resilience and heroism in 1940.

***

If –

"Brother Square-Toes"

'If –' is probably the best known and most beloved of Kipling's poems and it was first published in *Rewards and Fairies* in 1910. The voice is that of a father giving advice to his son about how a man should live his life.

> If you can keep your head when all about you
> Are losing theirs and blaming it on you;
> If you can trust yourself when all men doubt you,
> But make allowance for their doubting too:
> If you can wait and not be tired by waiting,
> Or, being lied about, don't deal in lies,
> Or being hated don't give way to hating,
> And yet don't look too good, nor talk too wise;
>
> If you can dream – and not make dreams your master;
> If you can think – and not make thoughts your aim,
> If you can meet with Triumph and Disaster
> And treat those two impostors just the same:
> If you can bear to hear the truth you've spoken
> Twisted by knaves to make a trap for fools,
> Or watch the things you gave your life to, broken,
> And stoop and build 'em up with worn-out tools;
>
> If you can make one heap of all your winnings
> And risk it on one turn of pitch-and-toss,
> And lose, and start again at your beginnings,
> And never breathe a word about your loss:
> If you can force your heart and nerve and sinew
> To serve your turn long after they are gone,
> And so hold on when there is nothing in you
> Except the Will which says to them: 'Hold on!'
> If you can talk with crowds and keep your virtue,
>
> Or walk with Kings – nor lose the common touch,
> If neither foes nor loving friends can hurt you,
> If all men count with you, but none too much:

If you can fill the unforgiving minute
With sixty seconds' worth of distance run,
Yours is the Earth and everything that's in it,
And – which is more – you'll be a Man, my son!

Kipling's 'If–' is drawn from the life and character of Dr Leander Starr Jameson (1853–1917), leader of the ill-fated Jameson Raid in 1895 against the Boer Republic of the Transvaal. Jameson was tried and imprisoned, but shortly thereafter released. He was a friend Kipling and of Cecil Rhodes, and he was the prime minister of Cape Colony from 1904–08. The poem contains 'counsels of perfection most easy to give' but exceptionally difficult to live.

***

When Earth's Last Picture Is Painted
1892
L'Envoi To *The Seven Seas*

This poem was published without a title in the *New York Sun* on 28 August 1892 following an article Kipling wrote called 'Half-a-Dozen Pictures'. The voice is that of a master artist reflecting on his time on earth and what comes after death.

When Earth's last picture is painted and the tubes are twisted and dried,
When the oldest colours have faded, and the youngest critic has died,
We shall rest, and, faith, we shall need it – lie down for an aeon or two,
Till the Master of All Good Workmen shall put us to work anew.
And those that were good shall be happy; they shall sit in a golden chair;
They shall splash at a ten-league canvas with brushes of comets' hair.
They shall find real saints to draw from – Magdalene, Peter, and Paul;
They shall work for an age at a sitting and never be tired at all!
And only The Master shall praise us, and only The Master shall blame;
And no one shall work for money, and no one shall work for fame,
But each for the joy of the working, and each, in his separate star,

> Shall draw the Thing as he sees It for the God of Things as They are!

This is an appropriate poem with which to end this book. *L'Envoi* is a French phrase indicating explanatory or commendatory concluding remarks to a poem, essay, or book. In writing *A Soldier's Kipling, Poetry and the Profession of Arms* I have 'drawn the thing as I see it.' Moreover, I have written the book 'for the joy of working'. As a member of the profession of arms and a practitioner of the art and science of war, Rudyard Kipling's military poetry resonates loudly in my consciousness. I carried a copy of the definitive edition of Kipling's poetry to every station that the US Army sent me to. Many times, after having read a particular poem a number of times, a new thought or connection would become obvious to me. I wish I had a dollar for every time I said to myself, 'Ah.... *That's* what Kipling meant! Now I get it.' I regret that there isn't room in this book to include every one of his military and naval poems.

Kipling's poetry has been an important part of my life and I found great value in what he had to say about so many topics that are relevant to the profession of arms – training soldiers, deployment, combat and peacetime garrison duties, returning home, considering the virtues of both enemies and friends, and what it means to be patriotic. On balance, the important 'take-away' from Kipling for me is a firmer understanding of the enduring and contentious relationship between soldiers and civilians. As I said in the beginning – I hope that you have enjoyed this book as much as I have enjoyed writing it.

Appendix I

Britain's Wars, Campaigns, and Expeditions

This list is not all inclusive and focuses on Queen Victoria's reign, much of which is drawn from Byron Farwell, *Queen Victoria's Little Wars*, (New York: Harper & Row, Publishers, 1972), 364–371.

1701–1939

1701-1714	War of the Spanish Succession
1740	War of the Austrian Succession
1744–1763	Carnatic Wars
1754–1763	Seven Years' War
1766–1799	Mysore Wars
1775–1782	First Maratha War
1775–1783	American Revolutionary War
1792–1802	French Revolutionary Wars
1802–1805	Second Maratha War
1802–1813	Napoleonic Wars
1812-1814	War of 1812
1815	Hundred Days
1813–1816	Nepalese War
1817–1818	Third Maratha War
1823–1831	Ashanti War
1824–1826	First Burmese War
1837	Insurrection in Canara, India
1837-1838	Mackenzie's rebellion in Ontario
1837-1838	Second Goomsore Campaign
1839	Operations in the Persian Gulf
	Kurmool Campaign
	Capture of Aden
	Jodhpur Campaign
1839–1842	First Afghan War
1839–1842	First Opium War
1840	First Marri War (Sind)
	Expedition into Kohistan
	Operations on the coast of Syria

1841	Expedition into Zurmatt
	Expedition against dacoits in Shahjehanpore district
1841–1842	Expedition against Walleng hill tribes on the Arracan frontier
1842	Expedition against Shinwaris
	Pirara expedition
	Insurrection in Shorapore district, India
	Bundlecund Campaign
	Industrial disturbances at Leeds
	Military occupation of Natal
1842–1843	Operations in the Saugor and Nerbudda territories
1843	Rebecca riots in Wales
	Sind Campaign
	Gwalior Campaign
	Pirates of Borneo chastised
	Disturbance in Malabar, India
1843–1848	First Maori War
1844	Mutiny of two native regiments on the Sind frontier
1844–1845	Campaign in southern Mahratta country
	Campaign against the hill tribes on northern frontier of Sind
1845	Expedition against Boers
	Suppression of pirates in Borneo
	Naval action against Argentines on Parana River
1845–1846	First Sikh War
1845–1872	New Zealand land wars
1846	Aden besieged
1846-1847	Kaffir War (War of the Ax)
1847	Capture of the Bogue forts, China
	Rebellion in Golcondah and Darcondah
1847-1848	Expedition to Goomsore
1848	Sherbo Expedition
	White Cloud expedition against the Braves
	Expedition against the king of Appolonia on Gold Coast
	Rebellion in Ceylon
	Action at Boomplaats against disaffected Boers
1848–1849	Second Sikh War
1849	Expedition against Baizai
1849–1850	Expedition against Afridis
1850	Mutiny of 66th Native Infantry, India
	Expedition against Kohat Pass Afridis

1850–1853	Kaffir War
1851	Expedition against Miranzai
	Occupation of Bahadoor Khail
	Bombardment of Lagos
	Siege of Dhasore
	Operations against Umarazi Waziris
1851–1852	Two expeditions against Mohmands
	First Basuto War
1852	Expedition against Umarzai Waziris
	Expedition against Ranizais
	Expedition against Afridis
1852–1853	Expedition to Black Mountains to punish Hasanzais
	Second Burmese War
1853	Expedition against Kasranis
	Expedition against Hindustani Fanatics
	Expedition against Shiranis
	Expedition against Bori clan of Jowaki Afridis
1854	Expedition against Mohmands
	Battle of Muddy Flat
	Rebellion of Burmese in Bassein district
	Operations against Rohillas, India
	Relief of Christenborg on Gold Coast
	Riots of Chinese in Singapore
	Eureka Stockade incident, Australia
	Operations against rebels in Tondiman Rajah's country, India
1853–1855	Malageah expeditions
	Crimean War
1855	Expedition against Aka Khel Afridis
	Expedition against Miranzai
	Expedition against Rubia Khel Orakzais
	Insurrection of Bedeers of Deodroog
	Storming of Sabbajee
1855–1856	Insurrection of the Sonthals suppressed
1856	Expedition against Turis
	Fights against hill Kareems in Burma
1856–1857	Persian War
1856–1860	Second Opium War (Arrow War in China)
1857	Operations on Canton River
	Operations against Shans and Kareens, Martaban province
	Expedition against Beydru Beluchis

	Expedition to the Bozdur Hills
	Expedition against the hill tribes in Rajahmundry district
	Expedition against villages on the Yusafzai border
	Occupation of Perim island in the Srtait of Bab-el-Mandeb (near Aden)
1857–1859	Indian Mutiny (Sepoy Rebellion)
1858	Expedition against Khudu Khels and Hindustani fanatics
	Expedition against Crobboes
1858–1859	Expedition against Singhbhum rebels
1859	Great Scaries River expedition
	Bundlecund campaign
	Expedition against Kabul Khel Waziris
	Expedition against the Dounquah rebels
1859–1862	The 'Blue Mutiny' in Bengal
1860	Expedition against Mahsud Waziris
1860–1861	Baddiboo War on the Gambia
	Maori War
	Sikhim expedition
	Quiah War in Sierra Leone
1861	Storming and capture of Rohea
	Disturbances in Honduras
	Attack on Madoukia
	Expedition against Porto Novo, Dahomey
	Bombardment and destruction of Massougha, Sierra Leone
1862–1863	Cossiah Rebellion
1863	Umbeyla campaign
	Action against Malay pirates
1863–1864	First Ashanti War
1863–1866	Maori War
1864	Operations against shore batteries in Japan
	Bhutan expedition
	Expedition against the Mohmands
1865	Insurrection of freed slaves in Jamaica
	Bombardment of Cape Haitian in Haiti
1865–1866	Expedition into interior of Arabia from Aden
1866	Fenian raids from United States into Canada
1867	Fenian troubles in Ireland
	Expedition to Honduras
	Expedition to Little Andaman Island
1867–1868	Abyssinian War
1868	Expedition against the Bizoti Orakzais

	Hazara expedition against Black Mountain tribes
	Basuti War
1868–1870	Maori War in New Zealand
1869	Expedition against Bizoti Orakzais
1869–1870	Red River expedition in Canada
1870	Fenian raid from United States into Canada
1871–1872	Lushai campaign
1872	Expedition against Dawaris
1873	Town of Omoa in Spanish Honduras bombarded
1873–1874	Second Ashanti War
1874–1875	Daffla expedition on North-West Frontier
1875	Naga Hills expedition
	Bombardment of villages on Congo River
	Rebellion in Griqualand
1875–1876	Rebellion of slavers against British anti-slavery laws in Mombasa and Kilwa
	Operations in Malay Peninsula
1877–1878	Kaffir War
	Expedition against Jawaki Afridis
1878	Pirate stronghold in Borneo bombarded
	Gaika war in South Africa
	Expedition against Zakha Khel Afridis
1878–1880	Second Afghan War
1879	Expedition against Zakha Khel Afridis
	Expedition against Suliman Khel Pawindahs and others
	Punitive expedition against Zaumukts
	Expedition against Mohmands
	Zulu War
	Expedition against Sekakuni
1879–1880	Naga expedition
1880	Expedition against Batanis
	Expedition against Marris
	Expedition against Mohmands
	Expedition against Malikshahi Waziris
1880–1881	The Gun War of the Fifth Basuto War
	First Anglo-Boer War
1881	Expedition against Mahsud Waziris
1882	Arabi rebellion (Anglo-Egyptian War)
1883	Bikaneer expedition, India
1883–1884	Akha expedition, India
1884	Metis rebellion in Western Canada

	Zhob Valley expedition
1884–1885	Expedition to Bechuanaland
	Gordon Relief expedition
1885	Bhutan expedition
1885–1887	Third Burma War
1885–1898	Wars with Arab slave traders in Nyasa
1888	Black Mountain or Hazara expedition
1888–1889	Sikhim expedition
1889	Tonhon expedition
	Expedition to Sierra Leone
1889–1890	Chin Lushai campaign
1890	Malakand campaign
	Mashonaland expedition
	Vitu expedition
	Punitive expedition in Somaliland
1891	Manipur expedition
	Hunza and Nagar campaign
	Samana or Second Miranzai expedition
	Hazara expedition
1891–1892	Operations in Uganda
	Campaign in Gambia
1892	Isazi expedition
	Tambi expedition
	Chin Hills expedition
1893	Confrontation with French in Sierra Leone
	First Matabele War
	Expedition to Nyasaland
1893–1894	Third Ashanti War
	Arbor Hills expedition
1894	Gambia expedition
	Disturbances in Nicaragua
	British expedition to Sierra Leone
	Expedition against Kabarega, King of Unyoro, Uganga
1894–1895	Punitive expedition to Waziristan
	Nikki expedition
1895	Chitral campaign
	Brass River expedition
1895–1896	Second Matabele War
	Jameson Raid
	Fourth Ashanti War
1896	Bombardment of Zanzibar

	Rebellion in Rhodesia
	Matebele uprising
1896–1899	Reconquest of Sudan
1897	Operations in Bechuanaland
	Operations in Bara Valley, India
1897–1898	Punitive campaign into Tochi Valley
	Tirah campaign
	Uganda mutiny
1897–1903	Conquest of Benin City and Northern Nigeria
1898	Riots in Crete, bombardment of Candia
1899–1902	Second Anglo-Boer War
1900	Boxer Rebellion
	Aden field force in fights with Yemen tribes
	Rebellion in Borneo
1900–1901	Ashanti War
1901–1902	Anglo-Aro War, Nigeria
1906–1913	Disturbances in South Africa (Ghandi)
1914–1918	First World War
1916	Easter Rising in Ireland
1917	Third Marri War
1919	Third Afghan War
	Amritsar Massacre and Non-cooperation movement, India
1919–1921	Irish War of Independence
1920	Iraqi Revolt
1923	Adwan rebellion, Trans-Jordan
1930	Salt March, India
1931–1939	Homespun Movement, India
1935	Yazidi revolts, Iraq
	Abyssinian Crisis
1935-1936	Iraqi Shia revolts
1936-1939	Arab revolts, Palestine

Appendix II

Brief Biography of Rudyard Kipling

Courtesy of the Kipling Society

Rudyard Kipling was born in Bombay on 30 December 1865, son of John Lockwood Kipling, an artist and teacher of architectural sculpture, and his wife Alice. His mother was one of the talented and beautiful Macdonald sisters, four of whom married remarkable men: Sir Edward Burne-Jones, Sir Edward Poynter, Alfred Baldwin, and John Lockwood Kipling himself.

Young Rudyard's earliest years in Bombay were blissfully happy, in an India full of exotic sights and sounds. But at the tender age of five he was sent back to England to stay with a foster family in Southsea, where he was desperately unhappy. The experience would colour some of his later writing.

When he was twelve he went to the United Services College at Westward Ho! near Bideford, where the Headmaster, Cormell Price, a friend of his father and uncles, fostered his literary ability. *Stalky & Co.*, based on those schooldays, has been much relished by generations of schoolboys. Despite poor eyesight, which handicapped him on the games field, he began to blossom.

In 1882, aged sixteen, he returned to Lahore, where his parents now lived, to work on the *Civil and Military Gazette,* and later on its sister paper the *Pioneer* in Allahabad.

In his limited spare time he wrote many remarkable poems and stories, which were published alongside his reporting. When these were collected and published as books, they formed the basis of his early fame.

Returning to England in 1889, Kipling won instant success with *Barrack-Room Ballads*, which was followed by some more brilliant short stories. After the death of an American friend and literary collaborator, Wolcott Balestier, he married Wolcott's sister Carrie in 1892.

After a world trip, he returned with Carrie to her family home in Brattleboro, Vermont, USA, with the aim of settling down there. It was in Brattleboro, deep in New England, that he wrote *Captains Courageous* and

The Jungle Books, and where their first two children, Josephine and Elsie, were born.

A quarrel with Rudyard's brother-in-law drove the Kiplings back to England in 1896, and the following year they moved to Rottingdean in Sussex, the county which he adopted as his own. Their son John was born in North End House, the holiday home of Rudyard's aunt, Georgiana Burne-Jones, and soon they moved into The Elms.

Life was content and fulfilling until, tragically, Josephine died while the family were on a visit to the United States in early 1899.

By now Kipling had come to be regarded as the People's Laureate and the poet of Empire, and he produced some of his most memorable poems and stories in Rottingdean, including *Kim*, *Stalky & Co.*, and *Just So Stories*.

At the museum of the Rottingdean Preservation Society, at The Grange in Rottingdean, there is now a Kipling Room, with a reconstruction of his study in The Elms, and exhibits devoted to his work. The Grange is open daily, and there is no admission charge.

Puck of Pook's Hill and *Rewards and Fairies*, which included the poem 'If – ', and other well-known volumes of stories, were written there, and express Kipling's deep sense of the ancient continuity of place and people in the English countryside.

Kipling's poem, 'The Absent-Minded Beggar' raised vast sums of money for the benefit of British soldiers in the Boer war.

Alfred Harmsworth, at whose request he had written for the fund, introduced him to the joys and frustrations of the pioneer motorist.

Kipling was a friend of Cecil Rhodes, of Lord Milner, and of Dr Jameson, on whose qualities the poem 'If –' is said to have been based. Kipling had written for the Army's newspaper in South Africa, rediscovering the familiar routines of journalism, and spent many winters thereafter in a house near Capetown.

Kipling foresaw the First World War, and tried to alert the nation to the need for preparedness. The Kiplings were to suffer a second bereavement with the death of their son John, at the age of eighteen, in the Battle of Loos in 1915.

Kipling continued to write, and some of the post-war stories (for instance in *Debits and Credits*) are counted among his finest.

He was also much involved in the work of the Imperial War Graves Commission, and King George V became a personal friend. The Kiplings travelled a great deal, and at the outset of one of their visits, in January 1936, Rudyard died, just three days before his King. He had declined most of the many honours which had been offered him, including a knighthood, the Poet

Laureateship, and the Order of Merit, but in 1907 he had accepted the Nobel Prize for Literature.

Rudyard Kipling's reputation grew from phenomenal early critical success to international celebrity, then faded for a time as his conservative views were held by some to be old-fashioned. The balance is now being restored.

More and more people are coming to appreciate his mastery of poetry and prose, and the sheer range of his work. His autobiography *Something of Myself* was written in 1935, the last year of his life, and was published posthumously.

Further Reading

Allen, Charles. *Kipling Sahib, India and the Making of Rudyard Kipling.* (New York: Pegasus Books LLC, 2009).

Callwell, Colonel C.E. *Small Wars, Their Principles and Practice.* (University of Nebraska Press, 2003 reprint).

Corvi, Steven J. and Ian F.W. Beckett (Eds.). *Victoria's Generals.* (Barnsley,: Pen and Sword Books Ltd, 2009).

Barthorp, Michael. *The British Army on Campaign 4, 1882–1902.* (London: Osprey Publishing Ltd, 1988).

Carrington, C.E. *The Life of Rudyard Kipling.* (Garden City: Doubleday & Company, Inc, 1955).

Carver, Field Marshal Lord (Michael). *The National Army Museum Book of the Boer War.* (London: Sidgwick & Jackson, 1999).

Chandler, David G. and Ian Beckett (Eds.). *The Oxford History of the British Army.* (Oxford: Oxford University Press, 1994).

Churchill, Sir Winston S. *A History of the English-Speaking Peoples.* (Four volumes) (New York: Dodd, Mead & Company, 1956–58).

Durand, Ralph. *A Handbook to the Poetry of Rudyard Kipling.* (New York: Doubleday, Page & Company, 1914).

Eby, Cecil D. *The Road to Armageddon, The Martial Spirit in English Popular Literature, 1870–1914.* (Duke University: Duke University Press, 1988).

Farwell, Byron. *Queen Victoria's Little Wars.* (New York: Harper & Row, Publishers, 1972).

Farwell, Byron. *Mr Kipling's Army.* (New York: W.W. Norton & Company, 1981).

Ferguson, Niall. *Empire, How Britain made the Modern World.* (London: Allen Lane, 2003).

French, David. *Military Identities, The Regimental System, the British Army, & the British People c. 1870–2000.* (Oxford: Oxford University Press, 2005).

Gugeler, Russell A. *Combat Actions in Korea.* (Washington, DC: GPO, 1954).

Holt, Tonie & Valmai. *'My Boy Jack?' The Search for Kipling's Only Son.* (Barnsley: Pen & Sword Books Ltd, 2007).

Junger, Sebastian. *Tribe, On Homecoming and Belonging.* (New York: Twelve, 2016).

Kipling, Rudyard. *Rudyard Kipling's Verse, Definitive Edition.* (Garden City, NY: Doubleday and Company, Inc., 1940).

Lycett, Andrew (Ed.). *Kipling and War, from 'Tommy' to 'My Boy Jack'.* (London: I.B. Tauris, 2015).

Masters, John. *Bugles and a Tiger, A Volume of Autobiography.* (New York: The Viking Press, 1956).

McElwee, William. *The Art of War: Waterloo to Mons.* (London: Purnell Book Services Limited, 1974).

McMunn, George. *The Martial Races of India.* (London: Sampson, Low, Marston & Co., Ltd, undated).

Packenham, Thomas. *The Boer War.* (New York: Random House, 1979).

Index